The Villages of Aberdeen
The Spital Lands

'Plans to continue Merkland Road East through to the Links were thwarted by the fact that someone had inconsiderately laid out a football pitch in its path.' In this the fourth of Diane Morgan's best-selling 'Villages of Aberdeen' series, the history of places that are familiar to every Aberdonian is written for the first time: Sunnyside, Sunnybank, Elmbank, Froghall, Bedford, Erskine, Merkland, Pittodrie, Linksfield, King Street. Not so long ago they were part of a vast estate, the Spital Lands, hailed as 'forming a large part of the City of Aberdeen'. *The Spital Lands*, is an amazing voyage of discovery; witchcraft in Sunnyside, a farm in Orchard Place, a mansion in Bedford Road and the Gibberie Wallie itself, moved, unnecessarily as it transpired, to a bowling green. Once again, Diane Morgan offers a refreshingly original, highly readable piece of local history, with a strong dash of humour. The Spital Lands is a sequel to The Spital, but is a complete and self-contained work in its own right.

By the same author

'Villages of Aberdeen' series

Footdee
and her Shipyards

Round About Mounthooly

The Spital

Front Cover
The Gibberie Wallie from Primrosehill
From the original watercolour by J A Sutherland

The Villages of Aberdeen

The Spital Lands
from Sunnyside to Pittodrie

Diane Morgan

Denburn Books
ABERDEEN

First Published 1997

© *Diane Morgan 1997*

British Library Cataloguing in Publication Data
A catalogue record of this book is available from the British Library

ISBN 1 898645 04 3

Design and Layout by
Jimmy and Pat Sutherland

Produced on the Xerox Docutech digital publisher by
Printagraph, Aberdeen

Acknowledgements

A great number of people have helped in the creation of *The Spital Lands*. Without their contribution, in the form of reminiscences, information, photographs, and often all three, this book would have been much the poorer. I would like to thank, in alphabetical order: Arthur and Wilma Abel, Stuart W Allan, Archie Baird, Elizabeth Bandeen, Margaret Birkbeck, Harold Bishop, Charlotte Booth, Jimmy Brown, Doreen Bruce, Ian B D Bryce, Tess Campbell, Billy Chalmers, Andrew Cheyne, Colin Clark, Edith Clark, Anne Cocker, May Cooper, Fred Crawford, Iain Davidson, Dorothy Dempster, Mike Dey, Tommy and Isobel Donaldson, George Elphinstone, Norman Fisher, Mary Forbes, Rachel Forbes, Margaret Fraser, Laura Galloway, Margaret Gemmel, Dorothy Gerrard, John Gillan, James Glennie, Stephen Henderson, Garth Jessamine, Anne Johnston, Jackie Kerr, Tony Kerr, Nancy McKidd, Ian McLaren, Stewart Matthew, Andrew May, Doug Mitchell, Gareth Morgan, Graeme D Nicol, David Paton of Grandhome, Stanley D Rennie, Charles Rettie, Hilda Robb, Ken Robertson, Sandy Robertson, John Ruddiman, Margaret Rust, Alexandrina Scott, Dennis Scott, Jean Simpson, Muriel and Alex Slessor, Jimmie Smith, John Souter, Alan Stalker, Molly Stephen, George Tait, Jim Thom, Arthur Tough, Elizabeth Weston, Colin and Elizabeth Wilson, Pat Wishart, Jimmy Yule, and Winram's Bookshop.

Many people, both at home and abroad have taken a great deal of interest in the project, and I must thank them for their encouragement and good wishes.

I owe a great debt to the staff at Aberdeen City Archives, Aberdeen City Libraries and the Special Collections, King' College, University of Aberdeen, who have provided me with much relevant material on an area where information is sparse. George Gordon has been most kind in allowing me access to his own superb archive and Frank Donnelly, yet again has given sterling support with his camera. Lynn Forbes at Printagraph has given whole-hearted assistance.

A special word of thanks to my husband, David I Morgan, who has patiently chauffeured me around Froghall on a number of occasions. There are less frustrating things to do on a Sunday afternoon than to seek out non-existent balcony flats in what was once known as 'the Jute Works Housing Scheme'.

I am grateful to everyone who has provided illustrations outwith the author's collection, and have acknowledged them individually. The front cover, maps and line drawings are by J A (Jimmy) Sutherland. And it is finally to the book's designers, Pat and Jimmy Sutherland, that I must express my warmest thanks. The success of the 'Villages of Aberdeen' series, is largely due to their enthusiasm, tenacity and expertise.

Diane Morgan, 1997

Contents

	Part One: The Spital Lands West	3
1	Sunnyside	5
2	Sunnybank	16
3	The Gibberie Wallie	30
4	The Sunnybank Enclave: Firhill and Primrosehill	43
5	More About the Sunnybank Enclave	57
6	The Urbanisation of Sunnybank	66
7	Modern Times	86
8	Sunnybank School	106
9	Sunnybank Football Club	121
10	Froghall Past	125
11	Froghall Present	139
12	The Froghall Granite Masters	153
	Part Two: The Spital Lands East	169
13	The 'Orchards': House, Cottage, Place and Lane	171
14	The 'Orchards': Street and Road	183
15	St Peter's Place	199
16	St Peter's Cemetery and its Residents	205
17	Around the King Street Road Dung, Sewage, Manure - and the Mill	223
18	Merkland to Linksfield A Granite Merchants' Mecca	236
19	Pittodrie	253
	Postscript - More About The Spital	265
	Select Bibliography	270
	Index	272

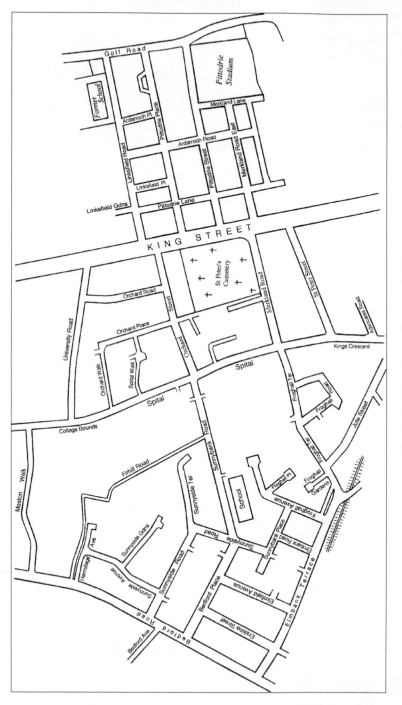

The Spital Lands as they are today.

Introduction

Sunnyside, Sunnybank, Elmbank, Froghall, Bedford, Erskine, Merkland, Pittodrie, Linksfield, King Street. Familiar names to every Aberdonian. But it was not so long ago that they formed a huge area known as the Spital Lands. It was while researching *The Spital*, the previous book in this series, that I came upon this mysterious-sounding domain. Where exactly was it? Help was at hand in the form of George Taylor's Plan of Aberdeen of 1773, (page 4). Here indeed were the 'Spital Lands' stretching out on either side of the Spital itself, surrounded by the Lands of King's College, the Lands of Powis with the Links to the east, while the south boundary of the Spital Lands marched with a part of the Freedom Lands of Aberdeen.

Nowadays, we would not associate the greater part of the Spital Lands with the Spital at all. But in Taylor's Plan, surveyed long before the city was parcelled out and built up, the relationship between the Spital and its lands was clear to see.

The Plan shows Sunnyside Farm in the west, 'A Well' at the Little Firhill - surely the Gibberie Wallie - and beside 'Ketty Brewster's How' (inside the Lands of Powis by a whisker), the long lost hamlet of Peterstown. In the east were broad, expansive fields and the great Whin Hill, which would be broached by King Street within a quarter of a century. Here too was the little Spital Kirkyard which developed into that great treasury of the granite mason's art, St Peter's Cemetery.

The first valuation roll of 1855-56 of Old Machar parish, reveals the rural nature of the Spital Lands. They boasted twenty-six farms, including ten in the King Street area. Later, the Spital Irrigation Farm arrived on the scene. It took me some time to suss that one out! Other clues about the Lands were provided thanks to a speech made at the opening of Sunnybank School in 1906. The estate of Sunnybank, one learnt, was carved out of the Lands of Sunnyside with dykes dividing it 'from that part of Sunnyside

1

called Froghall'. The jigsaw was slowly coming into shape, piece by piece, but not helped by the fact that the lairds of these Lands, the Moirs and their successors the Knight Erskines, left us little information, either about themselves or their estate. By the time I eventually got the pattern of the Lands figured out, I chanced on a plan of the Spital Estate as it was in 1883. To my relief, the boundaries I had toiled over for so long were reasonably accurate. The data accompanying the map described the estate of Spital as 'forming a large part of the City of Aberdeen', as indeed it did at that time.

This then is the story of how these lands developed into the streets familiar to us today. It is a voyage of discovery, rich in variety, from the early days of witchcraft at Sunnyside Farm to the post-war acquisition of that very same piece of land by the builder, Donald C Stewart.

We travel in time from the meetings of the Wise Club in the old Red Lion Tavern, where Aberdeen's contribution to the Scottish Enlightenment was hammered out to meetings of the Froghall Pals two hundred years later, and just a stone's throw away, battling away to achieve renown at a Commonwealth Games of modern times; we move across to Pittodrie, where Aberdeen FC are, well, battling away, as they have done for nearly a hundred years.

The rise and fall of the granite industry is encompassed; the Jute Works are found to be still partially intact and making paint; a farm is discovered in Orchard Place, a mansion in Bedford Road, and the Gibberie Wallie in a bowling green, whither it was removed, quite unnecessarily as it transpired, before the war. There is some sadness too, for in the course of this history, the green fields of the Spital Lands go under concrete forever. And at last, we are standing, metaphorically speaking, at the gates of Old Aberdeen .

The Spital Lands is a sequel to *The Spital,* but is in itself, a complete, and a very different piece of urban history from its predecessor.

Part One

The Spital West

The Gibberie Wallie

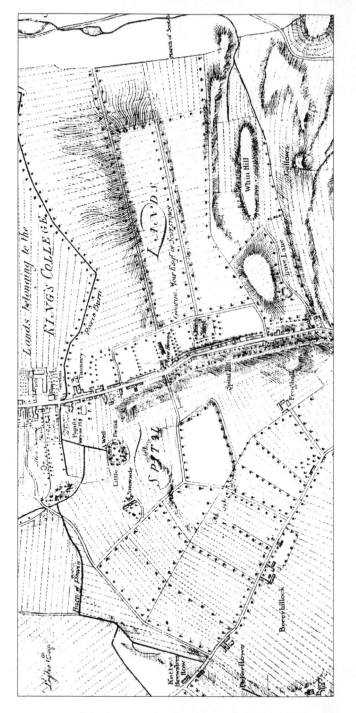

Taylor's Plan of 1773 showing the Spital Lands described on page 1. The Powis Burn near the top of the page divides these Lands from those of King's College to the north-east and the Lands of Powis to the north-west. Just east of Kittybrewster, the line of the march turns to run south-eastwards. The boundary then goes cross country, south of Froghall, to Love Lane (St Peter Street), the boundary with Aberdeen. This southern march of the Spital Lands, which continues to the Links, was marked by key-stones, a relic of the ancient parish of St Peter's. The eastern boundary, (today's Golf Road) continued northwards along the edge of the cultivated land, to meet the Powis Burn. This makes an interesting comparison with the same area as it is today, shown opposite page 1.

4

Chapter 1

Sunnyside

Sunnyside: adjoining Spittal, three minutes' walk west from the Red Lion Inn.
Aberdeen Post Office Directory: 1854-55.

The Spital Lands stretch far and wide on both sides of the Spital, to Kittybrewster in the west, to the Links in the east and they include places that we would not normally associate with the Spital. The Lands originally formed the parish of St Peter's, whose Chapel or Spital Kirk as it was sometimes called has vanished into the mists of time. The site of the Kirk remains, though, shared with the site of the twelfth century St Peter's Hospital which gave the Spital its name. That's the raised ground just inside the Spital Kirkyard, at the Spital end

In 1883 the Spital Lands were put up for sale and a useful map was supplied with the schedule of particulars which shows exactly where they were. If we translate the map into modern topography, looking at the west side first, we can take the boundary as starting behind Viewton Place, now No 33-35 King's Crescent, then striking cross country north-west to Isaac Spencer's paint works - Spencer Coatings Ltd as it now is - in Froghall Terrace. The boundary then dips to run south-west to the Froghall Railway Bridge (the Tarry Briggie) then along Elmbank Terrace, Bedford Road, Hermitage Avenue and the Firhill Road. About three-quarters way along that latter road, still a country lane rather than a road, the boundary strikes east to run behind the Primrose Centre above the Spital, then along the boundary wall to No 177, the last house on the west side of the Spital. This extensive area was known as the Lands of Sunnyside, and in the early days it included Froghall as well.

The story is told in *The Spital* of how the 'toun and lands callit the Sonny Syde, Spittelhill and others,' had, by 1604, been acquired by William Moir,

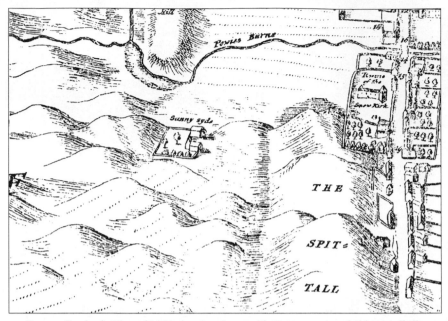

Parson Gordon's Plan of 1661 showing Sunnyside Farm, surrounded by sandhills.

burgess and Treasurer of Aberdeen. One of the treasurer's sons, William Moir, Principal of Marischal College took sasine or possession of the Spital in 1628, while that same year, another son, John, took possession of Sunnyside. It passed to his son, John Moir of Barnes and by 1679, the latter's daughters had became co-heiresses of Sunnyside. Eleven years later, in 1691, one of the younger sisters, Christian, married Alexander Fraser, then a regent (master) at King's College, later, Professor of Greek and sub-principal there. Part of Christian's tocher or dowry of 5000 merks was secured on her share of Sunnyside. In that year of his marriage, Fraser acquired a parcel of land opposite King's College, and it was from these small beginnings that the Frasers and their successors, the Leslies, developed the Powis estate. The Fraser-Moir marriage was a satisfactory arrangement, not in the least because the estates of Sunnyside and Powis marched together.

What sort of land had the Moirs of Barnes acquired at Sunnyside? Parson Gordon's *Plan of Aberdeen* of 1661 shows only one settlement in this extensive area, the farm of Sunnyside of Spital. Gordon shows three biggings surrounded on three sides by a tree-studded enclosure - or are some of these trees really hayricks? No other settlement in his Plan, not even Cotton, from which Woodside eventually grew, nor Upper Torry, have Sunnyside's aura of prosperity. The fairm toon sat in a hollow, almost

6

surrounded by sandhills. Just to the north-east lay the Little Firhill, whence the famous Gibberie Wallie sprang. Moving counter-clockwise was a larger hill round whose base the Powis Burn flowed. Parson Gordon called it the Broom Hill, but it was better known as the Firhill, and it used to be covered with valuable plantations. The Old Aberdeen Council Minutes for 4 March 1693 record a piece of opportunism following a spring gale. Many of the Firhill's fir trees, broken 'at the tyme of this present storme', had been 'cutted and taken away aff of the firhill'. They were subsequently traced to the house of Robert Lillie, a College Bounds tailor. The baillies fined Lillie according to 'the acts of parliament maid anent the cutting and stealing of greene wode'. When

The Firhill. Detail from an aquatint after a painting, by Alexander Nasymth, 1798. The Hermitage in its original form crowns the wooded hill.

the Hermitage, that legendary observatory-cum-summerhouse of Powis House was built on the Firhill in 1781, it became known as the Hermitage Hill, while within living memory local children called it the Miser's Hilly, for it was popularly believed to be the haunt of a miser. It was later sold for its sand.

Beyond the Firhill lay the Manse or Glebe Hill. Though a sand pit was worked on the lower slopes during the nineteenth century, it is still recognisable as a hill with the University's Chemistry Building, (or the Meston Building as it became in 1988) and the Queen Mother Library on its summit. Moving counter-clockwise again is the Broad Hill, the last and largest in the semi-circle round Sunnyside Farm. Powis Crescent skirts its foothills, and Powis House, now the Powis Community Centre sits atop of it. Of these sandhills, the Little Firhill alone lay within the Lands of Sunnyside. The Firhill and the Broad Hill both were part of the Powis estate, while the Glebe Hill in Old Aberdeen belonged to the Church. Sunnyside Farm itself was considered part of the Aulton, and as late as 1949 its site was still described as 'ground at Old Aberdeen, part of the Lands of Spital'.

One of the earliest Sunnyside residents of whom there is a record was

Arthur Craig. On 5 January 1662, the Old Machar kirk session minutes record an allocation of 'dasks'- desks or pews - for 'the more comfortable hearing of the Word'. (It must have been a relief, for the well-to-do, not to have to stand up throughout the long sermons of the day). One group, 'all water men on Don' apart from 'Arthur Craig in Sunniesyd' were to have their dasks at the east end of the Church between those of the Gibsons of Murcar and the Spital cordiners (shoemakers). Why Arthur Craig was sharing a pew with the water men is not explained. 'In Sunniesyd' indicated a tenant of substance, and it is likely that Craig, who was admitted a burgess of Old Aberdeen in 1666, was the farmer of Sunnyside.

Another to be admitted as a burgess some years later, on 8 March 1686, was James Baverlay or Beverley, described as both cordiner and mason in Sunnyside. His entry fee was waived, so the Burgh Records report, in respect of 'measson work wrought by him at the hie cross'. The high cross of Old Aberdeen must have been a fair age when Baverlay carried out his repairs. In the sixteenth century it had been the Bishop's girth cross, where fugitives could claim sanctuary from the law. In those days it was sited on the Bishop's Green, in what is now Seaton Park. After the Reformation, instead of smashing to smithereens something so tainted with popery, the magistrates thriftily pressed it into duty as the Mercat Cross of Old Aberdeen and sat it outside the forerunner of the Old Aberdeen Town House; its subsequent history belongs to that of the Aulton.

In the *List of Pollable Persons within the Shire of Aberdeen*, printed in 1696, (the poll tax of recent times was nothing new), a James Baverlay is noted as mason in West Spital, but it was probably the same man, and he may not have flitted. There was likely to have been a 'grey area' between West Spital and Sunnyside and the decision of where to place him would have lain with the magistrate drawing up the lists. But in view of the four shoemakers in the 'West Syde of the Spittel', not to mention the fourteen across in 'Spittel East', it was understandable, than some ten years on, Baverlay had re-stricted himself to mason, of which skill he was the sole exponent in the area.

The *List of Pollable Persons* followed from the Pole Act of 1695 by which the Estates - the Scottish Parliament - in order to strengthen the defence of the realm did 'freely and chearfully', so they said, 'offer to his Majesty an Subsidy to be uplifted by way of Pole-money'. The basic poll-tax was 6/- Scots, but there were a number of increments, depending on one's status. Tenants, for example, had, in addition to pay a proportion of the hundredth part of the 'valued rent' payable by them to the laird. *The List* reveals that Sunnyside, in Old Machar parish, then held by the heirs of John Moir of Barnes and had a 'valued rent' of £45, of which a hundredth part was 9/-. By this time Sunnyside had two tenant farmers. The principal farmer, 'Andrew Aberdeen in Sunisyde' paid 17/6, that is 6/- from himself, 6/-

from this wife, plus 5/6 as his proportion of the hundredth part. The other farmer, 'Robert Chalmer in Stankyaird', paid 15/6, that is 12/- from his wife and himself, and 3/6, the remaining proportion of the 'hundredth part'. (I now began to suspect that Stankyaird might be the same place as Froghall, of which more anon). John Gibb, the Sunnyside shoemaker, polled highest of all at 18/-, the usual 12/- plus an additional 6/- which was levied on cottars with a trade.

The other 'pollable persons' in Sunnyside, Alexander Guthrie, John Summer, Jannet Brow, William Black and Anna Black were all servants. In addition to the basic 6/-, a fortieth part of their annual wage had to be contributed. Thus William Black, Sunnyside's highest paid servant at £20 paid the basic 6/- plus 10/-, fortieth part, so he polled more highly than Chalmer, the Stankyaird farmer. However, the Act decreed: 'That for Each Servant shall be payed by the Master', so it was really a tax on the employer. Altogether, eleven folk were deemed pollable in Sunnyside though that would not have been the entire population. Exempted 'Poor Persons and Children under the Age of Sixteen' would have swollen the numbers. If the Sunnyside poll tax was collected in full, the contribution to the Exchequer would have been £5 13 2d Scots or about 9/6 sterling.

Jean Nimbrie is not on the *List*. She may have been a pauper, or perhaps dead by then. Or she may have evaded the poll tax by vanishing into thin air. Her story begins in May 1681 when the minister of St Machar's was visiting a sick member of his flock in Sunnyside, probably at the farm itself. The minister was told that Helen Collie, one of the servants there, had earlier been ill with a fever and Jean Nimbrie had cured her by charming. Charming, or casting spells, for good or evil, was rife at this time, and though the minister, Dr George Garden, described as 'very amiable and estimable' was no witch-hunter, the church was anxious to stamp out even the sort of harmless rite practised by Jean Nimbrie. It was looked on as 'unwarrantable healing' which was 'particularlie forbidden by the word of God' since it involved truck with the devil. Jean and Helen were both cited to appear before the Session the following week, and both were quite forthcoming about how the charm worked. Jean Nimbrie had taken:

a hose and tying a threed about it, then putting the hose about the said Helen and saying, 'the Lord Jesus Christ by the sea rode and the fevers on his side and buried them in a grave, in the name of the Father, Son and Holy Ghost'.

The hose - woollen stockings - and the thread were considered power-ful aids in curing fever, especially if the thread was spun from black wool. Using both together would have doubled their strength. The chanting of a few words over the patient, with a Christian reference thrown in, was also part of the rite, and the mumbo-jumbo used by Jean Nimbrie was a mangled version of a charm then in circulation.

Over a year passed before the church's verdict was announced, the delay perhaps caused by the hiatus between the death of Bishop Scougal and the enthronement of Bishop George Haliburton in July 1682. (St Machar's Cathedral was at this time in its Episcopalian phase). The Bishop's 'thinks fitt', Garden reported, that Jean Nimbrie 'being ane ordinarie charmer shall satisfie in the habite' while Helen, who had been ignorant of any wrongdoing, was to appear before the pulpit in her usual attire. This was to say that both must do a spell on the stool of repentance with Jean having to don the penitent's habit, the garment of sackcloth. It was the church's responsibility to provide 'the habite' and she was lucky in that a new one had been made up the month before on the orders of the Master of Kirkwork. The previous garment of sackcloth must have been sweaty, smelly, filthy and ragged before the session went to the expense of ordering a new one.

Could it have been Andrew Aberdeen, the farmer of Sunnyside who originally clyped on Helen Collie and Jean Nimbrie? In March 1689 his name, with the designation, 'in Sunisyd', appears on a list of various pillars of the kirk including the Principal and other members of King's College, and local lairds such as Sandilands of Cotton and Patton of Grandhome from which a new kirk session could be selected. Patrick and George, two Aberdeens of a later generation, are both described as farmers in Old Aberdeen. Patrick is buried in St Machar's graveyard.

By the eighteenth century, a couple of loanings or paths ran through the fields of Sunnyside, both of them passing the farm, as shown on Taylor's *Plan of Aberdeen* of 1773 opposite. One track, the Road to Sunnyside, led from that section of the old Inverurie highway beyond Canal Road - the modern Elmbank Terrace - and headed north-east through a tree-lined path beside open fields. After about four hundred yards the track turned north-west for another few hundred yards to give access to Sunnyside Farm. The Road to Sunnyside then continued on to meet the Road to Oldtown or Kittybrewster Road which linked Old Aberdeen with the old Inverurie highway at Peterstown.

The second track leading to Sunnyside Farm began in the Spital, at the old Red Lion Brae where the original Red Lion Tavern was sited, and whose modern equivalent is Firhill Place. This track ran west to meet the Road to Sunnyside at the junction where that road turned north-east towards Sunnyside Farm. For many years this was the route recommended by the street directories.

Down the years there are occasional glimpses of life at Sunnyside Farm. In October 1798, a roup was held 'at Sunnyside near Old Aberdeen',

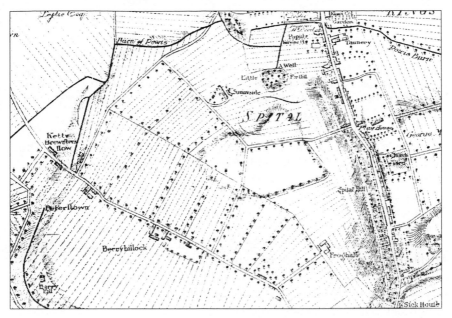

Detail from Taylor's Plan, 1773 showing the paths leading to Sunnyside Farm. The 'Road to Sunnyside' can be traced from the old Inverurie Highway, bottom centre, past Sunnyside Farm to the 'Road to Oldtown' just below the Powis Burn. The second track, via the Red Lion Brae, begins opposite the Play House, right, centre. Note also 'A Well' at the Little Firhill. This was the famous Gibberie Wallie. Sunnybank House was built in the blank feu.

perhaps taking advantage of the recent road improvements which made the nearby Firhill Well or Gibberie Wallie more accessible. Going up for auction, at what sounds like a displenish sale were: 'Six strong draught horses, several good milch cows, 100 bolls of bere and various farm utensils', with eight month's credit given.

In the late 1820s, Sunnyside Farm may have been occupied by the same James Sheriffs who between 1813 and 1825 had run a lunatic asylum in the Spital, almost opposite the Red Lion Brae. By 1826, Sheriffs was bankrupt, so he may have taken the short walk to Sunnyside and turned farmer for a time. The name was not a common one in the area. If indeed it was he, another trauma was in store. The *Aberdeen Journal* reported on 27 March 1827:

On Wednesday last, 14 March, the poultry house, stable and byre on Sunnyside Farm near the Firhill was broken into. Thirty birds stolen, three pea fowls, three turkeys, eight muscovy ducks, bantams etc. A dog on a chain failed to raise the alarm and there was no trace of the thieves.

11

Two years later, in May 1829, the farm then 'possessed by William Campbell and James Sheriffs' was offered on an eleven year lease, so if this was indeed our man, it seems that farming was not to his taste. The laird at this time - between 1824 and 1867 to be precise - was Dame Isabella Bruce, daughter of Alexander Moir sixth of Scotstown and Spital, and wife of Sir Michael Bruce of Stenhouse. The Bruces owned twenty-six farms throughout the Spital Lands, of which Sunnyside was the largest.

A new tenant, Peter McRobbie, came on the scene in 1845, and according to the 1851 census returns was running a farm of thirty-two acres. The 1871 returns reveal that 'Sunnyside Farm, Spital Lands' had expanded to sixty-three acres. McRobbie, by then sixty, was employing four men and two boys. He is noted in the Old Aberdeen directory as 'farmer', but after the Spital Lands became part of Aberdeen in 1883 he appears in the Aberdeen Directory as 'gardener'. Part of the farm, it seems, was being worked as a market garden. McRobbie ran a stall at the Market Hall - Archibald Simpson's New Market buildings at the top of Market Street which had opened in 1842. His three sons were following a variety of careers; one, John, was a general medical practitioner with a surgery at 160 Gallowgate, another, Alexander, was a fish curer and the third was a farm servant who would have worked Sunnyside with his father. Of his four daughters, three were living at home at that time, all spinsters. McRobbie also farmed the Irrigation Farm in King Street, which was not quite what it sounds.

Towards the end of his life Peter McRobbie witnessed considerable changes in the area, which he may have noted with apprehension. Almost a century earlier, in 1799, the neighbouring Powis estate had feued a sliver of land running north-westwards to the Aberdeenshire Canal Company whose waterway soon became part of the rural scene. The coming of the railway was another matter. By the mid-1850s the tracks of the Great North of Scotland Railway (GNSR) had replaced the canal. The GNSR's original Aberdeen terminus, its engine shops, marshalling yards, goods yard and passenger station were all based nearby at Kittybrewster. And it was from here that the line was extended, south-east to Waterloo Quay terminus in 1855, then during 1865-67, south to the Joint Station via the Denburn Valley.

The erosion of the Powis estate in the Kittybrewster area was an inevitable consequence of the GNSR's expansion, but it would initially have had little impact on Sunnyside Farm, some distance to the north-east. In 1879, however, further land was sold off to allow massive expansion at the railyard. The Kittybrewster end of the Road to Oldtown was swept away, to be replaced in 1880 by a new thoroughfare, which we know as Bedford Road. It was laid out parallel to the Road to Oldtown, and a little distance further south. At its north-east end, Sunnyside Farm was now only a stone's throw away. Tenements built in Bedford Road some years later, near the junction with Sunnyside Road overlooked the outbuildings of Sunnyside Farm, sitting in the hollow below. Peter McRobbie moved to nearby Elmfield Farm on the Inverurie highway, leaving Sunnyside to the care of the younger generation. It was there that he died in 1885, at the age of seventy-five. A plaque in St Peter's Cemetery commemorates his life.

Interesting changes are reported in the 1891 census. Sunnyside now has Alexander McRobbie, farmer and fishcurer as head of the family. Brother John, the doctor, is still in residence and Annie Beattie one of the sisters, possibly widowed, is housekeeper. Her two sons Alex and Peter, both at school, live on the farm. Also 'living in' was Agnes Watson, a general servant, while Adam Taylor, farm servant, his wife and Elizabeth Geddes stayed across at the servants' building. But there were boarders in the farmhouse itself, two grooms, Charles Pirie and David Mathers. This is unusual. On a farm one would expect horsemen rather than grooms, and in the bothy rather than the farmhouse. But Alex McRobbie was an unusual farmer. Before taking over at Sunnyside, he had carried on successful businesses both as a fish merchant in George Street, and as a fish curer, one of the oldest established in the city, at Point Law, and for some years ran both businesses in tandem. His great passion, however, was Clydesdale horses. These were a familiar sight at Sunnyside, and he exhibited them all over Scotland. Alex McRobbie died on 24 March 1912 and his obituary recorded:

Many an excellent animal he purchased. He was recognised as a sound judge, and his services in this direction were frequently and most willingly given and greatly appreciated. His stallions which travelled in some of the districts in the north and north-eastern counties had done a great deal in improving the breed in these parts.

Thus is the mystery of the grooms, Charles Pirie and David Mathers solved. They would have looked after the stallions and walked them to meet the local mares. Katherine Trail leaves a memory of them in *Reminiscences of Old Aberdeen* (1932).

Just off the Kittybrewster Road was the farm where the stallions were kept, and it was one of the thrills of our childhood to meet four or five of these beautiful horses, each with a man at its head, being taken out for exercise.

The expanding city was edging closer. Since time immemorial 'the Road to Sunnyside', had been the farm's access road and down the years had been improved from a simple loaning to a substantial cart road. In 1898 the Spital laird, Henry W Knight Erskine - his mother, Mary Anne Moir, was a cousin of Dame Isabella who had been childless - was developing a network of roads throughout his Lands. One of his proposals was the replacing of this section of the Road to Sunnyside with a new road to be given the more modern title of Sunnyside Road. It would share a similar though not identical alignment to its ancient predecessor, passing the outbuildings of Sunnyside Farm as of yore, but would be nicely tarmacadamed, with sewers in place, awaiting the attentions of the speculative builder. This was duly carried out and a long drive was laid out linking the farmhouse (a new one was built in the late nineteenth century), and Sunnyside Road. For generations the residents of Sunnyside Farm had been almost encircled by fir-clad sandhills. By the early twentieth century, tenements were taking over as those on Bedford Road were matched by a block on the south side of Sunnyside Road, opposite the farm.

After the laying out of Sunnyside Road, development around the farm ceased for the time being. The fields of Sunnyside Farm, and the many neighbouring market gardens stretching east to Firhill Road, gateway to the Gibberie Wallie, and north to the Powis Burn, remained an agricultural

Sunnyside Farm from No 58 Bedford Road, courtesy Laura Galloway.

oasis for many years to come. The greater part of the Spital Lands, including the farm itself was acquired in 1900 by the City of Aberdeen Land Association, known as 'the Association', then or CALA nowadays, and its plans, for the time being, did not include further development in that area.

After the death of Alex McRobbie, his widow stayed on at Sunnyside Farm until 1914 when George Killah, nurseryman, took over the tenancy. The Land Association was still the landlord. The farm was run as a market garden at this time. Mrs Alexandrina Scott (Nina Milton) who has lived in the area all her life recalls buying vegetables at the farm from Mrs Killah.

The well known local farmer, Willie Weir, whom we met in *The Spital* succeeded the Killahs at Sunnyside. While carrying on with the dairy business at Merkland Place, Weir, who already grazed his cattle in the Sunnyside fields, leased Sunnyside Farm in 1928. The market gardening side of the business was developed at Sunnyside, and Willie and his mother lived there. Mrs Jean Simpson (Jean Nelson) born and brought up at one of the Weir houses at No 90 the Spital, recalls Sunnyside Farm as larger and rather nicer than the one at Merkland Place, with a parlour lighted by a chandelier of paraffin lamps. There was a glass porch at the back door, and a sink that was the only water supply to the house. She recalls numerous outhouses, stables, henhouses, and a pigsty as well as fields of barley and corn and several grass parks. The farm lying in its hollow, was a splendid sun trap, excellent for cultivation. Berries and soft fruits grew in the large garden and vegetables and potatoes in the plots near the farm, all of which provided the Weir vegetable carts with a steady supply of produce. Willie drove one cart and Mr Dod Mann, who lived in St Mary's Place, Old Aberdeen, the other. Brother Harry Weir did the dairy round with the two-wheeled milk cart.

Sunnyside Farm, with Willie Weir at the helm, survived until after the Second World War. Fred Crawford, a former Head of the English Depart-ment at Ellon Academy, was brought up in Elmbank Avenue and recalls visiting his cousin whose house in Sunnyside Road was directly opposite the farm entrance. They would wander across to the farm and watch Willie feeding the pigs. 'Mostly I remember smells like manure and pigswill,' he says. Dennis Scott, well known for his work with vintage fire engines, who spent his childhood in Bedford Road, recalls the local sweep leaving soot in one of the outhouses for Willie to use as fertiliser. The piggery stood a little isolated from the main farm buildings and Dennis used to play there with his friends even after the farm itself had gone.

Chapter 2

Sunnybank

Major Mercer and his family, after many wanderings, built and settled at Sunny Bank, a suburban residence situated between the old and new towns of Aberdeen.
Margaret Forbes: Beattie and his Friends, 1904.

In 1789 James Mercer, soldier, scholar and poet, acquired land in Sunnyside described as 'a pendicle of the Kirklands of Kirktown of Spital'. A pendicle is a small piece of ground forming part of a larger holding, but Mercer's pendicle was a respectable pocket estate of five acres. It was bounded on the east and south by dykes dividing it from 'that part of Sunnyside called Froghall', and on the north by a dyke which divided it from 'that part of Sunnyside once possessed by William Wildgoose'. In today's terms from the rear of Sunnybank Primary School at the south, to the wall between Sunnybank Road and Sunnyside Terrace to the north. The janitor's house at No 18 Sunnyside Road marks the line of the western boundary, while the eastern boundary was only about eighty yards from the Spital. The feu is clearly visible on Taylor's Plan on page 11, that blank square south-east of Sunnyside Farm. The Wildgoose family were perhaps successors to the Aberdeens as farmers at Sunnyside and their distinctive name was for long a familiar one in the area.

James Mercer, born in Aberdeen in 1733, was not so much a Wildgoose as one of the Wild Geese who had fought on the Continent as a soldier of fortune. He was the younger son of Thomas Mercer, Jacobite laird of Auchnacant in the parish of Foveran, 'a gentleman of private fortune' and a merchant burgess of Aberdeen, who was aide-de-camp to the aged Lord Pitsligo during the Forty-five. After Culloden, Thomas Mercer fled to Paris

16

and spent the rest of his life in exile.*
His sons remained in Aberdeen,
looked after by relatives, and the
younger, James, was educated at
the Grammar School and Marischal
College where he developed a passion for the classics which remained
with him all his life. One of his
classmates, James Beattie, the son of
a Laurencekirk shopkeeper, was to
become a close friend.

After graduating MA in 1754,
James joined his father in Paris, who
as 'Thomas Messer, Garde du corps'
was in receipt of a pension of 600
francs. Here James completed his

After a portrait of James Mercer.

education and acquired his Parisian stylishness. He took up arms and saw
active service in the Seven Years War under Prince Ferdinand of Brunswick.
On one occasion, Mercer and his Scots company were captured after a
skirmish with a larger enemy force. Their Highland dress intrigued their
captors who took them to be barbarians. To their surprise, they discovered
Mercer's French to be more fluent, his manners more polished and his
knowledge of the classics more profound than theirs. They treated him as
a distinguished guest until an exchange of prisoners was arranged.

Mercer fought bravely at the Battle of Minden. This was noted by a
cousin by marriage, General Graeme, who presented him with a company
of his own in the newly-raised Queen's Regiment. Mercer returned briefly
to Aberdeen after the Peace of Paris of 1762, and renewed his friendship
with James Beattie, who, two years earlier had relinquished his teaching
post at the Grammar School to become Professor of Moral Philosophy at
Marischal College. Mercer also took the opportunity to court the lovely
Katherine Douglas, a lady of Jacobite stock, whom he married in 1763.

---

* Thomas's cousin, Hugh Mercer, who graduated in Medicine from Marischal
College in 1744, served as surgeon's mate to the Jacobite army and after Culloden
fled to the American Colonies, became an associate of George Washington and
fought as a brigadier-general in the War of Independence, at the head of a flying
column renowned for its night attacks. At the Battle of Princeton (1777) he was
unhorsed and bayoneted by redcoats and died of his wounds. A statue was raised
to his memory at Fredericksburg, Virginia where he had settled. His daughter Anne
Gordon Mercer married Robert Patton and their great-great grandson was the
distinguished US general, George S Patton (1885-1945).

Katherine's brother, Sylvester, Lord Glenbervie, was also a friend of Mercer's and a member of the circle of scholars and aristocrats that Beattie was gathering around him.

Mercer returned to soldiering soon after his marriage. The Queen's Regiment had been slimmed down at the end of the Seven Year's War, so he purchased a company - the routine method of advancement in those days - in the 49th Regiment, and was posted to Ireland where he served for the next nine years. He corresponded with Beattie, bemoaning his homesickness and missing the learned 'confabulations' they had as they strolled along the banks of the Dee. In 1770 he became a major, but two years later, although he had the funds in hand, was passed over for a lieutenant-colonelcy. Somewhat miffed, he left the army and returned to the North East with his wife and two daughters.

The Major was warmly welcomed into Beattie's circle which included the Duke of Gordon and Duchess Jean, Cosmo Gordon of Cluny Castle, the influential Mr Robert Arbuthnot, the learned Thomas Reid, Professor of Moral Philosophy at King's College, and Reid's maternal cousins, the medical and scientific Gregories, geniuses all. Mercer was by no means out of his depth in such a gathering. He had continued his classical studies after leaving the army and Beattie, in a letter to the Duchess of Gordon, 'doubted if there were six gentlemen in Scotland who knew Greek as well as the Major'. Beattie declared Mercer 'the pleasantest companion he ever met' and an account survives of both families setting off in their chaises in the summer of 1777. Mrs Mercer had become a chronic invalid and the Major was taking her to the south of France in the hope of improving her health. The Beatties kept them company as far as London.

At this time, Beattie was one of the most famous people in the kingdom, the lion of the London *literati* counting Johnson and Boswell among his friends as well as the poet Thomas Gray, and the actor, David Garrick. George III, though not without some persuasion, had bestowed a state pension on him in 1773. Beattie's popularity derived from the publication of his philosophical work, the *Essay on Truth* in 1770 while *The Minstrel*, his great 'landmark' poem, published between 1771 and 1774 would run to over fifty editions by the 1820s and English poetry would never be the same again. The minstrel of the poem's title, the solitary Edwin, is Beattie himself 'as I was in my younger day', seeking inspiration and knowledge from nature. The landscape of the North East is dramatically portrayed:

> *Oft did the cliffs reverberate the sound*
> *of parting fragments tumbling from on high;*
> *And from the summit of that craggy mound*
> *The perching eagle oft was heard to cry...*

After the constrictions of Pope's verses, *The Minstrel* struck a fresh chord. Wordsworth, whose poem *The Prelude*, on a similar theme, written thirty years later, was much influenced by Beattie's work, as was Lord Byron, who was a pupil at the Grammar School where Beattie's father-in-law, Dr James Dun was headmaster. The young Byron lived in Broad Street, and must have seen Beattie many a time, entering the Marischal College close.

At Beattie's request, Mercer had been appointed Dean of Faculty at Marischal College, but his appetite for things military had not deserted him. The country was gripped by a war scare when it was learnt that the French were joining forces with revolting American colonists. Mercer organised a recruiting drive in Aberdeen, the highlight of which was a parade through the town. The magistrates and the principal citizens including Beattie took in the parade, and the operation had a satisfactory conclusion. The *Aberdeen Journal* of 22 June 1778 reported:

several stout fellows entered with the Major. And when the Procession was over, the Magistrates ordered a Hoghead's of Rigg's fine home brewed Porter to be distributed among the Populace.

Mercer remained a stalwart of the fencibles, 'sound-headed, sensible and much to be relied on', until the end of the American War of Independence in 1783.

In 1787 he inherited the family estate on the death of his bachelor elder brother, David. He could now style himself 'James Mercer of Auchnacant', though that estate in the windswept parish of Foveran would have seemed remote from Aberdeen in those days. He had the means now to acquire property nearer town and another friend, George Moir, fifth Laird of Scotstown and Spital, 'a gentleman of good estate, excellent understanding and classical knowledge', as well as being an acknowledged 'Improving' farmer, feued him the pendicle, a part of his estate of Sunnyside, and by far the biggest piece of land he had given out. Moir and Mercer shared Jacobite sympathies and a European background; both were members of Beattie's circle; and both were landed gentry with interests in the same part of the county. Auchnacant was only some six or seven miles north of Moir's Scotstown estate.

Mercer's new property had the ambience of a small country estate, as well as the convenience of being only a short ride from Aberdeen, and a short walk from Old Aberdeen where a number of county families overwintered in their townhouses. An additional bonus was that not only were the approach roads, previously only used for access to Sunnyside Farm, in place, but were in the process of being improved to allow easier

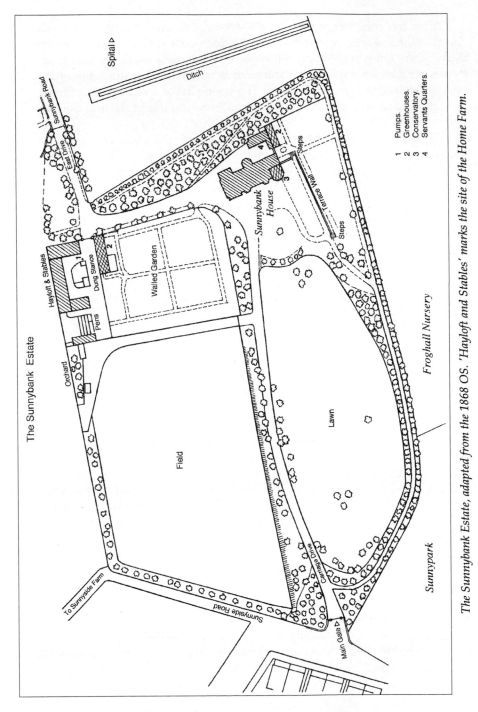

The Sunnybank Estate, adapted from the 1868 OS. 'Hayloft and Stables' marks the site of the Home Farm.

The Sunnybank Estate

1   Pumps.
2   Greenhouses.
3   Conservatory.
4   Servants Quarters.

Spital ▷

Ditch

Sunnybank Road

East Drive

Hayloft & Stables

Dung Stance

Pens

Orchard

Walled Garden

Sunnybank
House

Steps

Terrace Wall

Steps

Froghall Nursery

Lawn

Field

To Sunnyside Farm

Sunnyside Road

Carriage Drive

Main Gate ▷

Sunnypark

access to nearby Firhill Well - the Gibberie Wallie - now gaining fame for its curative powers.

In the south-east corner of his property, Mercer built 'a good house in an inviting situation' a 'pleasant little villa, to which, from its warm southern aspect he gave the name Sunny Bank', wrote his brother-in-law, Lord Glenbervie. A walled terrace, ran out southwards from the house offering views over the countryside which in time would be covered by the Froghall and Sunnypark nurseries. From the terrace, banked up against the sloping land - hence perhaps, the name - two flights of steps gave access to wooded walks around the policies and an elegant oval lawn stretched from the front of the villa almost to the Road to Sunnyside. A central, tree-lined carriage drive separated the oval lawn from a field which was part of the neighbouring home farm and stabling complex, as shown on the plan

Sunnybank House.

opposite. This central band of trees would have hidden grazing cattle, sheep or horses from the house. The situation was the same at the Seaton estate, where the home parks were used for grazing, but where four-legged beasts were not permitted to present themselves in front of Seaton House itself.

Visits to Auchnacant would have taken Mercer past the Seaton estate which lay just south of the Brig o Balgownie, which was then owned by the Middleton family. The handsome Seaton stables, built some years earlier, would have caught his eye, as would the walled garden, enclosed by Scotch bond brickwork. Was he inspired by these developments at Seaton? Certainly, the walled garden at Sunny Bank was something special. It probably was enclosed with the same local brick, perhaps from the nearest source at Fountainbleau, long since covered over by Seaton Place East. The garden was extensive, measuring some 170ft by 150ft and was laid out in four large beds, separated by pathways, with broad flower borders. Fruit trees would have been planted along the sunny east wall. A 50ft long greenhouse stood in the north-east corner where tomatoes, geraniums, vines, even orchids may have been grown. A small enclosure was attached, possibly to grow melons and cucumbers on a 'hot bed'. This is speculation, but the late eighteenth century was a golden age in Scottish gardening and even small lairds could dine off asparagus and artichokes as well as commonplace peas and beans if they were so minded. The Mercers, thanks to their trips to the south of France, were well aware of the existence of Mediterranean produce.

The small home farm and stables sat close to the north wall, forming a three-sided open courtyard where a large dung stance was handily placed both for receiving manure from the stables and fertilising the walled garden. A pump beside the stance provided water for man, beast and for the nearby greenhouse. West of the courtyard were cattle pens and sheep fanks and a south-facing orchard.

According to Lord Glenbervie, Mercer surrounded his property 'with shrubberies and plantations according to his fancy'. He greatly valued his privacy. The eastern boundary, the frontier with the Spital the nearest population centre, was densely planted, and a great ditch ran north to south in the empty ground between estate and Spital. The east entrance to Sunny Bank, only a short walk up the Red Lion Brae, and its continuation, 'old' Sunnybank Road, was barred by gates, as was the entrance from the Road to Sunnyside at the west side. In spite of these precautions, Mercer found it necessary to set up man traps. On 17 October 1797 the *Aberdeen Journal* reported that his ground had been broken into and a number of young trees destroyed. A reward of three guineas was offered to anyone who could name the culprits and a warning was also given that the Major was setting steel traps and spring guns at Sunny Bank to deter any further vandalism. 'Any person being injured by these contrivances has no claim against the Major'.

The last decade of Mercer's life was also taken up with more peaceable pursuits. He had scribbled the occasional poem over the years, but was embarrassed when his *Lyric Poems* first appeared in 1794, edited and published, without his permission, and against his wishes by his brother-in-law. He had nothing to fear. His poems were pronounced 'everywhere elegant and sometimes charming' and went through two further editions, in 1804 and posthumously in 1806. His poetry was not the pioneering stuff of Beattie's *Minstrel* but was gentle, often vapid, with much invoking of the

Muses. But there is a cheery ode of 1798, *To a Young Midshipman,* whose dedicatee, his grandson, would have been about twelve, and had already seen active service in Nelson's navy.

> *While thy compeers, at school confined*
> *Plod o'er the weary task assign'd*
> *Or snatch the short liv'd sweets of play*
> *Enfranchis'd on some holiday:*
> *Thine is, my boy! a manly game ,*
> *Doom'd by thy fate on seas afar,*
> *To wing the thunderbolt of war*
> *And share thy country's fame.*

'Decreppit aul age' was now taking its toll. Mrs Mercer was unable to move without the Major's assistance, while he was plagued with rheumatics. Beattie had been a valetudinarian all his life, and now his health was growing worse. His declining years were tragic. His two brilliant young sons had died, while his wife, Mary, the daughter of James Dun, had inherited that family's streak of insanity and had long been cared for by others. Both men retired from society but compensated by meeting frequently. 'One evening I call on the Major and the next evening he calls on me,' Beattie wrote to his old friend and biographer, Sir William Forbes. And in 1799 Mr Arbuthnot wrote to Beattie: 'That Major Mercer's company and conversation should afford you great comfort I can easily believe...I declare I never knew a human being on whose friendship, on the day of adversity or distress, I could have greater dependence than on Mercer's.' That would have served as a fitting epitaph.

Mrs Mercer died in 1802, and Beattie, who had been crippled by a series of strokes, in 1803. Mercer followed them to the grave in 1804. He and his wife were buried together in St Nicholas Churchyard in Aberdeen.

The Sunnybank estate went on the market after the Major's death, and owners in the early nineteenth century included A N McLeod Esq who lived there in the early 1820s, and a Colonel D Forbes, whose family by the 1830s was advertising Sunnybank - now spelt as one word - with its five acres of gardens and grounds, as 'an excellent family residence near Aberdeen, pleasantly situated within fifteen minutes walk of the city and five minutes walk from King's College'. It was purchased by a reverend gentleman, the splendidly named Hartcourt Norris Terriano Bushfield and tenanted by the Misses Paton of Grandhome, daughters of the laird, John Paton and his wife Mary Lance. The girls' childhood had been a traumatic one. Their mother had borne three sons and seven daughters in little more than ten years, to the lasting impairment of her physical and mental health. John Paton devoted himself to nursing her until the end, turning against his children whom he regarded as responsible for her death. He eventually abandoned the family and went to live in London, a recluse. The sons all went abroad, chiefly to India, while the girls were cared for by the eldest sister, the formidable Mary.

Papers at Grandhome show that the Misses Paton were at Sunnybank by 1839, the year their nephew John, the young laird, came of age. His four surviving maiden aunts must have withdrawn to give him the run of Grandhome, where he added considerable extensions. An inventory and valuation of the ladies' furniture at Sunnybank was made in 1840, indication that residence of a permanent nature had recently been taken up. The 'Misses Paton of Grandholm' are noted at Sunnybank on Gellatly's Plan of Aberdeen of 1855, but by that time the ladies were away. Three of the sisters had died, the third, Sarah in 1854. Bathia, the fourth, had no wish to live alone at Sunnybank it seems, and gave up the tenancy soon after. She then lived at No 48 Skene Terrace, until her death in 1871.

Alexander Stronach, a well known advocate in Aberdeen (of Stronach and Grainger, not Stronach and Sons, for he had none), was in residence by 1855, and he bought the estate in 1859. During the period that the Misses Paton were there, Stronach had lived at No 53 the Spital, where the rear windows would have afforded him a fine view of Sunnybank House and its policies. He must have decided it would do nicely for him.

By the 1860s a north wing had been added to the house, which was now embellished by bay windows to the front and a conservatory built in the south-west angle. Elegant villas were going up in the west end of Aberdeen at this time, and a fellow advocate, Francis Edmond, had recently acquired Kingswells estate and handsomely enlarged the plain old house of Kingswells. Stronach may have been anxious to keep abreast of fashion, though his household, by the standards of the time, was not a particularly large one. It consisted, according to the census returns of 1861, of himself, his wife, sister-in-law, niece and three servants. By this time Sunnybank House had a new, if humble, neighbour. Sunnybank Cottage, now No 26 Sunnybank Road, beside the south end of the present Firhill Road, may have been built as a lodge for the east entrance to the House. The 1861 census shows a gardener in residence, but by 1891 the tenant was Thomas Fullerton, an agricultural labourer whose son William was a stockbroker's apprentice.

Alexander Stronach had died childless in 1881 and Sunnybank passed to his niece and co-heiress, Miss Anna Stuart, who was to marry James Smith-Shand, Professor of Medicine at Aberdeen University, a widower with a sizeable family. The professor had started off as plain Smith, but had added his wife's name at the time of his first marriage. The census returns of 1881 show the opulent if mysterious Thomas L R Shand in residence, possibly some connection of the first Mrs Smith-Shand, with his wife, family of five, governess and servants. A gentleman of leisure, his occupation was 'none', and his income derived from land.

Professor Smith-Shand, 'a placid, reflective man, carrying a whole world in his head and not finding it too heavy' died suddenly in 1891. No one above stairs was in residence that year when census forms were delivered. The housekeeper, Jane Gilbert, and Jane Craib and Grace Rennie, laundress and under-laundress were holding the fort. The widowed Anna Smith-Shand retained Sunnybank, renting it out to a succession of genteel lady tenants, to Mrs Principal Pirie, the widow of William Pirie, Principal of Aberdeen University, then to Lady Geddes, widow of Pirie's successor, Sir William Geddes.

In the 1890s, when the Spital laird, H W Knight Erskine, was laying out streets over the green fields of Sunnyside to the specifications required by Aberdeen Town Council, there appears to have been something of a falling out between himself and Mrs Smith-Shand. On 15 June 1896, the Council Minutes noted that 'the proprietor of the Spital' had been 'unable to arrange with the proprietor of Sunnybank for having the levels of (Sunnyside Road) fixed as required by the Town Council...' Knight Erskine's architects had to put forward an amended scheme. Three years later, in May 1899, the Council bought the Sunnybank estate, 'for the behoof of the Common Good of the burgh of Aberdeen'. The price was £3,500. The motive for the purchase was 'to create a new road to run eastward from the junction of Sunnyside Road and Bedford Place through the Lands of Sunnybank', in effect linking Sunnyside Road with the Spital. This new road, the Sunnybank Road we know today, ran through the grounds of Sunnybank House with a vengeance, right up the carriage drive, bisecting the walled garden and marooning the home farm and stables, as shown on our plan on page 26.

Some months before the purchase of Sunnybank was finalised, Dr Mitchell, a member of Aberdeen School Board, got wind of the Council's plans. He had previously stressed to his fellow Board members, the need for a new school in an area that was rapidly filling up with housing and the Sunnybank estate seemed to him the ideal place. He egged the Board into action. By 1901 they had secured a two acre site - the gracious oval lawn itself - at an annual feu duty of £70. Sunnybank School, whose story is told in Chapter Eight was completed by 1906.

What was the fate of Sunnybank House? In spite of having a wide new road driven through its policies, it had survived and even retained its terraced gardens to the west and south. 'Though the amenities of the place have been severely curtailed,' wrote J F George in 1906 in *The Powis Book*, 'Sunnybank House is still occupied by a citizen of distinction, Professor

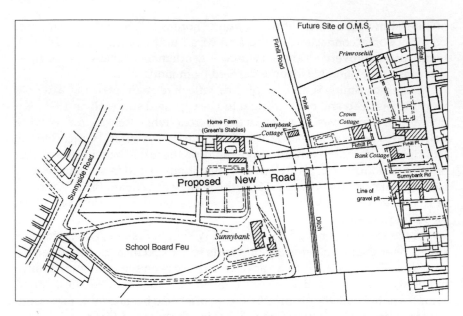

Plan for the proposed new road (Sunnybank Road) which goes straight through the walled garden of Sunnybank House, cutting off the farm and stable block. Note the narrow version of Sunnybank Road which has developed from the Spital end.

Neil J D Kennedy of the Chair of Scots Law.' The Professor was in luck, for a new amenity was added that year. The House was linked to the new sewers of Sunnybank Road and its cesspool was removed. Robert Booth, a teacher at Robert Gordon's College was the last private resident. Being a master at one school and the near neighbour of another was perhaps more than human flesh could endure. He gave up his lease in 1910 and the Council placed the following advertisement in the *Free Press*: on June 17:

> To Let: Sunnybank House belonging to the Town Council. Annual Rent, £50'.

The last tenant now appeared on the scene. Aberdeen Endowments Trust traces its more recent origins to the Aberdeen Educational Trust, an amalgamation of charities dating from 1888, one of whose obligations was the running of a 'Home for Girls and a School of Domestic Economy'. Both were located at the handsome premises at No 352 King Street, custom-built twenty years earlier by William Smith to house the Boys' and Girls' Hospital, whose own roots went back to 1739. In a reorganisation of 1910, the Home for Girls was taken under the wing of the newly established Endowments Trust, which in that first year had at its disposal the sum of

26

£1075 towards the maintenance and education of sixty girls, the endowments foundationers. Thirty outdoor foundationers lived at home and received grants towards their schooling, while the girls from the Home at No 352 King Street became the first indoor foundationers. At this point, their King Street co-occupant, the 'Dough' School had expanded to such a degree that the Home for Girls was in danger of being squeezed out. Sunnybank House came on the market at just the right time. A ten year lease was entered into and the Home for Girls transferred to Sunnybank with their matron, Mrs Sinclair, where, with assistance from the Town Council, the Trust had set up a new home for them.

And so in September 1910 Sunnybank House entered on the final phase of its career, as Sunnybank Home - the 'Homey' as it was called locally. Professor J W H Trail as Chairman of the Trust presided at the opening ceremony, and over the years the trustees were a roll call of Aberdeen's great and good; in the 1930s for example Baillie John D Munro, Councillors George Duncan LLD and Sir Thomas Mitchell, and G R McIntosh, joiner, trade unionist and future city treasurer; the solicitor W D Esslemont of Esslemont & Cameron, Professor A S Ferguson of the Chair of Logic, Patrick McGee, the gents' outfitter, and Mrs Katherine Trail of Old Aberdeen fame who had succeeded her husband on the Board of Trustees. And there was always an abundance of prominent city ministers.

For many years to come, an annual Endowments Trust notice in the local press would invite applications for five indoor foundationer places 'in the Home in Sunnybank Road until they attain the age of sixteen. Candidates must have lost either or both parents and be not under ten years of age'. There were many sad cases, applications from a domestic servant and a charwoman whose late husbands had been respectively a stone cutter and a crofter. Neither woman could afford to keep her daughter. Applications from widowers were more common; one from a tramway repairer whose wife had recently died and who was living in lodgings with his children boarded out. Another from an unemployed labourer, whose two little girls aged seven and eight were accepted. One applicant was a grandfather whose son, a carter, had died, and whose daughter-in-law had deserted her family.

But the records indicate that a number of girls were reunited with their families. One mother wrote to say that she had remarried and was 'now in position to provide a comfortable home and good education for Nettie.' Others had gained responsible positions after widowhood, as housekeeper for example, where it would be possible for a daughter to join them. And there were cases of foundationers going to live with uncle and aunts, sometimes in Canada or New Zealand. All such applications were carefully checked out by the House Committee.

The records of the early years at Sunnybank show the girls settling in. After the building of the Sunnybank School, it seemed that some reinstatement of the House's still substantial garden was required. Grass seed was bought from Messrs Reid & Leys; vegetables were planted and a swing was purchased and erected at a cost of £7. In 1913, rose bushes (not to exceed 30/-) were purchased and Mr Walker of the Victoria Park was to superintend cropping of the garden. In 1918 Reid & Leys supplied seeds to the value of £5 3s 6d.

Careful management and thrifty maintenance were the order of the day: repairs to settee carried out in 1913; dining-hall relaid with linoleum in 1918; a good second hand carpet to be purchased at reasonable cost by the Clerk and the Matron in 1919; distempering and wall-papering in 1930. Keeping the girls well and neatly dressed was very important. Mrs Muriel Slessor remembers a uniform of cloaks, fawn-brownish frocks, ecru pinafores, and buttoned boots. The girls would have been very handily placed for Sunnybank School, quite literally, was at the bottom of the garden, but in 1924 it gained intermediate status and Old Aberdeen School became the primary for the Sunnybank girls. Mrs Iris Donald recalls the girls at a later period, marching to Old Aberdeen in a crocodile, and as she lived in Sunnybank Road she would march along with them. At that time they wore navy coats and green berets. The cost of the uniform features regularly in the records. In the 1920s summer hats cost 2/11, winter hats, 4/2. Gloves for Sunday wear cost 1/-. Material for uniforms came from Esslemont & Macintosh and boots and shoes from John A Dunn. Other local suppliers in the 1920s included Messrs McIntosh Ltd, butchers, AB Hutchison, bakers, Ellis & McHardy, coal merchants, the Balgownie Dairy and John E Esslemont, but that was for groceries rather than sweeties. The 'Homey', like other institutions in Aberdeen in those days, was good for local businesses.

By the early 1920s, separate rooms were allocated to juniors and seniors. The House Committee had interviewed the girls and Mrs Sinclair about how the spare hours of the evenings were spent, and it was decided that the young girls should go to bed a little earlier than the seniors, allowing the latter a quiet time to read. A library was set up, lists of suitable books and magazines drawn up and a sum set aside annually for their purchase. Mrs Sinclair also taught penmanship and letter writing to those girls who were interested.

Every Christmas there was special entertainment and a visit to the pantomime at His Majesty's. There were visits to the Majestic Cinema in the course of the year, and a month's summer holidays, at Dinnet for example, during July. This was after the summer picnic, which in the 1920s, was held at Paradise, Monymusk, by courtesy of Sir Arthur Grant. The Sunnybank party, including the House Committee, who took afternoon tea at Paradise, would leave the Home by charabanc at 2 o'clock, returning about seven. In 1926 the summer picnic was held on a glorious day, one of the best in the year.

At Sunnybank the girls were trained for domestic service and the Walker Gold Medal was awarded annually to the best girl at the commencement of her last year. Aberdeen Endowments Trust still retain the medal, a golden oval pendant, in their archives. It bears the legend:

The Best Cook
Tidiest House Maid
and Kindliest Girl of
the Year

The Home kept in touch with its charges, and congratulations were sent to those who did well in later life.

By 1936 Sunnybank's days as a 'Homey' were drawing to a close. The minutes of 31 December 1936 state: 'some endeavour should be made without delay to find more suitable accommodation than Sunnybank House for housing the foundationers.' By then two houses in Polmuir Road, Ferryhill Lodge at No 9, on the Devanha Gardens' corner, once the home of the weaver-scholar, Professor Alexander Bain, and No 19 had already been looked at with a view to purchase. Then in April 1937, the Aberdeen Town Council gave the Trustees notice 'to vacate Sunnybank Home not later than Whitsunday 1938, as the whole site would be required in connection with extensions to Sunnybank School.' With so many councillors on the Board, this was no bolt from the blue. Trustees were well aware of what was afoot, hence the urgency to find new accommodation even before the notice to quit was issued. Ferryhill Lodge was purchased and the foundationers left for their new home on 5 June 1938 though without Mrs Sinclair who had recently retired. Mr George Gordon, the King's Crescent historian, had joined the Shore Porters at the beginning of that year, and still can remember the flitting which his firm carried out at a cost of £15 10/-. Sunnybank House was demolished soon after, though its site has never been built over. The extension to Sunnybank School stops some yards short of where the House used to be.

Chapter 3

The Gibberie Wallie

The Firhill Well whaur aul Babie Courage eest tae sell her gibrie.
Glimpses of Olden Days in Aberdeen, W Buchanan, 1870.

Scarcely one hundred yards north-east of the site of Sunnyside Farm the Gibberie Wallie once bubbled forth. The Wallie's official name was, and still is, the Firhill Well, though it sprang, not from the Firhill itself, but from its neighbour, the Little Firhill. It was a chalybeate spring, iron-rich and in his little book *A Medical Treatise on the Fir-hill Well*, published in 1800, Dr J Taylor, graduate of Marischal College and Fellow of the Royal College of Physicians of Edinburgh tells us a little of its history:

About the year 1721, John Forbes in Old Aberdeen, and one of the name of Catto, who is alive at the present time in the Spital, in the winter time when there was a great storm on the ground, they had gone out a-shooting hares and small birds about the hedges, when by mere chance, Mr Forbes observed a spring of water issuing from the bottom of the round hill near the Well; a vapour arising from the spring made it more discernible.

Forbes, as it chanced, had long been 'afflicted with a calculus or gravely complaint' - gallstones. He drank some of the spring water, 'and soon after was very sensible of its giving him ease'. He drank more and 'passed a considerable quantity of gravel and small calculi in his urine'. For the rest

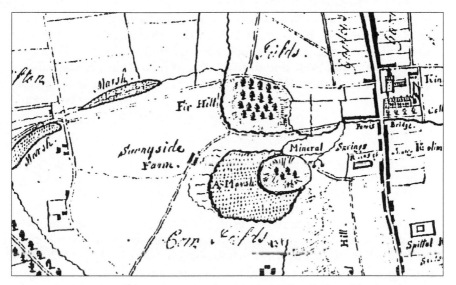

Logie's Plan of the early 1750s, showing the Well as 'Mineral Springs.'

of his life 'it never failed to bring him relief'. Locals had been aware the existence of the spring, but, in spite of its 'red okery (ochrey) substance', had not tumbled to its medicinal qualities. Moreover, it would 'be often so choaked with mud, that it could not be discovered'. Storms and rain must have swept away the mud and made the spring clearly visible when Forbes chanced to take a drink.

The Firhill Well continued in its natural, unprepossessing state for some years, oozing up and creating a morass around itself. G & W Paterson in their Plan of Aberdeen of 1746 show the 'Bogg of Sunnyside' and that was probably it. Baillie Andrew Logie, plotted the well as 'Mineral Springs' on his Plan of the early 1750s, issuing from the Little Firhill, surrounded by a sizeable marsh. The usually accurate Captain Taylor in his Plan of 1773 identifies 'A Well' at the Little Firhill, as shown on page 11.

Dr Taylor, his namesake, tells us in his *Treatise* that the water filtered through a sloping sandy hill, just like the famous chalybeate well at Scarborough. He gives us some Firhill success stories. Mr John Dothwell who worked at the Battery (on the shore near Footdee), was 'afflicted with a strangury', a prostate complaint. He drank deep of the Firhill Spring and was cured. William Urquhart and Andrew Duncan 'both respectable farmers in Old Aberdeen', were respectively cured of the calculus and the strangury. William Cooper, confectioner in Old Aberdeen, 'a thin spare man with a dry cough', was cured of asthma; the mineral water strengthened his lungs. (Dr Taylor notes that confectioners, millers, hairdressers

31

and chemists, because of the nature of their work, were prone to asthma). Jean Harvey, aged eighteen, niece to Mr Cruickshank at the Red Lion Inn was cured of what sounds like conjunctivitis after she went 'of her own accord to the Firhill Well, and drank a chopin (half a pint) of the mineral water, at the same time bathing her eyes daily'. Another cure was successfully completed by a spinster afflicted with stomach pains for many years. Taylor has identified the cause of the lady's problem and makes the comment:

Intemperance in tea-drinking, and drinking it too hot and too sweet, accompanied by a sedentary life is the general cause of stomach complaints; all of which are removed by the tonic and strengthening powers of the mineral water.

Major and Mrs Mercer were resident at Sunnybank House from 1789, and given that both had poor health it seems probable that at some point they would have tested the iron-rich waters on their doorstep. Alas, they do not appear among the success stories of Dr Taylor's *Treatise*. But during their years at Sunnybank they would have been aware of environmental improvements in the vicinity of the springs. On 17 July 1798, the *Aberdeen Journal* reported:

It has long been known to invalids in the neighbourhood of the city that a chalybeate spring was situated at Fir-hill *(sic)* between New and Old Aberdeen. But the superior excellence of its waters was perhaps not fully discovered till a beautiful stone fountain, into which the springs have been carefully collected, has been recently erected on the site. A public subscription has not only produced an elegant fountain but excellent roads have been constructed leading to the place in all directions.

And Dr Taylor commented:

The water runs from a brass spout, into a stone bason, well secured from all extraneous matters, This work has been done, and well done it is, at the sole expence of a few public-spirited Gentlemen, whose voluntary contributions do them great honour.

Major Mercer may have been one of the 'public-spirited Gentlemen'. Another was almost certainly Hugh Leslie, Laird of Powis. His accounts show the following entry under 'Miscellaneous';

June 21, 1798: By Mr Jaffray, 3rd Subscription to Improvements... £14 14s 0d.

The name of the mason who constructed the elegant well-head has not been handed down, but George Jaffray, the Old Aberdeen wright who oversaw the building of Old Aberdeen Town House, Powis House and the Hermitage, is certainly a candidate.

The *Journal's* report that 'excellent roads have been constructed leading to the place in all directions' is perhaps an exaggeration. Sunnyside was already crossed by loanings, and Dr Taylor's comment 'a pleasant access (has been provided) to the well by repairing the roads' confirms one's suspicions that these paths were improved rather than replaced. But one new access to the well, the Firhill Road, was laid out at this time, replacing the more northerly reaches of the old west back road, the existing access to the spring. The journey began at the Spital, at the Red Lion Brae, now Firhill Place, and it led straight on to 'old' Sunnybank Road that had originally given access to Sunnyside Farm, and had served Sunnybank House since the late eighteenth century. This was the preferred route of the street directories of the 1850s:

Firhill Well: Spittal: half a mile west from Old Aberdeen. Approached by foot-road leading from beside Red Lion Inn, Spittal.

The Firhill Road proper began just short of the east entrance of the newly built Sunnybank House, turning sharply north. To the west was a newly constructed wall and fields, to the east, a hedgerow and beyond that, the humanist's glebe, the glebe of Humanity Manse, home of the Professor of Latin at King's College. (Humanity was the old name for Latin which was taught by the humanist. Humanity Manse is now numbered No 19 College Bounds). And so to the well itself of which Dr Taylor wrote:

The appearance of our well is somewhat romantic, environed with pleasure-grounds, a grove, an hermitage, and the lofty tower of King's College, highly ornamented with a stately imperial crown.

The Firhill Road continued on past the well, wound round the Firhill where the Hermitage was perched, and on to meet the 'Road to Oldtown' near the junction with what is now Meston Walk. For much of this northern part, the Powis Burn kept company with the little road. In her *Reminiscences of Old Aberdeen* , Mrs Katherine Trail, approaching the well from the 'Road to Oldtown' recalled the Powis Burn as 'comparatively broad and deep' and, 'coming out under the Powis wall with a rush that was almost a miniature waterfall'.

Even before Dr Taylor published his *Treatise*, the pilgrimage to the spring was so popular that the semi-circular stone benching on either side of the well-head had to be supplemented with wooden seats. Such was the reputation of the water's healing powers that its consumption was rationed by the superintendent, Andrew Angus, seeing to it that there was no jumping the queue. But not everyone came to drink the waters. It was a favourite rendezvous for young folk, and Sunday was the great day for the tryst. Indeed it was the only day, for until the mid-nineteenth century, the working day lasted from six in the morning till eight at night, with no half holiday on a Saturday.

The Firhill Well boasted the services of the famous, or perhaps infamous, Baubie Courage who from around 1815 to 1830 sold the gingerbread that gave the well its popular name. Folk would have pronounced it 'ginnerbreid' which got shortened to 'ginbried' and then to 'gibrie' or 'gibberie'. It was baked by Robert Murray of Castle Street and his speciality was the production of gingerbread in a variety of shapes. His Parliament cakes or parleys, were thin, small cakes with crimped edges and at two for a halfpenny were the most popular. There were superior cakes at a halfpenny or a penny each, as well as a luxury fourpenny cake for the gentry. According to William Smith writing in the *Bon Accord* of 29 January 1903, these were 'rich in colour, fragrant with spices of the Orient and ornamented with whigmaleerie designs and orange peel on the top'. They were wrapped 'in tissue paper, hermetically sealed with an outer covering of thicker paper'.

It was rumoured that Baubie kept something in her basket for those

The Gibberie Wallie in its heyday.

34

brave enough to mix spirits with potent taste of the water. It seems that she was granted a monopoly to sell her wares at the well, including, according to some reports, the spring water itself. That she fed sparrows on morsels of gingerbread reveals a kind heart, yet she was a martinet. Alexander Inkston McConnochie discussing the well in the *Book of Powis* (1906), writes:

> Dressed in white aprons and mutches, Baubie and her assistant, another old woman, were regarded as priestesses of the spring, and they made a profit accordingly, Baubie making it hot for any trade rival who dared to appear on the scene.

And so, in spite of the delightful surroundings and the well's healing powers, all was not sweetness. In his *Bon Accord* article William Smith mentions a Mrs Davidson who would have been contemporary with Baubie Courage, and shared her less desirable qualities, terrorising would-be rival vendors 'with a unique vocabulary, rich and rare in terms of abuse and delivered with great vehemence and rapidity'. She sounds too formidable to have been Baubie's assistant and the Little Firhill would not have been big enough to hold two such termagants. Courage may have been Baubie's maiden name, so she herself may have been Mrs Davidson. That lady clashed angrily with 'Old Prosody', the Reverend Patrick Forbes, that 'dour, sour, old deil', who had been called to the second charge at St Machar's in 1816. He strongly disapproved of Sabbath-breaking and threatened to remove her from the list of communicants if she continued selling gingerbread on an Sunday. Mrs Davidson, would have none of it. Sunday was the day when she sold by far the greatest quantities of gibberie.

'Old Prosody' himself worked an amazingly varied seven-day week. In addition to preaching at St Machar's of a Sunday and presumably tending on his flock through the week, he was appointed humanist at King's in 1817, and was required to lecture five days a week. That same year, he became lecturer in Chemistry and Natural History which involved lecturing six days a week. It was he who occupied Humanity Manse at the time, whose glebe marched with the Firhill Road, and whose grounds were separated from the well itself by a mere wall. The noise of young folk daffing about of a Sunday may have triggered off his feud with Mrs Davidson. There was vandalism too. On 4 June 1817, the *Aberdeen Journal* reported:

> During the night the Fir Hill Well was totally shut off. The ornamental building which was erected some years ago at considerable expense for giving access to a spring was thrown down and rendered a heap of ruins. Several persons must have been engaged in this piece of wanton outrage.

In time the well was repaired and looked as good as new. And so

35

closely had it become identified with the sale of gibberie that its original name was abandoned except in formal documents, and it became the 'Gibberie Wallie'. Even the stretch of the Powis Burn that ran so near the well acquired the name by association, for 'Gibberie' sounds more like a burn chattering as it flows along, than a piece of gingerbread.

Barbara Courage died on 18 November 1830, after fifteen years' service at the well, clearly a retirement job for she was by then aged eighty. She left £126 sterling in silver, a reasonable legacy for a 'gibberie wifie' of those days. Baubie was succeeded by other gibberie wifies for Katherine Trail, born in 1863, recalled that in her childhood the well:

> had quite lost its healing powers (but) it was popular with us on account of its quaintness and because of the 'Gibberie Wifie', and most delicious gingerbread cakes did she sell, as well as flat ginger biscuits called 'parlies'. I seem still to see the basket, covered with an immaculately white napkin which she carried over her arm, and which was full of the cakes so dear to children.

Dr Taylor in his *Treatise* of 1800 had described the Firhill Well as 'pleasantly situated at the foot of a round hill covered with firs' but the natural spring had vanished by Mrs Trail's time. The Little Firhill's sand had been removed for building purposes by the 1860s and the spring disturbed. The valuation rolls reveal that for some years in the later part of the century a sandpit at Sunnyside was worked by Alexander Anderson and that was probably the remains of the Little Firhill. This is borne out by the 1868 ordnance survey where no hill is marked at the site of the Firhill Well. Nor is there any sign of the house beside the well which is clearly marked on the anonymous 'Plan of the City of Aberdeen' of six years earlier, which was likely to have been the cottage of Firhill-well.

As the nineteenth century wore on, the Gibberie experienced many setbacks. In September 1878 it was reported to be in a poor state and the Water Committee decided to repair 'the old well in Old Aberdeen known as the Jibberie Well at a cost of £60'. By 1894, however, both the well and its approaches had become, according to the press, 'disgraceful'. That February, Councillor George Sinclair urged 'that a supply of water be introduced to the Firhill Well and the footpath leading from Sunnybank Road to Bedford Road (which had replaced the 'Road to Oldtown) be repaired'. The Water Committee 'did not see their way' to recommend any improvements, alarmed by the cost, another £60. They had gone on a site visit and afterwards commented rather peevishly that no one went to the well but local children who could get water in their own homes. Sinclair, a shipowner who lived at St Clair House in the King Street Road, had been the last provost of Old Aberdeen before the union with the city in 1891. He

An early photograph of the Gibberie Wallie showing the stonework in poor condition.
Courtesy, G R & M Winram.

persisted, and the Town Council on 16 April 1894 voted by sixteen votes to fourteen that the necessary improvements be carried out. Water was piped in from the River Dee and the well was reprieved - but not for long.

The years that followed saw the fields of Sunnyside going under concrete, and though the well-head and benching remained intact, the water supply was finally stopped. In 1910 Robert Anderson, writing in *Aberdeen in Byegone Days*, noted that:

dry and deserted (the Gibberie Wallie) still stands at the bend of a lane leading from what is now Sunnybank Road to what is now Bedford Road, for thus quickly is the town encroaching on what not so many years ago, was quite a rural spot.

The Sunnybank Road he refers to was the new one, laid out by 1906 and meeting Firhill Road beside Sunnybank Cottage, No 26 Sunnybank Road. The old route via the Red Lion Brae/Firhill Place and 'old' Sunnybank Road, though perfectly usable, was rendered superfluous. Mrs Jean Simpson, who played around the well in the 1920s recalls that it was always a popular spot for children. There were plots all around both on the humanist's glebe, and west of Firhill Road, near Sunnyside Farm. Mrs Nina Scott recalls the plotties and the little market held there regularly beside the well with vegetables as well as eggs and farm produce on sale.

Then there came great changes. After the First World War, it had been Aberdeen Town Council's policy to lay out playgrounds and sports fields in every ward of the city, wherever there was suitable ground. It was now the turn of St Machar Ward of which the Spital Lands was part. In December 1930, the Council announced plans to feu over three acres of land between Sunnyside Road and the Firhill Road from the City of Aberdeen Land Association. Here a sports ground would be laid out complete with bowling green, four bitulac tennis courts, an 18-hole putting course, a pavilion, and a children's playground, 'with swings, maypole etc,' and a shelter, at a cost of £4616. This announcement marked the end of a long search to acquire a suitable site in the Sunnyside-Froghall area. Ground adjacent to the Jute Works had been under consideration at one point, but the Aberdeen Jute Works Company would not play ball.

Thanks to the lie of the land, the development of the St Machar Sports Ground was not easy. The Council had to lay out, plant, maintain and 'retain as a feature', the slopping bank forming the south boundary of the sports ground for its whole length from Sunnyside Road to the Firhill Road. It would, however, remain Land Association property. Some of the neighbouring plotties would have to be absorbed and their tenants compensated.

Greenkeeper Stewart Matthew contemplates his immaculately kept greens. Note the slopping bank which the Council had to lay out, plant, maintain and 'retain as a feature' The rooftops of Sunnyside Terrace are glimpsed behind.

Having at last secured a site, the Council did not waste time. By January 1931, the convener of Links and Parks, Councillor James Hay and the superintendent of Public Parks, Mr W B Clark, were off 'to visit the Lancashire marshes to select suitable turf' for the bowling green.

The St Machar Sports Ground was formally opened on Saturday 27 June 1931, a day of blazing sunshine. In his speech, Councillor Hay said he hoped this would be something for the good of the people, physically and morally. When every industry was depressed a little recreation helped to keep people going. Mr George Robb, secretary of the Land Association was thanked for the help given. CALA had done 'everything in their power to promote the project'. With a large crowd looking on, Mrs Hay then threw the first jack and Miss Beaton, daughter of Councillor Beaton played the first ball, on the tennis court. Bowling at the St Machar green proved so popular that in December 1936, the Council feued a further two acres from CALA to create an extra green.

At this time the Land Association was in the throes of further develop-

The' 1994 Sunnyside Ladies' team throwing the first Jack of the season. Above, left the OMS building and right, the Primrose Centre in Sunnybank Road can be glimpsed. Their story is told in Chapter Four, courtesy, Sunnyside Ladies' Bowling Club.

ment in the Spital Lands and had permission to lay out a new road and a *cul-de-sac* between Sunnybank Road and Bedford Road. The new road would start beside No 26 Sunnybank Road, snake round the sports ground, incorporating a sizeable chunk of Firhill Road before exiting in Bedford Road. It looked as though the Gibberie Wallie would end up precariously in the middle of the carriageway. In the following month, the Council, aware of the well's popularity as an Aberdeen totem, wrote to CALA whose ownership of well-head and benching had come with their acquisition of the Spital Lands in 1900. It was suggested that they might allow the well 'to be removed from its present position' and re-erected within the St Machar Sports Ground 'in suitable and artistic surroundings'. The directors of CALA, showing that they too were no slouches when it came to local traditions, offered 'no objections to the proposals, providing the Town Council erect an appropriate tablet on the well, giving its historic connections'. The gentlemanly exchanges continued. On 1 February 1937, the Council recorded its thanks to the Land Association for allowing the well to be moved and also thanked the City Librarian, Mr G M Fraser who had been asked 'to fix the wording to be inscribed on the tablet to be erected on the well'. And so the Gibberie Wallie, well-head, semi-circular stone benching and small forecourt, was moved some forty-seven yards southwest, to the north side of the new bowling green, to surroundings arguably more sporting than artistic. The tablet was affixed. Fraser had written:

The Gibberie Wallie today, with the houses of Hermitage Avenue in the background.

Firhill Well.
The 'Gibberie' (Gingerbread) Well so called as persons sold gingerbread
there especially on Sundays.
Noted from 1721 for its curative qualities.
Removed by the Town Council from its original site 40 Yards to the north
east of this point for the making of a new street and rebuilt on its present site
1937.

In the years that followed the Gibberie Wallie, fell out of sight, out of mind. It was overgrown with bushes and its stonework started to deteriorate. Things improved when it was Category-B listed as a monument of architectural or historic interest, and in June 1990 it underwent a £1200 refurbishment, The stonework was repointed and cleaned and low-growing shrubs were planted around it. So here, at the immaculately kept St Machar Bowling Green, or the St Machar Outdoor Centre as the notice board says, the Gibberie Wallie, dry for the best part of a century now, and with not a gibberie wifie in sight, rests in peace - and features on our front cover. And the Firhill Road remains a popular walk for local folk and their dogs, even without its well.

But what of the new road which was responsible for the well's upheaval in the first place? It was never built. The war intervened and at its end, a different road pattern was implemented to which Sunnyside Farm fell victim. As our photograph below shows, the well need not have been moved at all.

The Firhill Road today looking towards Sunnybank Road with the original site of the Gibberie Wallie, right foreground and the St Machar Bowling Green behind. To the left is the old boundary wall of the former humanist's glebe.

41

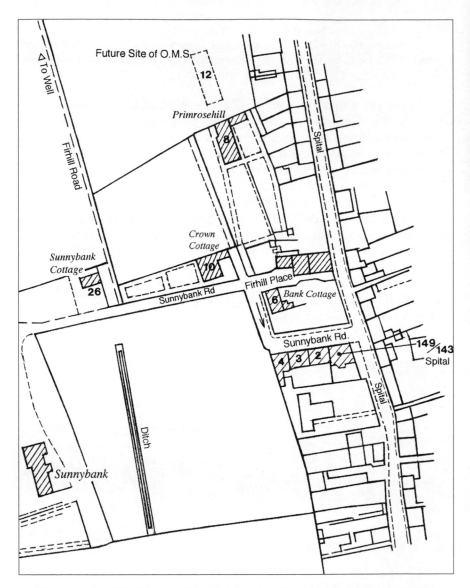

The Sunnybank Enclave: a guide to locations mentioned in Chapters 4 and 5. The numerals relate to house numbers. Firhill Place is the successor to the Red Lion Brae where the Inn was sited. OMS is now Liberty Occupational Health.

Chapter 4

The Sunnybank Enclave:
Firhill and Primrosehill

The Aulton folk were content to call slight eminences by the name of hill...Primrose Hill, Little Fir Hill, Fir Hill...

Alex Inkston McConnachie, Book of Powis, 1906.

Between the Spital and the old Sunnybank estate there was, and there remains, an interesting enclave. The earliest access to it was by the Red Lion Brae which took its name from the Red Lion Inn, the first of them, which sat near the junction with the Spital. The inn is named on the 'Plan of the City of Aberdeen' of 1862, but in 1773 Captain Taylor had already noted the inn and its neighbours on his Plan as a rectangular shape. Across the road, just north of the present Orchard Street, Taylor had also noted the Play House, whose history was traced in *The Spital*. The Red Lion would have served as an eighteenth century dress circle bar when this theatre was in session.

Between 1758 and 1773, the Aberdeen Philosophical Society, nicknamed the Wise Club, met at the Red Lion. The leading light among the founding members was Dr Thomas Reid, whom we met briefly in Chapter Two. Born in 1710 at Strachan near Banchory where his father was minister, Reid, a Marischal graduate, was elected Professor of Moral Philosophy at King's College in 1752. 'His lectures are extremely sensible and perspicacious,' commented a student, 'but his language is unmusical and his manner ungainly.' Such undergraduate strictures did not inhibit his career for in 1764 Reid was appointed to the Chair of Moral Philosophy at Glasgow University in succession to Adam Smith who later wrote *The Wealth of*

43

Nations and is credited with establishing the 'dismal science' (economics) as an acceptable course of study. Another founder member was George Campbell, Principal of Marischal College, who insisted on the use of the hard 'C' in Latin, and was consequently known as 'Prinkipal Campbell', hence the origin of 'the Prink', the nickname for the head of Aberdeen University that is still in use. Another early member was Dr David Skene, a noted physician whose great passion was botany and who corresponded with the pioneering Swedish botanist, Linnaeus. Thomas Reid's cousin, Professor John Gregory, one of that amazing medical and scientific family was another leading member of the Society. He held the Chair of Medicine at King's from 1755 until 1766 when he became Professor of the Practice of Medicine at Edinburgh. John Gregory's death in 1773 was lamented by James Beattie in the closing verse of *The Minstrel,*:

> *Art thou, my Gregory, for ever fled?*
> *And am I left to unavailing woe?*

Beattie himself was made a member on becoming Professor of Moral Philosophy at Marischal in 1760. His daybook of 23 February 1773, the Society's final year, notes:

Yearly contribution to Philos. Society......................... £1.

The Club met on the second and the fourth Wednesday of every month at five in the afternoon, and the serious business came first. The eighteenth century was a time of religious and philosophical controversy in Scotland sparked off by David Hume, the Edinburgh agnostic, whose *Treatise of Human Nature* of 1739 and *Philosophical Essays* of 1748, challenged accepted Christian beliefs. The Wise Club entered the fray, responding to Hume's arguments in a series of essays, famous in their day, which first saw the light at the Red Lion. These essays, which members took it in turn to present, would be chewed over, analysed, amended, and polished by the Club prior to publication. 'Prink' Campbell struck an early blow with his *Dissertation on Miracles* in 1763 (the great debate proceeded at a leisurely place), responding to Hume's attack on the existence of miracles. Reid followed by denouncing Hume's philosophy in his *Inquiry into the Human Mind upon the Principles of Common Sense* of 1764 with which Hume himself was much impressed. He and Reid entered into a courteous correspondence. John Gregory, doctor and botanist contributed too, with several philosophical works, such as *A Comparative View of the Faculties of Man*.

Most renowned of all the contributions to the debate was Beattie's *Essay on Truth* which we would nowadays regard as long and boring, but in 1770 was an instant bestseller going into twenty editions by the end of the

Sir Joshua Reynold's allegorical portrait of Professor Beattie, 1775.
Courtesy, Aberdeen University.

century. Of all contemporary writings it was regarded as having most vigorously taken up the cudgels on behalf of basic Christian beliefs and reinstated them as the orthodox principles of philosophy. Reid's 'Common Sense' philosophy is studied to this day, but among contemporaries it was Beattie rather than Reid who was hailed as the greatest philosopher of the age. But if Beattie is remembered at all nowadays, outwith academic circles, it is as the subject of the famous allegorical portrait by Sir Joshua Reynolds, shown above, in which Beattie as 'Truth', primly holds his *Essay* to the fore while a formidable winged lady representing 'Justice' looms from behind, dinging doon a clutch of hobgoblins, caricatures of the philosophers Hume and Voltaire, with the one hand while tilting her scales heavily in Beattie's favour with the other. *Sic transit gloria.* Nevertheless, in his day Beattie was the great star of learned London society while his colleagues were head-hunted by the Universities of Edinburgh and Glasgow. Aberdeen in the eighteenth century was far from being the remote and parochial backwoods that some might have assumed, and the Philosophical Society was responsible for Aberdeen's formidable contribution to the movement later known as the Scottish Enlightenment. But it was not all learned debate at the Red

Lion. At half past eight, after some three hours serious discussion, the philosophers adjourned for supper, pipes were smoked, and there was after-dinner chat until ten o'clock.

We know the names of some of the tavern's later landlords, Thomas McFarlane and James Ross who was succeeded by his wife, or possibly his widow Margery Ross for the 1861 census returns name her as innkeeper. She had a son and daughter of ten and twelve. About this time the Red Lion Inn flitted to the east side of the Spital near St Peter's Gate, where it appears on the 1868 ordnance survey, a little to the south of its present site. The rectangular shape on the Red Lion Brae has now separated into three distinct dwellings and the Red Lion has probably reverted back to being the house that it once was. In 1810 the *Aberdeen Journal* had advertised 'that house in the Spital called the Red Lion to be let as a tavern'. The map of 1868 names the most westerly of the three buildings as Firhill Cottage. It sometimes called Firhillwell Cottage, and should not be confused with the cottage at the Firhill Well. Both cottages appear on the 1851 census, the latter occupied by William Adam, market gardener, while Andrew Knox, a retired labourer and his nephew, a joiner, were at Firhill Cottage. Ten years on, a salmon fisher, Alexander Rae was in residence at Firhill Cottage and would remain there until well into the twentieth century. This area of the Red Lion Brae was now more formally known as the Firhill-well Lane or the Firhill Lane. In 1840 Alexander Scott was to be found in Firhill Lane, Spittal, and in 1849, Thomas Chambers, feuar, was in Firhillwell Lane. Title deeds indicate this as being virtually one and the same place.

By 1869, this area 'Firhillwell Cottage and others' was rouped to Daniel Macandrew, the versatile head of the Loch Street building firm that bore his name. During this period he was working on a wide range of contracts in the area including joinery work at the Militia Barracks, the pioneering concrete buildings in Jute Street, King's College Library, and the tenements at Hillhead Terrace, and at Boa Vista Place for George Troup, the iron moulder who had made his pile in Brazil. In 1870 his acquisition of the Firhill Lane subjects was confirmed by a feu charter granted by Henry Knight Erskine of Pittodrie 'with the consent of his wife Mary Anne Moir'. Firhill(well)Lane now became the more upmarket-sounding Firhill Place. In 1875-76 for example, we have Captain William Colville at 2 Firhill Place, Spital, and in 1879-80, John Buchan, Merchant, 1 Firhill Place. Macandrew had three tenants at Firhill Cottage and by the mid-1880s the houses of Firhill Place had four tenants each, solid artisans, stonecutters, mechanics, combmakers and masons.

The Firhill Place houses continued to be multi-tenanted well into the twentieth century. There were five in the group. By 1925, No 159 the Spital, the gable-end that fronts on to the Spital, sharing the same building as No

Firhill Place looking west. Its steepness reflects its ancestry as the Red Lion Brae.

1 Firhill Place, was a grocer's, then a baker's shop. No 1 Firhill Place had six tenants, No 2 had four. There was also a No 2a, while No 3, the original Firhill Cottage, had only two tenants including Alexander Rae, salmon fisher who was still there. In *The Spital*, Harold Bishop recalled some of the tenants of later years, the Bowers, the Wrights and the Breslins. One Firhill resident, Mr William Webster, lost his life during the air raid of 12 July 1940, when so much damage was done to Hall Russells shipyard. In the post-war era, the Firhill houses, by then in poor condition, were acquired from Daniel Macandrew's trustees by Aberdeen University and attractively restored as Nos 1 and 2 Firhill Place along with No 159 Spital,

Firhill children enjoy an outing in the early 1930s, courtesy Mrs Jean Simpson.

though Firhill Cottage did not survive. In 1979, Aberdeen Civic Society awarded the University a commendation for the quality of the restoration.

At the top of Firhill Place we will turn right and enter the long garden that leads to a most interesting cottage. Here, in 1853, Alexander Watkins, linen manufacturer, who until that time had been living 'over the shop' in the manager's house at the Broadford Works, started to carve out an attractive property that would provide plenty of fresh country air for his wife and three young sons, one of whom had 'Holland' as his middle name in honour of the owners of Broadford. At a cost of £100 Watkins bought three pieces of ground which came as one package from an Aberdeen merchant, Alexander Mennie. At the north end his new domain reached as far as 'Professor Gordon's glebe, belonging to King's College' - the humanist's glebe; at the south, down to 'a lane leading from the highway to Sunnyside' - Firhill Lane - and to the neighbouring Red Lion Tavern and Hall, though he was forbidden to erect any buildings within twelve feet of the back wall of the Red Lion without the consent of the proprietor. On the east Watkins' land was bounded by the Spital, on the west by a part of the Lands of Sunnyside.

Within this extensive area he laid out his own patch, a sizeable rectangle perched high above the last houses of the Spital. At the north end Watkins built, not the grand house as one might have assumed, but a substantial, west-facing cottage, its door and windows stylishly embellished with consoled cornices, and a long garden running down towards the Red Lion and Firhill Place. West of the garden, a leafy drive led to the house, while on the Spital side was a greenhouse and kitchen garden. Watkins called his new property Primrosehill. The 1861 census reveals a household that has grown to seven children, with housemaid and nursemaid. His sixteen-year-old son was now 'a clerk at Linen factory', presumably Broadford, while his fifteen year-old was a university student.

Watkins later bought Andrew Sutherland's woollen mill at the top of Canal Road where Stephen Goodbrand, whom we met in *The Spital*, was the long-serving cashier and manager. (Whilst still employed by Watkins & Co, Goodbrand found time to establish his own factory, the Mounthooly Ropeworks on the site of the old leper colony). Then something drastic happened, which, by 1866 caused Watkins to make his Primrosehill property over to James & George Collie, Advocates, probably as security against a loan. Watkins may have overreached himself, and we do know that the woollen mill subsequently failed. The loan if such it was, could never have been repaid, for Primrosehill was subsequently acquired by the North of Scotland Banking Company and rouped in its original three sections in 1869. It was at this time that Daniel Macandrew acquired the Firhillwell

Primrosehill.

property which was Lot 2, while Primrosehill itself, Lot 1, was successfully bid for by George Rezin, a master tailor from Huntly who employed four men and two boys, so his business must have been a sizeable one.

The Rezins had a lodger, Margaret Primrose, 61, unmarried, and a fundholder. The name, age and means of livelihood tie in perfectly with that Miss Primrose, whose mother had founded Primrose School in the Spital and who had paid for the building of a new school on the same site in 1863. Miss Primrose was peripatetic in her later years, staying at a variety of lodgings, and perhaps was attracted to Primrosehill because of its nearness to 'her' school - and its name. She would now be Miss Primrose of Primrosehill - or Primrose Cottage, as it was sometimes called. The 1891 census shows George Rezin at Primrosehill, still tailoring away. His wife, Jane, daughters Elizabeth and Frances, are there, and two sons have gone into the family business. George was a tailor's cutter and Augustus, a tailor's shopman. His third, Edwin, was still at school. Miss Primrose was long gone, and six years later would die at her Holburn Street lodgings.

The remaining lot of Watkins' property 'that Dwelling House numbered Ninety-three Spittal' went for £224, successfully bid for by John Henderson, 'pensioner residing at the King Street Barracks'. No 93 was the tall house that sits back from the road, subsequently No 89, and now No 177, all part of the fun of Spital house numbering. (It was flatted in 1953).

Henderson is subsequently styled as 'sculptor and granite polisher', conjuring up an alarming picture of an elderly man forced to take up a physically demanding job after retirement. But Henderson, who signs his name with a flowing hand, must have been an ex-soldier with an army pension. It is interesting that he and his wife and children were able to lodge at the recently built Barracks until they found a home of their own. Primrosehill and Henderson's house shared a mutual wall which ran south to the back of the Red Lion Tavern and Hall and was the cause of an ongoing feud between the neighbours. In 1876, Henderson without seeking Rezin's permission, built a drying loft whose 'roof and rhones' rested on the wall. Rezin complained, Henderson admitted fault, and agreed to remove the loft if Rezin so requested. Twenty years on, the loft was in a bad way and Rezin told Alexander McAllan, Henderson' successor, to remove it. Peace broke out again when McAllan agreed to carry out repairs. That is not the last we will hear of the wall.

The Rezins remained at Primrosehill till the end of the century, when they were succeeded by the city's gas engineer, 'the indefatigable Alex Smith', as Dr John S Reid called him in his excellent work *Mechanical Aberdeen*, though by this time Smith was nearing retirement. Born in 1837, he served an engineering apprenticeship at William McKinnon & Co, the Spring Garden ironfounders, and later become foreman there. He was employed by the city's gas works in the days when it was still privately run, and in 1871 transferred with it to Aberdeen Corporation where he remained for thirty- two years. He not only supervised the building of the municipal generating station at the Cotton Street gasworks between 1892 and 1894, but was responsible at the same time for the famous Gallowhills gasholder which overlooked Pittodrie Stadium for a century. Smith was 'a thorough master of all the details of

The man who built the Gallowhills gasholder. Alex Smith, Aberdeen's gas engineer from 1871-1903.

gas-making', his obituarist recorded, 'too engrossed in his work as manager of a large and growing concern as Aberdeen Gas Works proved to be', to be involved in public life. He did find time to teach drawing at the Aberdeen Mechanics' Institute of which he was a director, and to have a family of six sons and a daughter. The careers of his sons were a blend of high tech and tradition; two were gas engineers, two were electrical engineers, one in

Durban, one was a chartered accountant and one, William McQueen Smith, was a solicitor who remained with his mother at Primrosehill after his father's death in 1905.

By 1907 Alex Smith's trustees had sold Primrosehill to the Committee of Management of Aberdeen Home for Widowers' Children. The Committee was formed from a group of local people much concerned about the welfare of those children who had lost their mothers, and whose fathers were out at work all day and struggling to bring up their young families decently. They recognised 'the need to provide a helping hand' and in 1903 had opened their first home at Berrybank House, Belmont Road, once the home of the famous Scottish Episcopalian bishop, John Skinner. But now applications for admission outstripped accommodation and Primrosehill, purchased for £800, offered ten rooms, a spacious garden and room to expand. Twenty-seven boys and girls made the move from Berrybank, and by 1919 there were thirty-six in residence.

The rules governing admission were strict in the early days: Every applicant, (ie the widower), 'must be respectable, hardworking and anxious to provide for his children to his utmost ability', as one would expect, but if he defaulted on weekly maintenance payments, his child would be returned to him, or sent to the new Poorhouse at Oldmill (Woodend). Were he to die, his child had to quit the home, for the remit was for the care of widowers' children, not orphans. Fortunately these rules were relaxed after the First World War. The children attended Sunnybank School, though occasionally a boy won a bursary to Robert Gordon's College.

A substantial granite extension to the north was built in 1928 the year before the death of Lord Provost Sir James Taggart, chairman of the Committee of Management from the beginning in 1904 and a great friend of Primrosehill over the years. He was one of a number of philanthropic citizens who provided treats for the children. These included visits to pantomimes at His Majesty's Theatre for the Donald family were also great benefactors of the Home. Summers until 1925 were spent at Linn Moor Home as part of the Aberdeen Children's Fresh Air Fortnight, and later the children boarded in the halls at Kirkton of Skene, Keig and Durris, travelling by charabanc with the bedding and luggage going by lorry.

By 1931 Primrosehill was home to forty-one children. Older residents of the area will tell you that the Widowers' Children were not so well dressed as the smart Sunnybank Foundationers down the road - the fathers had to provide clothes - and sometimes the regime was hard. All this changed when Taylors took over in 1949. Mrs Elizabeth Weston, née Hutton, who lived in Froghall Road as a girl, recalls: 'The Taylors came from Keith where we used to stay with them for holidays during the war. Mr Taylor had worked for the railways and Mrs Taylor had been a children's nurse. The widowers' children could not have been in better hands when Nanny Taylor took over'.

Mrs Taylor retired in 1961, and was succeeded as matron by Mrs Hilda Robb, who gave up her nursing post at Cornhill to take over at Primrosehill. Here she created a happy home for all the children and her own family. Her

Mrs Robb, left and Mrs Taylor in 1961. Courtesy, Mrs Hilda Robb.

husband, James, suffering from back trouble, was only too happy to give up his job in the building trade, and though he originally came as caretaker, in no time at all became house father to a family of eighteen.

Hilda Robb's photo albums are crammed with pictures of the children playing in the spacious garden, setting out for Sunday School in their Sunday best and of James with 'his' boys, immaculate in their Boys' Brigade uniforms. There are snaps of everyone having fun at Halloween and Christmas parties, round a table piled high with delicious food where everything was home baked. Joining in the festivities and thoroughly enjoying themselves, (though not all at once) are James R Donald of HMT fame, the solicitor J Scott MacLachlan, (there is a splendid snap of 'Scotty' cycling round the grounds), and Professor Philip Love, successive chairmen from 1962 until 1993; of Stephen Henderson, treasurer from 1957 until 1993; of Lord Provost Norman Hogg and his wife Elizabeth, both of whom had Spital connections. It was during Norman Hogg's provostship in 1965 that a Primrosehill girl, Patsy Whyte, switched on the city's Christmas lights clad in a splendid Red Riding Hood outfit. Many others gave of their time, among them the Reverend John Birkbeck, minister of John Knox, Gerard Street at that time. He was much impressed with the warmth and homeliness of Primrosehill compared with the large orphanage in Capetown where his own childhood was spent.

The committee were first class, recalls Mrs Robb. They let her get on with running the place without interference, but were always there when needed. She consequently had the freedom and the authority to make her own decisions. 'I was never in a hurry to put out a child who had reached the age for going it alone.' She did not like to see families being split up, and would put up an extra bed if need be. Primrosehill children were allowed

The Reverend John Birkbeck and Mrs Robb with the Primrosehill children.
Courtesy Mrs M Birkbeck.

to bring school friends to play in the garden. One lad who was left hanging around the streets with a bag of crisps when his parents went out drinking would be taken to the Home for his tea by his Primrosehill friends. Visiting children from other, more institutional Homes were reluctant to return. Others returned to their parents by social workers would run back to the Home. These situations could prove embarrassing but Hilda Robb, with tact and diplomacy, handled it all.

During these years, there were many improvements in layout, furnishing and equipment, with donations coming from a from a wide range of organisations. That infamous mutual wall, such a trial to the tailor George Rezin, continued to cause problems, and a section of it collapsed in September 1963, taking the Home's rabbit hutch with it. Mrs Robb's album has memorable photographs of the children sitting amidst the ruins, tending their rabbits, all of which survived.

As the sixties and seventies wore on, ideas about the care of children were changing. By the end of 1977, with child care authorities opting for fostering in private homes, there were five vacant places, and that marked the beginning of the end for Primrosehill as a Home for Widowers' Children. In February 1982, with only five children left, it was decided that the Home should close. Provision was made for the remaining children and at the beginning of 1983 Mr and Mrs Robb retired after twenty-one devoted years. Sadly Mr Robb died the following year and a bearer party of 'his' boys carried the coffin from the church. Today, Mrs Robb's home is full of mementoes from the children. Many still visit or keep in touch, including one girl now married and living in Oklahoma. Many have done well and several boys have distinguished themselves in the Services - they would often board at Primrosehill during leave - though unfortunately one serviceman was killed by an IRA sniper in Belfast in 1973. One of Mrs Robb's former charges became a Royal Navy champion boxer, another, a Royal Navy diver.

The Primrosehill committee felt that the premises, now consisting of twelve rooms, a garden and play area, should continue to benefit children, particularly in view of the fact that there were many families in the surrounding area of Froghall, including one-parent families, who needed help and support. The cottage was leased as a Family Centre to St Katherine's Centre, which had recently lost its own day nursery. Initially Primrosehill Centre, as it became, was managed by a committee with representatives from Primrosehill, St Katherine's and the Aberlour Child Care Trust. (Aberlour had closed its famous orphanage in the 1960s and now the Trust ran homes for small groups throughout Scotland). Alterations including an extension in 1985 made the cottage more suitable for its new role. By 1986 Primrosehill and St Katherine's had withdrawn from the management committee and responsibility for running the Family Centre rested with Aberlour. 'Having seen the Family Centre running so successfully, it seemed sensible that the Primrosehill Association should consider handing over the house to Aberlour Child Care Trust. In 1991 the House was duly conveyed along with a gift of £20,000 to fund activities at Primrosehill during the first year.' So wrote Stephen Henderson in his excellent account, *The Story of Primrosehill*. The balance of Primrosehill's investments was then realised, and the magnificent sum of £57,393 was distributed mostly to locally based children's charities.

The Primrosehill Centre continues to give good vibrations. The main staircase retains its original Victorian banister and wrought iron balustrades while the former public rooms remain intact and still have their handsome mouldings, one decorated with scallops, the other in vignette style with trailing flowers. One is a meeting place for parents, the other for project leaders. Jackie Kerr, appointed project leader in spring 1997, straightway began to develop plans for adult and parenting groups as well as adult educational courses. Work with the children continues. Although Froghall is no longer the designated catchment area and the Centre is casting its net wider, the majority of children still come from that locality, fifty-two all told, from thirty-two families. There are three activity-based pre-school groups and an after-school club where various themes are explored. Play schemes operate throughout summer. The spacious grounds

around Primrosehill are a great boon, for there are no gardens to speak of in the Froghall flats, apart from a small strip at the front and mothers worry about syringes and needles left lying about that locality. And so growing vegetables has proved popular at Primrosehill, not to mention the creation of a wild life garden where an environmentalist has been on hand to give advice.

A number of Asian children, particularly Bangladeshi, whose fathers are post-graduate students at Aberdeen University, attend. There is multi-cultural programme and the children integrate readily. 'It's about making life better,' says Jackie Kerr, who originally trained as a social worker.

Jackie Kerr, project leader at Primrosehill.

The nursery group at Primrosehill, 1997 with project worker Morag Nicol. The upper windows of No 177 Spital are visible to the right.

55

Primrosehill is No 8 Sunnybank Road, and just to the north is No 12. (The fate of No 10 is revealed in the next chapter). No 12 sits in the old humanist's glebe and is perhaps not what one would expect to find in Sunnybank Road. A modern building, it began life as Aberdeen University's custom-built Computer Unit and later became the headquarters of Offshore Medical Services. Since health and saftey services are now provided on a worldwide basis the establishment was simply known by its initials. The Director, Dr Graeme D Nicol, explains that OMS a joint venture between Shell, Esso and BP, started off in premises in Ashgrove Road West, outgrew them, and in 1982 moved to Sunnybank Road. The former computer building was converted to provide company headquarters as well as facilities for medical screening. In the late 1980s, ownership passed to University of Aberdeen by means of a gift of the equity held by the three oil companies. In 1996 the University sold OMS to Liberty Manual, the largest workers' compensation insurer in the United States, and the centre was renamed Liberty Occupational Health.

The story of OMS, which in the 1990s began operating in Siberia and Georgia, has been one of initiative and growth. When the company first established itself at Sunnybank Road it had seventeen employees, purely devoted to the provision of emergency medical and screening services to the North Sea oil industry. It now has over 120 employees and provides a specialist range of services both to the oil and gas industry as well as other sections of industry and commerce. Courses on offer include First Aid at Work, Specific Hazards and Offshore Medic Courses while the Travel Clinic offers health advice and vaccinations. It undertakes statutory fitness assessments for offshore and onshore employment and offers around-the-clock emergency services to meet any foreseeable offshore emergency including diving medical emergency support. And speaking of divers, Allan Stuart, Primrosehill's Royal Navy diver, made a point of popping in to visit the Home en route to get his check-up at OMS. A small world.

Liberty Occupational Health headquarters today, perched in the old humanist's glebe.

Chapter 5

More About the Sunnybank Enclave

'The Dungers was a tip and a favourite playground of local children...'

In 1871 a mysterious address appears in the census returns. Hope Terrace, Spital, apparently situated close to Primrosehill, is the home of Andrew Marshall from Edinburgh. It must have been newly built at this time. It does not appear on the 1868 ordnance survey, and according to the 1869-70 street directory, Andrew Marshall, a brewer, (of T M & Co) was living at No 5 Powis Place. T M & Co was Thomson Marshall & Co, Brewers to the Queen and successors to Smith Irvine & Co at the Old Aberdeen Brewery which sat north of King's College. The 1871 census also notes that Andrew Marshall had a lodger at Hope Terrace, William Martin, Professor of Moral Philosophy at King's from 1846, and of the united University from 1860 until 1876. 'It is difficult to do justice to Professor Martin', wrote W Robertson Nicoll, journalist, author and minister:

> What his claims to be a professor of philosophy were I have not the least idea. His only publications I can trace are two tiny pamphlets...The professor must have been fairly old by 1870, but it would have been hard to tell his age. He had a long brown beard, only slightly whitened and a wig. His wig was no specious production of art. Everybody could see what it was.

Martin's class was filled with noisy students who indulged in frantic and prolonged applause which he never considered to be other than a genuine response. 'One student in the class had an extraordinary gift of whistling in such a manner that nobody could detect the culprit,' said

Robertson Nicoll. And at one point, Andrew Marshall had to take firm measures with his eccentric paying guest. Robertson Nicoll explains:

Out of the goodness of his heart, Dr Martin held a Bible Class on Sunday evenings. It used to be conducted at his lodgings, but the scenes became so violent, that it was transferred to a room in the Music Hall.

Marshall had little need to take in lodgers. He and his partner Andrew Thomson were doing so well for themselves that Thomson was able to acquire a fine house in Banchory, Tor-na-Coille, long since converted into a hotel, while Marshall left Hope Terrace for the west end and was settled at Mile End House by 1883. Hope Terrace then vanishes as mysteriously from the records as it had appeared - or does it? Mr George Gordon has come across an item in the *Aberdeen Journal* of 16 December 1882:

The large double cottage, Hope Terrace, Primrosehill, Old Aberdeen, belonging to Mr A Marshall has been sold at a reduced price of £700 to Mr Adam Pratt of the Crown Clothing Co.

We learn from the advertisement that the mysterious Terrace was a house rather than a street, and confirms that it was sited at Primrosehill. But where exactly was it? Mr Gordon comes to the rescue again. He noted that by 1883 Hope Terrace had disappeared from the street directory, but that Adam Pratt who had just bought it, was living at Crown Cottage. It seems obvious that Pratt had changed the name, a nice piece of advertising for his clothing company. Crown Cottage features on the 1901 ordnance survey, and at last we can tell where it, (and Hope Terrace) were located- opposite the west end of Firhill Place. Its long garden stretched along 'old' Sunnybank Road as far as the start of the Firhill Road.

'I remember Adam Pratt and his shop very well,' recalls George Gordon. 'It sold seamen's clothing and the sort of clothes that Millet's sell. Crown Clothing was on the east side of south Market Street at No 101, at the corner of Jamieson's Quay. It's difficult to realise that until fairly recent times, there were a number of shops and businesses there - several coal merchants such as James Gordon and Archibald McKenzie and fish houses, like John Hector and Ben Allenby, with Gorrod, Davie, Kemp and Walker wedged on the centre.'

Crown Cottage, Spital, alias Hope Terrace, Primrosehill, later became No 10 Sunnybank Road and the Pratt family were associated with it for the rest of its existence. But over the years the house also had a number of tenants, including, early in the century, John F Neave, a once well known name in Aberdeen hairdressing circles. George Gordon recalls Robert Robb an insurance agent who was there from the early 1930s until the early 1950s.

Homes for the elderly on the former site of Crown Cottage, with Bank Cottage, No 6 Sunnybank Road in the distance. This photograph indicates the steepness of Sunnybank Road here.

'His wife ran the shop at the corner of Orchard Walk and College Bounds and was probably the last shopkeeper there. Another tenant was my old friend, Willie Oliver, a noted sea swimmer and Dee to Don record holder, who saw in Hogmanay in the sea, down at the Beach.' Dennis Scott who used to deliver mail there recalls it as a fine, granite-built two-storey building, sitting on a slope with an attractive garden. Two charming elderly ladies, probably Adam Pratt's granddaughters, always had a present for him at Christmas. Charles Rettie, whose family were long resident in the area remembers the house with its stained glass fanlight above the door, the lovely garden, and Miss Pratt, who lived there until the late 1960s. Crown Cottage was taken down around 1970 and replaced on the site by a cluster of homes for the elderly, Nos 14-24 Sunnybank Road whose little front gardens change colour with the seasons. The old wall of Crown Cottage remains.

Nearby, Sunnybank Cottage, No 26 Sunnybank Road had become the home of Mrs Falconer, who kept hens there. Some time before the old people's homes on the Crown Cottage site were built, No 26 had been threatened with demolition to make way for a new road (yet again), this time planned by Grampian Region. Aberdeen District Council, the owners of No 26, refused to sell. It was felt that this road would be too close to the vulnerable elderly folk who would soon be in residence nearby. While the

This boundary wall is all that remains of Crown Cottage. The wall sloping off to the right indicates the line of the Firhill Road with the council-built houses of Sunnybank Road behind.

contretemps continued, Sunnybank Cottage became derelict. Fortunately, the threat of the road passed and the cottage was renovated.

Until the 1890s, the stretch southwards of Crown Cottage and Firhill

Sunnybank Cottage, No 26 Sunnybank Road, after restoration. The start of Firhill Road is extreme right.

Place was something of a desert. A huge ditch ran below the east end of Sunnybank House, and beyond, a vast gravel pit stretched down to the Spital. Its raw materials were much in demand for building purposes and a little path allowed barrows to be wheeled in and filled up. By 1892, however, a new cottage was being constructed across the way from Crown Cottage, backing on to Firhill Place and neatly missing the gravel pit. The land had been feued to a monumental mason, William Macdonald, by Daniel Macandrew. This was part of the Firhill land rouped to Macandrew back in 1869, and as an architect and builder he had firm ideas about the kind of development he wanted. The house had to be of stone and lime, covered in slate, and at least £200 in value. Moreover, 'the said house shall be built so that the front thereof shall face Sunnybank Road.' This sounds a trifle curious, but 'old' Sunnybank Road had at this time been extended, forming a Z of sorts, turning south at Firhill Place for some yards, then turning east to form a junction with the Spital, where, in a few year's time, it would find itself facing across to Orchard Street. Macandrew intended that the new house should face the middle section of the extended Sunnybank Road.

William Macdonald's house, Bank Cottage, he called it, with its pedimented-porch, and semi-circular fanlight sits there, neat, crisp and double-fronted. It has something of the look of a rural station master's cottage, yet as befits a house built by a mason, the stonework with its

Bank Cottage, No 6 Sunnybank Road, with Elizabeth Wilson at the door. The front garden is both inside and outside the boundary dyke. Courtesy, C&E WIlson.

The back garden of Bank Cottage, showing the dormers of Firhill Place behind.
Courtesy, C&E Wilson.

distinctive use of sandstone, its sneck-coursed granite, and its mullions of red Corennie, set it apart. Bank Cottage became No 6 Sunnybank Road, and later residents included Captain G Forbes, Charles Rettie's great-grandfather who was a shipmaster, Miss Marion Welsh, and Mr and Mrs Cox, of the well known Froghall boxing family. Colin and Elizabeth Wilson bought it from the Coxes in 1981. Colin is a gardener and Elizabeth a scientist and they have done much to reinstate the cottage, restoring the original pine where possible, renewing it where necessary. They replaced the parlour with a spacious double bedroom and created a small bedroom and a sitting-room leading to the kitchen beyond where Colin grows cucumbers and melons, transforming the ceiling into a leafy raft. They added a custom-built conservatory-cum-dining room which offers a green vista of the garden beyond. What had once been the backyard, a bit of a dump looking across to Firhill Place, is now a cottage garden with a hint of the exotic, and they have planted a front garden both inside and outside the boundary dyke.

Gravel pit or no, building at the Spital end of the Sunnybank enclave began in the 1880s with the erection of handsome tenements at Nos 147-151 Spital, put up by Mr James Gammie, a builder, over a part of the pit. A little terrace now attached itself, turning into the new section of Sunnybank Road. It took the shape of two similar tenements, Nos 2-3 Sunnybank Road, in granite rubble and more modest than their corner neighbour. No 2 was owned and in all probability built by George Stott, the granite merchant who lived in King's Crescent and had his yard across at Merkland Road East. For No 3, a pleasant russet granite was used. George Hutchison, the proprietor, lived there with three tenants, a custom's officer, a seaman and a stonecutter.

By 1892, plans for another house for the little terrace, this time for

No 4 Sunnybank Road, formerly Deer Cottage, with No 3 to the left.

Arthur Hunter, a New Deer mason and builder, were passed by the Town Council. It joined itself on to No 3. Hunter, I suspect, attempted to make Deer Cottage, as he called his new home, doubtless in fond memory of New Deer, a show piece for his building and granite cutting skills. Like Crown Cottage it was not a cottage at all but a grandly built pocket tenement in rough cast granite, a riot of string courses, tympana, skewputs, corbie stepping and ball finials. Arthur Hunter had two respectable-sounding tenants, George Kelman, boot manufacturer and John L Williams, clerk.

The name Deer Cottage has long been forgotten and these days it is simply No 4 Sunnybank Road. George Gordon recalls that at his old partner in the Shore Porters' Society, William Ross, lived there from 1929 until his death in 1967. 'Amiable, irrepressible, Willie Ross was undoubtedly one of the great personalities of the Society in recent times,' he writes. 'Of farming stock, he sallied forth to the Castlehill Barracks in 1915 at the tender age of fifteen, determined on joining the Gordon Highlanders only to be met by a wary recruiting sergeant, who suspecting that he was under age, turned him away. His wife, Jessie, was a member of the gifted Irvine family, and a contemporary of Leslie Mitchell (Lewis Grassic Gibbon) at Arbuthnott School.' Mrs Dorothy Dempster and her family were also long time residents at No 4. The little terrace ends here for immediately to the west was the termination of the path that came up through the Froghall Plotties, giving access to Sunnybank. This right of way, originating in the Spital's ancient west back road, was not built across. By 1906, as already noted, the new Sunnybank Road had been laid out through the policies of Sunnybank House to link up with this relatively new section of road which was widened out in front of the little terrace as we see it today.

Between the little terrace at No 4 and Sunnybank School there lay open ground, a part of it stretching back and overlooking Froghall. This area, long known as the Dungers, was a tip, and a favourite playground of local children. Here they could find a chalky, clay-like substance which was used for marking out beddies. This substance had already been used in the granite yards as a cutting aid. The clay was laid in a thick strip on top of the block about to be cut, and shot was added as an abrasive. The saw was then pulled back and forth, grinding away, cutting the block in two. After use, the clay was dumped at the Dungers to the delight of local bairns.

This area, became, roughly speaking, No 19 Sunnybank Road, and was occupied by a haulage contractor, John C Fiddes. It was a base for J. Leith & Sons Contractors, and for Nu Style Products (Aberdeen), asbestos cement specialists. It then served as the depot of the Aberdeen Grocers' Buying Group and the subsequent use of heavy goods vehicles to make deliveries caused problems for the neighbours. Mrs Dempster at No 4, the Wilsons at No 6 Sunnybank Road and other local residents were worried that the ensuing vibrations were causing structural damage to their houses. At time of writing, the grocers have gone, the gates of the depot are closed, all is quiet, and the Wilsons hope that this area may now go over to housing.

A little nearer Sunnybank School, another industrial development went ahead. Joseph Shirras, the well known Aberdeen builder had started up in Cattofield in the late nineteenth century, moving his yard to Froghall

The warehouses at No 19 Sunnybank Road, the old site of the Dungers with Sunnybank School, top left.

The 'neat row of bungalows' Nos 21-39 Sunnybank Road. Sunnybank School is hidden by the trees.

before the First World War. By the 1930s he had flitted up the hill to Sunnybank Road. The firm remained there until the mid-1970s, when it was taken over by Chap Construction Ltd who continue to use these premises. This industrial aspect of Sunnybank Road is largely out of sight, hidden by a neat row of bungalows which went up before the last war, Nos 21-39 Sunnybank Road, between the School and the little terrace.

Meanwhile, 'old' Sunnybank Road linking Firhill Place and the east entrance of Sunnybank House was rendered redundant when that entrance was swept away by the creation of the 'new' Sunnybank Road. In time it too vanished. Some of the 'Crown Cottage' homes for the elderly are now built over it. The Firhill Road, cut off from its old access, is still easily attainable from 'new' Sunnybank Road, and survives as a rural lane amidst the flats and bungalows of Sunnybank and Sunnyside. Firhill Place, once the Red Lion Brae, still takes you from the old site of Hope Terrace and Crown Cottage, now the site of the old people's homes, down to the Spital. It is a pleasant walkway, with an air of privacy, its ancient steepness long ago tempered by steps.

Chapter 6

The Urbanisation of Sunnyside

Though the scenic beauties of Sunnyside have been sadly marred of recent years by the operations of excavators and builders, who touch nothing in nature that they do not disfigure, the district is still passingly picturesque.

J F George, The Book of Powis, 1906.

Quite early in the nineteenth century Sunnybank House had a neighbour. In June 1813, Robert Davidson, a Gallowgate soap manufacturer and uncle of the Robert Davidson of Canal Road who discovered electrical traction, took possession of 'part of Sunyside', the feu charter granted by Alexander Moir, sixth laird of the Spital. According to the first post office directory of 1824, Davidson's house, Elmfield, lay 'half a mile above Mounthooly, east side of Canal', within easy strolling distance of Sunnybank. Elmfield House overlooked the old Inverurie highway and Split-the-Wind, recently created when the new Inverurie turnpike forked to form George Street and Causewayend. It was L-shaped and a little larger than Sunnybank, and though the policies were less extensive, they were still spacious. While Sunnybank was a plain house of an earlier generation, Elmfield was elegant. The carriage drive led through wooded grounds to a semi-circular terrace at the front of the house where a portico, also semi-circular and supported by pillars, provided a handsome entrance. The façade was flanked by two gables, set forward, and a substantial north-east wing commanded fine views of ornamental gardens, lawns and woodlands. In this part of the grounds there were three conservatories, small - a hexagonal summerhouse - medium, and large, the latter over 40ft long, with a pavilion attached. At the rear, steps led down to a rectangular enclosure running the

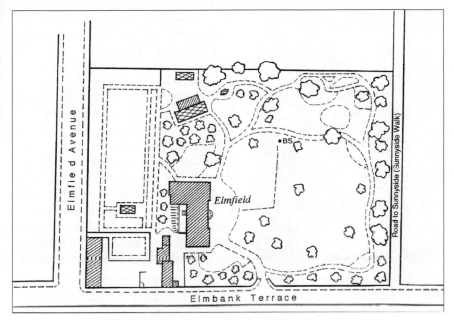

Plan of Elmfield House adapted from the 1901 ordanance survey.

breadth of the house where kitchen garden, stables, coachhouse and greenhouses were located. Elmfield was surrounded by trees, elms no doubt among them, and while the house itself had the distinction of being out of town the northern part of the garden was not. The city boundary ran through it, marked by March Stone ABD 58, a nineteenth century interloper which sat amidst trees north-east of the house. The Road to Sunnyside, or at least the part of it that is now Sunnyside Walk, defined Elmfield's eastern boundary. Just beyond lay Sunnypark where James Cocker began his career as a nurseryman, and the Lands of Froghall.

By the 1840s, the proprietor was a Footdee merchant, David Copland. He was succeeded by Thomas Hogarth whose name appears in the first valuation roll of 1855-56. He too was a merchant, a member of a family that had fingers in many commercial pies. The census returns of 1861 find him in residence there, with wife, daughter and six servants. He had gone upmarket by this time, describing himself as 'landed proprietor'.

After Hogarth's death, the house, now technically the property of his heirs, was tenanted by his son-in law, Captain, later Major Henry A Crane, who had earlier been resident at Willowbank House. As a young officer, Crane had served with the 72nd Regiment of Foot, the Duke of Albany's Own Highlanders, but by the time he moved into Elmfield, he was Adjutant of the First Aberdeenshire Rifle Volunteers, later the First Volunteer Battal-

Major Henry Crane, courtesy, the Gordon Highlanders' Museum.

ion the Gordon Highlanders. (Rifle Volunteers were more socially orientated than the Militia). According to the 1871 census the Crane ménage consisted of the thirty-one-year-old adjutant, his wife, the former Elizabeth Hogarth, their two daughters, his mother-in-law, his sister, the lodger, William Butler, and the six servants - they must have come with the house. Mrs Crane's interests were well protected by her marriage contract and decisions regarding the property were not taken by her husband as was normal at that time, but by the trustees of that contract. No matter, the Major cut a stylish figure in his gig, and as late as the 1980s, folk then in their nineties could recall the family driving to church with coachman and footman. Frederick Evans was the groom at the Elmfield House stables for many years and would have been responsible for the smart turnout. When it came to modern warfare, the Major was not such a hot shot. Lachlan Mackinnon who enlisted as a private in 1871 and ultimately commanded the Volunteer Battalion recalls that :

The Adjutant, Major Crane, appointed under the old regulation for an indefinite time, retained office until 1890. The practice of renewed periods of command was a bad one. Commanding officers without modern training or knowledge continued to peg away at close-order drill long after magazine rifles, machine-guns, and improved artillery had made close-order movements under fire so deadly dear that they were ultimately ruled out altogether.

The third grand residence of the Spital Lands was Elmbank, a short distance to the north of Elmfield and 'near Kittybrewster toll bar', to quote the street directory. It makes it first appearance in the directory of 1854-55, with James Henderson, builder and architect in residence. The first valuation roll of 1855-56 confirms him as owner and given his qualifications, it seems likely that he would have built Elmbank himself, though he had to borrow to do so. An extract from the Index of the Register of Sasines reveals that in 1857 James Henderson, Architect, raised a loan of £700, offering as security 'one and a half acres of ground with the Dwelling House and other buildings thereon...'

Elmbank House. Note the giant stone inverted 'fork' on the south-west gable
Courtesy, Alastair Colbeck.

Though Henderson had given up his studies at Marischal College in 1826 after his father's death, he was running a successful builder's business at No 120 Loch Street by the 1830s and studying architecture at the Mechanics' Institute at night. Elmbank itself was a tall, sprawling yet elegant lodge in granite rubble, a riotous assembly of gables, bays, steep pitched roofs, a gabled porch with fish scale tiles, half-dropped dormers, overhanging eaves, some fancy iron work on the roof, some dressed granite here, a dash of sandstone there, giving the impression that he used what materials came most readily to hand. While Sunnybank and Elmfield had carriage drives which led to the front of the house in the usual way, the approach to Elmbank was via the west-facing servants' quarters. Mr Ken Robertson, who bought a flat here in 1983, puts forward the interesting theory that in order to impress guests driving up to the house, the servants' façade was designed almost as grandly as the frontage, its central portion flanked by gabled bays, the lower windows embellished by dressed granite surrounds, the flue enlivened by a giant inverted fork.

Unlike Elmfield which was quite close to the Inverurie highway, Elmbank sat well back, behind a great expanse of lawn, encircled by a tree-lined drive. Two gates, flanked by stone piers guarded the property, one at the north end, one at the south. Opposite the latter, the drive linked with a little bridge which straddled the Kittybrewster-Waterloo Quay railway

69

Ken Robertson outside his flat at Elmbank. The windows of the former servants' quarters have dressed granite surrounds.

The railway bridge opposite Erskine Street. Its original purpose was to provide access to Elmbank House and Elmfield House years before Erskine Street and Bedford Road were laid out. This explains why there are now two railway bridges close together.

line as it still does, though is no longer unique to Elmbank. Behind the house, and banked up at a higher level were stabling, an octagonal kitchen garden and a conservatory. Elmbank's next door neighbour to the north was Sunnyside Nursery which was not connected with Sunnyside Farm, and like the neighbouring hamlet of Peterstown had become part of the Powis estate at the end of the eighteenth century.

James Henderson owned Elmbank for about eight years, but did not live there very long. By 1860, and now designated purely as architect, he concentrated his business at Belmont Street where he had his office for many years. Daniel Macandrew, none other, took over his Loch Street yard. Elmbank was tenanted by Henry Cooper, wincey manufacturer, his wife Sophia, his three charmingly christened daughters, Charlotte, Sophia and Amelia, and two servants. Cooper, then forty-two, was a businessman of some consequence employing 300 weavers at his wincey or lindsey woolsey factory in Exchange Street. He also had a silk mercer's, linen and woollen drapery business at No 47 Union Street where he kept on twelve salesmen. For several years the Coopers had been as peripatetic as Miss Primrose, staying at addresses in the better parts of town. True to form, in a year or two, the roving family left Elmbank, and eventually moved to a new home of their own, Homewood, 'a dwelling-house on the Countesswells Road', now the Palm Court Hotel. The original building is very reminiscent of Elmbank, its gables and roofs facing all the points of the compass.

James Henderson continued to do fine architectural, and even some civil engineering work, designing church buildings for the Free Kirk, buying nursery land at Westfield, laying out Westfield Terrace there in 1874, developing feuing plans for Pitmuxton - the Allan Street, Pitstruan Place area - and laying out the approach roads to the Duthie Park on its being gifted to the city in 1883. He and his brother, Baillie William Henderson, who served on Aberdeen Town Council between 1849-57, founded the firm of builders' merchants, J & W Henderson Ltd, well known in the city for many years.

He never returned to Elmbank. By 1862 he had sold it to the Kemnay-born William Mitchell who at thirty-six had already been Postmaster of Aberdeen for ten years, and would remain so for another thirty. At Elmbank his five children must have enjoyed playing in the gardens and woodlands, where there were indeed elms. Soon after the Mitchells took up residence, the description of Elmbank underwent a change in status in the street directory, from 'house' to 'mansion'. But no one was going to challenge that, the directory, was, after all, published by the Post Office. Mitchell, an eident public servant, had started as a lad on the lowest rung of the ladder. During his era, the Post Office nationally and locally enjoyed a remarkable period of growth and by the time he retired in 1891 his workforce had grown from seven to 400.

The last laird of the Spital Lands was Henry William Knight Erskine of Pittodrie and Spital who inherited through his mother, Mary Anne Moir, wife of Colonel Henry Knight Erskine, commanding officer of the Royal Aberdeenshire Highlanders and one of the moving spirits behind the building of the King Street Militia Barracks. Their marriage would unite the Moir estate of Spital and the Knight Erskine estate of Pittodrie near Chapel of Garioch. Mary Anne succeeded to the Spital Lands on the decease of her cousin, Dame Isabella Bruce in 1867, and when the Colonel died only three years later, Henry William became responsible for running the estates on his mother's behalf. Some sixteen years younger than her husband, she survived him by twenty-six years.

In the mid-1870s, Henry William embarked on an extensive pro-gramme of feuing out the Spital Lands. He was well aware of Aberdeen's burgeoning population, and the urbanisation of the northern area of the town that had been going on for seventy years and more. The need for new homes was now given fresh impetus by the GNSR's increasing presence at Kittybrewster. Given that feu duty was a substantial form of income in those pre-inflationary days, it was not surprising that Knight Erskine opted to cover the green fields of Sunnyside with streets. But the housing that he had in mind was of a different order from what was available in the Mounthooly area, for example, where the factory or mill owner had provided only basic tenement accommodation for his workers. Certainly there would be tenement houses, though of a superior sort, for skilled artisans, but much of his development would be similar to what was on offer in the west end of Aberdeen; houses for foremen and middle management. A popular style was the two-flatted granite villa favoured by the builder Joseph Shirras, each flat with its own entrance.

A different system of urban development operated in those days. Knight Erskine and his architects would propose to the relevant Town Council Committee the laying out of new streets on his lands. Approval was usually granted, though Knight Erskine's roads at widths of 40ft to 45ft were frowned on by the Streets and Works Committee, and nearly always upped to 50ft. The provision of services, such as water and sewerage, was the responsibility of the Police Commissioners, and later of the Town, but often the developer was called on to share and in some cases to bear the full burden of costs. Builders, stonemasons and joiners - often in a small way of business - would then (it was hoped) feu two or three building stances in one of the new streets and submit plans for the houses they intended to build, often one for themselves. Though a row of houses would be built by a number of different firms and individuals, the feu charter ensured they were of a like standard. It is this system which has given Aberdeen's older streets character, variety and an overall feeling of harmony.

A start was made in the early 1870s with the development of the present Elmbank Terrace and Erskine Street. The former, the old Inverurie highway, was transformed from a country lane to a city street, though still a narrow one, making its first appearance in the street directory in 1875-76 as Elmbank Terrace 'near Kittybrewster station, east of the railway line' taking its name, of course, from Elmbank House. The first stretch, between Erskine Street and the future Elmfield Avenue, was feued to two building concerns, Mowlen & Co and Messrs Bisset & Son and the fruits of their labours presently appeared in the shape of a terrace of large houses. The first house, which stood alone for a time was occupied by James Marsden, Mowlem's manager. By 1880 there were seven more with the builder James H Bisset, replacing the Mowlem man at No 1, and a member of his staff at No 8. James Hay Bisset now headed the firm his father Peter had founded. It had carried out numerous major building contracts over the years, including Gilcomston Free (now South) in Union Street, several North East harbours, the laying out of the Duthie Park, and the construction of Aberdeen Jute Works. Indeed Bisset built No 5 Elmbank Terrace for the Jute Company and here they installed their manager, William Aberdein. In these early days the terrace was popular with granite merchants, but there was a drawback.

Elmbank Terrace. These houses were the original Nos 1, 2, 2 $\frac{1}{2}$ and 3. The tenemental block, left, was built in the 'front garden' of Elmbank.

Though Kittybrewster was already within the city boundary, thanks to the Aberdeen Municipality Extension Act of 1871, Elmbank Terrace was fractionally beyond the pale. Water and a sewerage system were being installed in the vicinity, but Elmbank residents initially had to pay to be linked up. By 1883 all was well. The Spital Lands became part of Aberdeen under the Extension and Improvement Act of that year.

The little farm of Elmfield, not to be confused with the Big Hoose, was swept away by the building of the Terrace, gone by 1889 when the architect George Coutts designed No 13 for the grocer and china merchant, David Anderson, decorating the facade with 'patera' or little rosettes. (There is a house similarly embellished in Fountainhall Road, another Coutts' stamping ground). Perhaps not to be outdone, James Bisset called in his architect John Rust Jnr the following year to carry out alterations and additions. In view of Bisset's considerable involvement in concrete work, was it he who at this time ornamented the gables of Nos 1, 2 and 2½ with corbie stepping and ball finials? He already owned the estates of Burnside, Rosehill and part of Ruthrieston, so why not a castle in town as well?

No 2 was the manse of the Congregational minister, John Duncan of the Ragged Kirk in Bool Road and later of the handsome Trinity Congregational Church in the Shiprow, now part of the Maritime

No 40 Elmbank Terrace designed by George Coutts. Note the 'patera' or rosettes between ground and first floors.

Museum. A brilliant exponent of the Doric, he was voted the most popular preacher in Aberdeen by *Evening Express* readers in 1898. His neighbour at No 3, was the Reverend James A Russell of Causewayend Church. These roomy houses long remained popular choices as manses - and as surgeries. Body and soul were well catered for in Elmbank Terrace. Nos 2 and 3 became No 50 and No 49 respectively when Elmbank Terrace was renumbered in 1903 from the Froghall end. No 49 was later the manse of a well-remembered minister, the Reverend T Maxwell McAuslane, of John Knox's, Mounthooly. Dr Douglas Dugan had his surgery at No 45 for many years, with Mr F G Mundie the dentist next door at No 46. Mr W G Mitchell the chemist lived at No 40, (formerly No 19, the George Coutts' house), but his shop was down in George Street. No 48 was the home of the baker Mr R B Jessamine who owned Bendelow's famous pie shop in Causewayend. Garth Jessamine has recalled 'its very large garden in which rumbustious boys' games were actively discouraged on a Sunday'. That was when family and friends gathered round the pedal organ to sing hymns after the evening meals. 'I can still recall my surprise at the number of people who would gather outside in the street to listen to the choral renditions from within.'

Erskine Street, 'from Elmbank Terrace eastwards' was also up and running by 1875. Taking a leaf out of the book of the Leslies of Powis who christened the roads on their lands either Leslie or Powis as often as the Town Council would permit, Knight Erskine named his first road in honour of his family. Erskine Street, though it did not initially continue very far, would offer a variety of houses. Among its earliest residents was the station master at Kittybrewster, William Morrison. By 1879 a third road was underway, replacing the Road to Oldtown further north, much of which had been swept away to accommodate expansion at the Kittybrewster railyard. The hamlet of Peterstown and Elmbank's neighbour, Sunnyside Nursery, both acquired by the GNSR back in 1866 largely vanished to make

Cottages and villas in Erskine Street.

way for the railway extensions and for a bridge, which would carry the new road over the railway to join with Powis Terrace. This new street was named Erskine Road, again in honour of the Knight Erskine family, and it made its way into the street directory of 1881, as running 'from Powis Terrace to Hermitage', which still crowned the Firhill. The Road to Oldtown may have been little more than a country lane - Mrs Trail found it 'exceedingly dark and narrow' - but the new road would accommodate both the industrial and the residential. Elmbank House, its policies still intact, now found itself sandwiched between Erskine Road and Erskine Street.

The GNSR served the cattle-rich North East, and given that its principal goods yard was based at Kittybrewster, it was logical that the auction marts, then still in their pioneering days, should locate in the area. First to go up, on the north side of Erskine Road, were the auction mart and cattle pens 'erections of the Great North of Scotland Railway' as they were described in the Valuation Rolls, tenanted by Reith and Anderson, auctioneers. There would be no further building on this side of the street for years, for beyond the cattle pens lay the approach road with its great arch, leading to Powis House and Estate. Further on, and sharing the same alignment as the new street, a small part of the Road to Oldtown had survived, curving eastwards towards Old Aberdeen winding round the Firhill as of old, and known at this point as College Lane. This stretch had earlier been called College Wynd and in the eighteenth century, 'the Common Wynd called the Doctor's Wynd that leads to the Broomhill', an early name for the Firhill. When Erskine Road was laid out, this little stretch now acquired a separate identity as College Road, described in the directory as running 'from High Street to Hermitage'.

Erskine Road did not last long. In October 1884 the Streets Committee of the Town Council stated that having had their attention drawn:

> to the names Erskine Street and Erskine Road in the same locality, resolved to recommend that for the purpose of preventing confusion the name Erskine Road be changed to Bedford Road.

In the years to come, Knight Erskine would continue to chose street names for his Spital Lands that were bewilderingly similar. Unfortunately the confusion thus caused was never again drawn to the attention of the Town Council!

By 1885 the south side of Bedford Road had seven 'fine tenement houses' as Mrs Trail called them, running east from the Elmbank stables. Nos 1-3 were owned by William Morrison, cashier. Was he any relation to the Kittybrewster station master? Probably. The back garden of William Morrison's house in Erskine Street exited onto Bedford Road just at this spot. The majority of tenants were porters, engine drivers, mechanics and

Original tenements in Bedford Road. It began life as Erskine Road.

Members of the GNRS workforce pictured at Kittybrewster in the 1920s with one of the Company's buses. The Bedford Road tenements across the street were popular as railwaymens' homes. Mr Alexander Milton, extreme left, lived at No 58. Courtesy, Dennis Scott.

railway servants, handily placed for their work across the road. Nos 4-5 were owned by George Stephen shipmaster, No 6 by Robert Smith of South Africa and No 7 by Mary Hepburn, a cork merchant with a business in the Upperkirkgate. By the end of the century, this side of Bedford Road was built up almost as far as it is today, and now incorporated little College Road. As a result, Bedford Road was described as running 'from Powis Terrace to High Street', thus emulating its predecessor, the Road to Oldtown, in linking Kittybrewster with Old Aberdeen. Hermitage Cottage near the Firhill found, no doubt to its surprise, that it had become No 151 Bedford Road.

In 1882, the Spital Lands of 139 acres was put up for sale. There was a little matter of £42,000 which had been raised using the estate as security, and Henry William and his mother would now have the opportunity to discharge the bonds over the property. Alas there were no takers. This was the first of a number of abortive attempts to sell. In 1883 an impressive 'Particulars of Sale' was prepared by Knight Erskine's Aberdeen lawyers, Marquis, Hall & Mill and the London auctioneers, Lumley's for a sale due to take place in the capital that June. It is a very upbeat document. The Spital estate according to the schedule, is 'a very valuable property ...forming a Large Part of the City of Aberdeen (which it did in those days), bounded and intersected by King Street Road, Spital Road, Erskine (Bedford) Road, Elmbank Terrace and other well known Business and Residential Thoroughfares served by Tramways and Omnibuses' ...High lying blocks of property command fine views of Old Aberdeen and the Sea, 'and 'the estate adjoins Kittybrewster Station where there is an immediate and pressing demand for building plots in those roads being marked out. Frontages are rapidly secured at a high rate of feuing'. The Spital Lands' yearly income was £2,016 16s 1½d of which £749 5s 4d was in feu duties 'secured on Hundreds of Houses and Business premises including the Residences of Elmfield, Elmbank and Sunnybank'.

At this time, with many roads still in an embryonic state, the bulk of feu duties came from the houses on the Spital Road, but given the 'prosperous state and natural growth of the City of Aberdeen' the authors of the schedule estimated that 'the growth in feu duties could rise to £4865' - more than double the current Spital Lands' income from a number of different sources. There was no sale that year in London. In 1884 the lawyer Norval Clyne acting on behalf of an anonymous client was told, 'the price now asked for the estate of Spital is £57,000. The Proprietor does not intend to sell it in lots. We may mention that the former price asked was £71,000.' Again, no sale.

So Henry William Knight Erskine continued to feu out his Spital Lands himself, at a leisurely pace. During 1884 his architect, J Russell Mackenzie,

Holmwood, No 7 Elmfield Avenue, home of Robert Mitchell. The name was on the fanlight and painted on the top left hand corner of the facade as well.

sought approval for a new street 'running eastward from Elmbank Terrace along the north boundary of the property of Elmfield for 113 yards or thereby' It was named Elmfield Avenue. It was wide and had style. Holmwood, No 1 Elmfield Avenue, (soon renumbered No 5-7), was in a class of its own, a handsome, well-proportioned two-flatted house with much excellent detail including mullions of dressed granite, an engaged arch of pink granite around the front door, and a monogram within the gablet of the centre first floor window amidst whose florid granite lettering an M can be discerned. Robert Mitchell, the first occupant, was a builder to trade. The other early resident, a sea captain, was soon succeeded by Charles McDonald, stonecutter, sculptor and one of the great Froghall granite masters. On the same side of the road was a terrace of two flatted houses of three storeys, the upper flat being originally on two floors. They had separate entrances and most of the bay windows carried up through all three floors. Mitchell had his builder's yard in the lane, Elmfield Place, which in those days marked the end of the Avenue. It was perhaps he who was responsible for the little row of buildings behind Elmfield Avenue, Nos 1, 2 and 3 (his own yard) Elmfield Place, and Nos 33-35 and Nos 37-39 Bedford Place which at that time were in open country.

In January 1888 J Russell Mackenzie again successfully presented plans for 'a new street running from Bedford Road to Sunnybank' - Bedford Place

The lane leading to Nos 33-39 Bedford Place.

- while Elmfield Avenue and Erskine Street were to be extended to meet it. Robert Mitchell must have been in his element, erecting houses along the extended line of Elmfield Avenue, even moving to one of them himself, No 34, directly opposite his works in Elmfield Place. Again he had a granite merchant as neighbour, this time Archibald A Brown who had recently set up his St Nicholas Granite works in Advocates Road.

Building also cracked ahead in Erskine Street with combinations of architects, carpenters, builders, stonemasons and plumbers, putting up different yet compatible types of houses. In the early years of the twentieth century, William Dove Paterson, Elocutionist and Cinematographer, lived at one of these new houses, No 38, which he christened Crichton Cottage. He had started out as a concert promoter, and as an enthusiastic film-maker himself, was among the first to bring the movies to Aberdeen. He presented the popular Cinematograph Carnivals at the Music Hall, opened Aberdeen's first permanent cinema, the Gaiety in the Shiprow, and later showed films at the Coliseum in Belmont Street, (the former Trades Hall, and future Media Centre), as well as at his little seasonal Beach Bijou. A stalwart of the temperance movement and a keep fit enthusiast, Dove Paterson, was if anything, even more peripatetic than Miss Primrose and Henry Cooper. After leaving Erskine Street his subsequent homes in Leslie Road and Powis Terrace (two of them) were all rechristened with the 'Crichton' cachet.

Knight Erskine's architect, Russell Mackenzie, had suffered financial problems for some years, and set off for South Africa where he died in 1889. A new team was employed, Messrs Smith & Kelly. William Smith, the architect of Balmoral Castle was the son and successor of John Smith, a creator of the Granite City, while William Kelly was then at the outset of a distinguished career. Unfortunately, through no fault of these distinguished architects, Knight Erskine's neat grid of streets now began to look ragged at least at the south-eastern side.

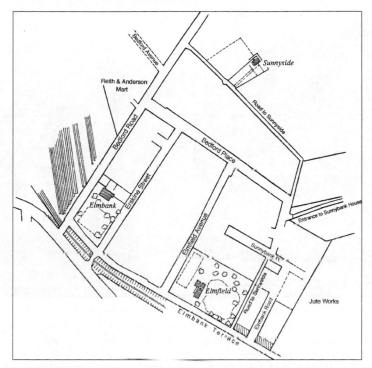

The Lands of Sunnyside go under concrete. The grid system of roads in 1899. Sunnyside Road has not yet been laid out, and is still the Road to Sunnyside, while Elmbank Road and Sunnybank Place are incomplete. Tenements built hard against Sunnyside Walk (the lower end of the Road to Sunnyside) prevented its widening as part of the Sunnyside Road development.

Erskine Street and Elmfield Avenue, running at right angles from Elmbank Terrace had marked a progression of the grid towards Froghall. Logically, it should have been completed by expansion of the narrow old Road to Sunnyside into a modern road, running along the boundary of Elmfield House and beyond to form a junction with Bedford Place. (The Plan above comes in handy here). But by 1893 two blocks of tenements had appeared in Elmbank Terrace, near the Froghall end, the first building of which was hard against the old Road to Sunnyside, ruling out a widening of its line. Smith & Kelly's plans of 1896 for three new streets, tried to make the best of the situation. The first, Elmbank Road, was to begin between these two new blocks of tenements and to run eastwards to meet the second new street, Sunnybank Place. This was to be a street of two halves, starting as a cul-de-sac behind the gardens of Elmfield Avenue and running as far as the boundary wall of the Jute Works, on whose parks Izzy Mason's cows later grazed.

In time Elmbank Road developed as a street of solid tenements, with

Causeyton House, No 20 Elmbank Road, left. No 16, right, was the birthplace of the composer Ronald Center. The houses are similar to those on Bedford Road but the string courses and larger windows create a more expansive facade.

consoled cornices over the doors, and gablets like those in Bedford Road adding welcome detail to the top storey. But even by 1900 it was still far from complete. The house on the west corner, No 19, proudly bearing the date 1898, stood in splendid isolation in open country until its opposite number, No 20, Causeyton House, eventually appeared. Mrs Harper for whom the house was built was born at Causeyton of Clunie. She entered from the front, her tenants from Sunnybank Plcae. No 18 was named Linstead, while No 16 next door was the birthplace in 1913 of the composer Ronald Center. The youngest of six children and a pupil at Robert Gordon's College, Center, with his father's encouragement, studied music locally under William Swainson and Julian Rosetti. In 1943 he moved to Huntly to teach part-time, but later devoted himself to composing. Geoffrey Atkinson, director of music at Queen's Cross Church, has described Center's music as:

Compelling and often uncompromising, but while of its time, not difficult to listen to. It is well constructed, has clear textures, exciting rhythms, bold harmonies and sometimes a disarming melodic sweetness.

There was some recognition at first. Lord Provost Sir Tommy Mitchell ensured that Warwick Braithwaite, conductor of the Scottish Symphony Orchestra, (later the Scottish National Orchestra), knew about Center and

Ronald Center.

his work, and as a result, his symphonic poem, *The Coming of Cuchullin* was performed in Glasgow in 1944. During the 1951 season, Walter Susskind included Center's *Divertimento for Strings* in the SNO's repertoire. But after that, interest seemed to slip away. Securing performances of his work became an uphill struggle and Center was anything but a self-publicist. He died in 1973. 'In the end he lost heart,' said his wife, Evelyn, a great champion of his music. In 1986, an LP which included his piano sonata, his cantata *Dona Nobis Pacem*, and three carols was produced, with generous funding from Aberdeen District Council. A plaque now marks his birthplace.

But we are running ahead of ourselves. Sunnybank Place, contemporary with Elmbank Road, was going well, and by the early twentieth century neat granite flats had gone up in the cul-de-sac section where back gardens on the south-west side of the street carried as far as the rear wall of Elmfield House. When Muriel and Alex Slessor first went to live there, an elderly neighbour would tell them how Major Crane used to come round regularly in his gig on tours of inspection. No building stances had as yet been taken up in the lower part of Sunnybank Place and the ground was laid out as bleaching greens.

Smith & Kelly's third street, running between Sunnybank Place and Bedford Place was intended to absorb a portion of the old Road to Sunnyside, north of the taboo section between Elmbank Terrace and Sunnybank Place. This was the beginning of the Sunnyside Road we know today. The old Road was a burgh road and its absorption within Knight Erskine's scheme had to be negotiated with the Town, not, perhaps too onerous a task, given that William Smith as well as being in private practice, was the city architect. That third street - just a short stretch - passed the west boundary of Sunnybank House and the dispute between Knight Erskine and Mrs Shand Smith of Sunnybank relating to levels, noted in Chapter Two, soon halted work. Amended plans were called for. Before long, however, it became known that the Council was minded to purchase the Sunnybank estate at some time, so the Knight Erskine team held fire and changed tack. In December 1898 they proposed yet another new road, in fact the upgrading of the upper section of the old Road to Sunnyside which passed the outbuildings of Sunnyside Farm, then turned south to meet Bedford Place. So far so good. Then two months later the Council approved a reworked plan by the Knight Erskine team for the Sunnybank Place-to-Bedford Place leg. Knight Erskine's new Sunnyside Road, its two sections meeting together at Bedford Place, had a similar alignment to the old Road to Sunnyside that it replaced, but problems continued. In 1903, the burgh surveyor, William Dyack, complained that the levels were too low. Joseph Shirras was contracted to carry out 5695 cubic yards of banking the following year, and a fair amount of man hours were expended in demolishing the old houses that still clung to the old Road, whose ghost was lingering on. To this day Sunnyside Road retains the quirky shape, imposed long ago by the difficulties of the terrain and the need to provide access *en route*, first to Sunnyside Farm and later to Sunnybank House as well.

In May 1899 the purchase of the Sunnybank estate was finalised and the Council subsequently engineered Sunnybank Road through the middle of it, linking Sunnyside Road at Bedford Place with the Spital. It was a broad avenue, and fine trees were planted on either side. The following year, the lower, untouched section of the Road to Sunnyside was officially named Sunnyside Walk. It gives us an idea of how narrow the old Road had been.

The great avenue of Sunnybank Road stretching towards the Spital, photographed from Bedford Place. Sunnyside Road runs between the two.

It was in 1900 too that the Spital Lands were acquired by the City of Aberdeen Land Association, set up in 1874 on the initiative of a former provost, the powerful and ubiquitous Sir Alexander Anderson, for the purpose of acquiring and developing land on what was then the city's outskirts. In 1895 the surveyors Walker & Duncan who acted for the Knight Erskines had valued the estate, more modestly than their predecessors, at £43,720. This sort of figure clearly appealed to the Land Association for whom Walker & Duncan also acted. Henry William Knight Erskine, his estate sold at last, retreated to the Junior Carlton Club in London's Pall Mall and remained there until his death.

The Houses of Sunnybank, Elmbank and Elmfield were still there in 1900, but in changed circumstances. Elmbank, after William Mitchell's death that year, became the Elmbank House Temperance Hotel, No 21 Erskine Street, later No 15. The great lawn and tree-lined drive went over to housing. The section fronting onto Elmbank Terrace was filled with lofty tenements and numbered Nos 55-63. Nos 3-13 Erskine Street and Nos 4-8 Bedford Road occupied the rest of the Elmbank 'front garden' and the direct link with Elmbank Terrace was lost. The Crane household was still in residence at Elmfield which emerged from the renumbering of 1903 as No 32 Elmbank Terrace. This underlined the fact that the old house was just part of a row, as it had been for the past quarter of a century. This was not the Major's style. By 1904 the family had beaten a retreat to Inverdon House at the Bridge of Don and Elmfield was demolished to provide ever more land for housing.

Though Elmfield had gone, and Elmbank had gone down market, J F George, writing in *The Book of Powis* in 1906, was still able to say:

Though the scenic beauties of Sunnyside have been sadly marred of recent years by the operations of excavators and builders, who touch nothing in nature that they do not disfigure, the district is still passingly picturesque. The trees have not been cut down, nor the whole of the once wide-spreading meadow and corn lands covered with monotonous architectural similitudes in grey stone and narrow arid strips of bleaching-green. The old-world air has not been 'improved' away nor will it so long as the farm 'toon' of Sunnyside and the quaint eighteenth century mansion-house of Sunnybank remain.

Chapter 7

Modern Times

A very valuable property, forming a Large Part of the City of Aberdeen.
Particulars of Sale, the Spital Estate, 1883.

And so the twentieth century brought new brooms to the Spital Lands. After Aberdeen Town Council had purchased the Sunnybank estate, their neighbouring 'lairds', the City of Aberdeen Land Association, were anxious to get on with the profitable business of feuing out the new areas that had now come 'on stream'. 'As soon as the agreement with the Town Council for the joint access through Sunnybank is completed, the Association's feuing plan will be lithographed,' their surveyors, Walker & Duncan, declared in 1902, adding gloomily, 'the delay in publishing the feuing plan has kept feuars off.' This seems to have been the case. Apart from Sunnybank School, only one substantial development went up at this time, a corner block opposite the school, which followed the usual pattern of shops on the ground floor and dwelling houses above. It ran from Sunnybank Road at Nos 60-66, then turned the corner into Sunnyside Road as Nos 40-42. In 1907 we find Alex Clark, detective, and Thomas Milne, chemist in residence at No 60. H W Flaws, 'tenor vocalist' lived at No 62 from 1918 until 1949. His widow later went to South Africa.

The butcher Mr George M Greig had his shop on the corner, at No 40 Sunnyside Road between the early 1920s and the late 1950s and his daughter, Mrs Isobel Donaldson, recalls that little group of shops. 'Kellys was owned by Edward and Bunty Kelly, and before them by Johnny Dey. At the corner was Harry B Forbes, the chemist. His brother, Charles, was my husband's maths teacher at Sunnybank School and he was also a

Mr Greig the butcher (wearing a wing collar)
outside his shop, with PC Louis Grant.
Courtesy, Isobel Donaldson.

director of Aberdeen Football Club. Harry Forbes was later taken over by a Mr Crombie. Round the corner was my father's butcher's shop. On the days he made potted head, my brother George and I used to go round to the shop with a couple of slices of bread during the school lunch break, and have a bowl of freshly made soup out of the big pot. Lastly there was a shoemaker, first George Mathieson, then Campbell Robertson, and latterly Stevenson.' The Greigs lived round in Sunnybank Road opposite the school and Mrs Donaldson says that it was not unusual for beggars to walk through the back green and sing 'something usually unrecognisable' or play the bagpipes and ask for a couple of slices of bread. She remembers 'Woodies', owned by Alice Wood, at the corner of Bedford Place and Sunnyside Road, just across from her father's. It was a general merchant or 'Johnny a'thing' well placed to sell sweeties to children on their way to school. The shop is now a hairdresser's. Fred's Mini Stores are at No 66 where the chemist's used to be while Mr Greig was succeeded by Robert Bannerman, then Alistair Ross, butcher and poulterer.

John McMillan, the licensed grocer, was down the brae at the bottom of Sunnyside Road, on the corner with Sunnybank Place,. This was the shop that had been originally owned by Mrs Harper of Causeyton House. 'It was not unusual to see well known worthies having a dram in the back shop outwith pub drinking hours,' recalls Isobel Donaldson. 'This was, of course, illegal, and the police kept a watchful eye on licensed grocers.' The shop, now Smith's is still a licensed grocer.

In the old days there was one other development, although not a permanent one. Sunnybank Skating Rink made an appearance in 1909 under the management of Alfred Gibb. These were the days of the city's short-lived roller skating craze, and in a couple of years the rink, like most of its contemporaries, had vanished. Nearer the Spital end of Sunnybank Road, the old home farm of Sunnybank House, though marooned when the new road went through, had survived. Muriel Slessor can still recall the farm with its apple trees and high wall. The buildings had a new lease of life as Green's stables, 'Greener's, we called them,' says Tommy Donaldson. Mr Robert Green, who did cartage work for the granite yards, was a familiar figure in the area, and the stables were a favourite gathering place for local children. 'We loons helped to groom the horses and cut hay to feed them,' recalls Harold Bishop. Gordon Cardno remembers the consternation when one poor beast expired outside the stables.

Further development in Sunnybank Road eventually took place in 1926 when three blocks of council houses went up in the empty ground between the corner block and the stables. These dwellings, each tenanted by four families, were built under legislation of 1923 specifically to house families left homeless as a result of slum clearance programmes. Each house attracted a fifty percent Government subsidy. Some years later, Mr Green and his stabling business flitted to Mounthooly, and the stables, council-owned since the acquisition of the Sunnybank lands back in 1899, were demolished to make way for a further batch of council houses. By 1937 they stretched almost as far east as Sunnybank Cottage.

Today this row of houses is painted in an attractive wash and have neatly-tended gardens. Mrs Bonner, whose younger days were spent in Froghall, has lived for a few years now just opposite the School and Community Centre, which share the same building. She finds it nice and quiet, with no one bothering them. Many of her neighbours have also spent a lifetime in the area. Their back gardens are bounded by the wall of the old stables, once the wall of Major Mercer's home farm, and all that survives from his Sunnybank estate.

Mrs Bonner and friend with the original wall of Sunnybank Home Farm behind.

The tenements of Elmbank Terrace which prevented the widening of Sunnyside Walk. Note the corner shop. The lower building extreme left, was the stables of Elmfield House.

Down in Elmbank Terrace, the change in direction which began in the 1890s with the building of tenements at the Froghall end, continued. By 1905 Elmfield House had been demolished to make way for housing and the omnipresent surveyors, Walker & Duncan, acting on behalf of the marriage contract trustees of Major and Mrs Crane, successfully lodged a plan with the Town Council, to lay out a new street, 50ft wide through the lands of Elmfield between Elmfield Avenue and Sunnyside Walk. The trustees were also permitted to build 'dwelling-houses of three square storeys in height, with attics, towards Elmbank Terrace', proof indeed that Elmfield House had already been taken down. A similar dwelling-house was to be built on the Elmbank Terrace-Elmfield Avenue junction. Finally, they agreed to give off land from the Elmfield site which would allow the widening of Elmbank Terrace. The stables would remain. Bar the building of the solitary tenement near the Elmbank-Elmfield junction, the lofty 'dwelling-houses of three square storeys with attics', failed to materialise. As it was, nothing higher than garden sheds appeared, used by the men who had the plotties across the road, beside the railway line. Local folk can recall heaps of stones lying where Elmfield House had stood, surrounded by a profusion of grass and weeds. Lottie Yule (Mrs Booth) who lived in Elmbank Road remembers picking wildflowers there and duly presenting them to her teacher at Kittybrewster School.

In 1912, the proposed street between Elmfield Avenue and Sunnyside

Right the square-shaped modern houses of Elmfield Terrace, the old 'Crannies' area. Front left, the Joe Shirras development of three villas. Sunnyside Walk is to the rear, with the backs of the Elmbank Road houses behind. Note the width of the road.

Walk at last made its appearance. It was laid out, 50ft wide as promised, where the wooded policies once had flourished and was officially named Elmfield Terrace. This area was already known as 'Crannies', inspired by the memory of the Major whose name locally must have been pronounced

March Stone No 58 at Sunnyside Walk.

'Cran'. Joe Shirras got the go ahead to build three dwelling-houses where Major Crane's largest conservatory and pavilion had once stood and two two-flatted villas went up straightaway. The First World War put the brakes on further development, and the third house did not appear until years later. Meanwhile 'Crannies' had filled up with wooden huts and garages where lads tinkered with motor bikes, and children played.

By 1925 things were on the move again. Elmfield Terrace was at last widened according to plan, the work carried out by the unemployed, with 75 percent of the funding coming from the Government's Unemployment Grants Committee. The Shirras flats stood in solitude in Elmfield Terrace until 1933 when the City of Aberdeen Housing Association Ltd (not to be confused with the Land Association), implemented a scheme for some thirty-six semi-detached houses. Square modern houses went up in Elmbank Terrace and Elmfield Terrace, the ground floor stone-built, the first floor of metal-covered wood framing, cement plastered and harled. March Stone ABD 58 was rescued from the Major's erstwhile policies and placed outside No 21 Elmbank Terrace, the last house before Sunnyside Walk, while a separate bungalow development eventually replaced the Elmfield stables. The original builders of Elmbank Terrace may have envisaged a latter day Rubislaw Terrace in the northern half of town, but what emerged was a mixter-maxter.

Two further housing developments took place in 1934. The Land Association developed ground between the steep south bank of the St Machar sports ground and the old wall of Sunnybank House - which in future years would cause problems for the new feuars. Danders from the Jute Works had been dumped in this area for many years, but no matter. The new road, Sunnybank Terrace, would curve southwards in a sort of inverted crescent forming a link between the upper part of Sunnyside Road and Sunnybank Road, exiting beside No 26, Sunnybank Cottage. John Bisset & Sons Ltd were to be the builders. The old days of houses going up in twos and threes had been superseded by one building firm taking charge of a complete sector.

In 1935, Forbes Ogston Rettie, Charles Rettie's father, a Merkland Road East granite merchant, flitted from his Shirras house in Elmfield Terrace, to become one of the first purchasers of the Sunnyside Terrace bungalows. The terms of CALA's feu charter dealing with this part 'of the Lands of Spital', were strict. The Rettie's bungalow which cost £550 was to be 'for the accommodation of not more than one family'... while 'the granite of which this house shall be built shall be subject to our approval before erection'...and 'the space between the dwelling-house and Sunnyside Terrace shall be kept in all time coming as an ornamental garden or grass plot,' and more in that vein. In 1937, with the Terrace only partly constructed, an amended plan was announced. It would now 'deviate' to join CALA's new road linking Sunnybank Road and Bedford Road, in effect, that expansion of the Firhill Road, which had been given approval at the end of 1936. Nothing happened for this was the road that was never built, the one that caused the unnecessary removal of the Gibberie Wallie from its ancient site to the St Machar Sports Ground. When Sunnyside Terrace was eventually completed, it joined Sunnybank Road, as originally planned, but only by a pedestrian path situated between No 26 and the Firhill Road.

The second new development in 1934 was carried out by the architect,

Adie's shop in Bedford Road, with the Scott Sutherland bungalows left.

Tommy Scott Sutherland, who would be a town councillor by the end of that year. He built thirty-two three and four-apartment bungalows on the north side of Bedford Road, a contrast with the plain tenements opposite. Behind these little bungalows lay a group of the area's numerous allotments and Dennis Scott remembers old men with wheelbarrows working away there in the 1950s.

On the Kittybrewster side of Bedford Avenue (the old approach road to Powis House) major changes had taken place. The Reith & Anderson auction mart had flitted across to the Berrybank site at Kittybrewster where there was room to expand. Their old yard subsequently became a mini industrial complex, occupied by the Cruden Bay Brick and Tile Company, an oil depot, Briggs the asphalt manufacturers and Nu-Style's Products, the latter two up a side lane. Back on Bedford Road was Mackenzie's taxis. Laura Souter (Mrs Galloway) who lived at No 58, remembers that Mr Mackenzie always wore gaiters. Galls - 'Gallies' - succeeded Mackenzie, and took over adjacent ground for a filling station.

At the far, Old Aberdeen, end of Bedford Road, the Firhill or Hermitage Hill or the Miser's Hilly - Mrs Galloway can still remember the hermit who made his home there - was sold for its sand in 1927 and began to vanish. The Hermitage, one of the most familiar landmarks in the area - its tale really belongs to Old Aberdeen - had already been demolished. In 1940 the Town Council finalised plans to carry Bedford Road on to Tillydrone and the

University Court suggested that the section that was being abandoned, the little road of many names, College Road, College Wynd, and before that, the Doctor's Wynd, be given a new name, Meston Walk. Lord Meston had been appointed Chancellor of the University in 1928 and would die in office in 1943. The proposal was not without opposition. 'Baillie Robertson', the Town Council Minutes record, 'dissociated himself from the recommendation', but his amendment, to rename the section College Walk, did not carry the day. Meston Walk still gives us some idea of the narrowness and country 'feel' of the Road to Oldtown.

Like the Sunnybank area, Bedford Road had its own shops. Mrs Galloway and Mrs Nina Scott who also used to live at No 58, both recall the Misses Morrison who had a drapery shop on the Sunnyside Road corner where Adie the general merchant is now. Nearby, on the Bedford Place

corner, Miss Joan Alexander and her mother ran an unlicensed grocer's shop at No 46 Bedford Road. Mrs Galloway remembers getting a penny for the Sunday School collection and spending a halfpenny of it at Miss Alexander's shop on the way there. The shop, now Scott's, is newsagent, grocer and off licence. Charles Davidson, and later Christopher Gray

Mr Wilson Ritchie on duty at Bedford Place.

had the licensed grocer's at the corner of Erskine Street and Bedford Place, at No 53. It is now a house. Further along Bedford Place, which had developed into an attractive street, were two little shops, Reuben Laing the Woodside butcher at No 27, and the Mastrick Dairies next door at No 25. Commercial

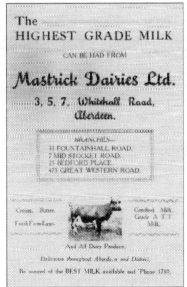

A 1936 advertisement for Mastrick Dairies.

premises are there now. Aden's dairy occupied the corner of Bedford Road and Elmbank Terrace for many years. It latterly became the Elmbank Dairy but had closed down by the mid 1990s. The hairdresser next door at No 61 Elmbank Terrace used to be a shoemaker. Near the Elmbank Terrace-Erskine Street corner there was a butcher at No 57 and though that shop is now occupied by catering services, the old signs, 'poultry' and 'game' are still visible. The corner shop No 55 Elmbank Terrace used to be a grocer and it too has become a house.

Moving along to the Froghall end, No 18, alias No 3 Elmbank Road, had been a grocer and general merchant's corner shop since the tenements were built there in the early 1890s. It was run by Alex Cruickshank, then A & A Cumming, and James Coutts It is now Bon-Accord Refrigeration. Across the way, there had been shoppies near the Tarry Briggie since the late nineteenth century, temporary at first, two in the early days, and later half a dozen, and now a familiar landmark. Over the years there have been baker's shops here including Mitchell & Muil, a fishmonger's, a Chinese takeaway, a hairdresser's and a bookie.

Shops, the great community centres of their day, were often the focal point of children's games. Isobel Donaldson and other local children, Betty and Gordon Robson, (later Father Robson), J D Gill of advertising fame, Shirley Gill, (Shirley Spain) and Betty and Hazel Thow used to play, 'I spy - something in Kelly's window'. 'We dashed across the road before coming back and naming the article. Sometimes we got it wrong!' One game of earlier times that involved covering a wide area was 'Hoist the Flag' enjoyed by Lottie Booth and her friends. It entailed following arrows and took the children all over the Sunnybank-Spital area. Laura Galloway recalls that she and her friends would pool their pocket money of a halfpenny each and spend it on hiring a Fairy cycle from the pram and cycle shop next to the Co-op at Split-the-Wind. They took it in turn to ride all over Elmbank and Sunnyside. Children in those days had a freedom to range widely.

Elmbank Road at the far end of Elmbank Terrace was the birthplace of Ronald McLeod, classics master at Aberdeen Grammar School, known to generations as 'Tarzan', and a near neighbour was Sheila Rae, wife of Bob Smith, the journalist and author. Fred Crawford was brought up in one of the tall tenements at the top end of Elmbank Terrace - the old Elmbank 'front garden'. Looking back to the postwar era he says: 'My friends from the same block were the Kynoch boys, David and Douglas. (Douglas, a well known broadcaster, is the author of *Teach Yourself Doric*). We played in all the places that would probably be forbidden in this age: the railway embankment, the goods yards in Bedford Road, Central Park and the Mart, and among the stones and debris of bombed houses.' Dennis Scott recalls

The cul-de-sac end of Sunnybank Place.

a great game in Bedford Road, dashing through the grounds of Elmbank House to Erskine Street without getting caught. The presence of the railway also added a little excitement to life. Cattle were regularly offloaded at Kittybrewster for the marts, and inevitably some poor beast would go berserk and career along the street, to the delight of children and alarm of adults. Circus trains were regularly unloaded and loaded at Kittybrewster and Dennis remembers in the 1950s, circuses parading along Bedford Road *en route* to pitching their big top at Seaton.

Margaret Gemmel (née Dow) who lived in Sunnybank Place recalls that the area was popular with railwaymen, among them Messrs Castles, Menzies, Burnett and Muir, tram drivers and policemen too, with Inspector Hill, and 'Bobbies' MacKenzie and Grant in Sunnybank Road and 'Bobbie' Lobban in Elmbank Road. The Maitland family who later lived at the old Mitchell house, Holmwood, No 7 Elmfield Avenue, are well-remembered. George Maitland, tall and grey-haired, was an elder at John Knox's Mounthooly for many years. The Maitlands owned the Balgownie Dairy which had about half-a-dozen branches in the north of the city in the 1930s, including three in George Street. The creamery was based at No 578 where dairying utensils were also made and repaired. This building was a sturdy, interesting piece of industrial architecture that sat gable-end on to the road. It latterly sold water sports' equipment, but was demolished in 1996.

The Hays lived in Rocklands Cottage, Sunnyside Walk, and Alice

This collage of some of the residents of Sunnybank Place reflects something of the style and sophistication of an earlier era. Mrs Christie wears her widow's weeds, while the ladies below are elegantly attired. The pinny was considered 'dressy' enough to be kept on for the photograph. The interesting 1930s interior shows Mr Duncan at ease by the range, left, listening to his Bakelite radio. The exterior picture of the Johnstons' well-stocked garden shows that garden furniture is nothing new. All photographs, courtesy, I B D Bryce.

◄ Mrs Christie , seated, and her daughter Mrs Dow, of No 49 Sunnybank Place.

▲ Mr Joe Duncan.

Mr and Mrs Joe Johnston with Toser in
▼ the garden of No 53-55 Sunnybank Place.

▲
From left, Mary Duncan (Mrs Bryce) her mother Mrs Joe Duncan of No 47 Sunnybank Place and Mrs Coutts of No 41, owner of the houses.

Margaret Gemmel, daughter of Mrs Dow, opposite, in her Sunnybank Place garden with the wall of Elmfield House behind. Courtesy, Margaret Gemmel.

Harvey in Elmfield Avenue. She married Ian McLaren who owned Bower & Florence, the last of the King's Crescent granite yards. One of the Bower & Florence masons, Mr J Primrose, whose home was in Sunnybank Place, was the father of the late Norman Primrose, the jeweller. Sunnybank Place was also famous as the home of two unrelated Duncan families. Mr John Duncan who lived at No 35 had a joiner's business and was factor for houses in Elmbank Road and Linksfield Road, as well as owning houses in Sunnybank Place. 'I recall that at different periods of time we had four generations of that family living in the cul-de-sac part of Sunnybank Place,' says Tess Campbell (née Burnett). Her old neighbour, Margaret Gemmel remembers that of the three sons, Painter Duncan lived in No 21 Sunnybank Place, Tailor Duncan lived on the corner of Sunnyside Walk and Joiner Duncan lived in Sunnybank Place before moving into his father's house. Their respective daughters were Mrs Brechin, Mrs Cowie and Mrs Allan. A married daughter, Mrs Barry, owned a haberdashery shop in George Street.

Mr Joe Duncan who was no relation lived at No 47 and the architectural historian, Ian Bryce, provides a glimpse of his grandfather, recalling his favourite, 'pannie tea' - 'a small pan with water and tea added which stewed on the fire until to his taste.' The block Nos 41-47 was bought by Mr and Mrs Coutts who moved into No 41 and rented out the other three, as was common practice. Near neighbours at No 49 were Mrs Christie and her daughter Mrs Dow, the mother of Margaret Gemmel. The Christies, like the Duncans were originally country folk who had come to the town for work.

The end house, No 53, was the home of Mr and Mrs Alex Cassels and their son, Alex a joiner. 'Mrs Cassels would give me a sweetie or a piece,' recalls Ian Bryce, 'and if I was very good, a shottie on the organ in the front room parlour. Young Alex worked in the joiner's yard off Elmfield Avenue later took over the business. He made me a train set, just wooden blocks hooked together with which I played for hours.' At No 55 were his aunt Jeannie Johnston, and her husband, Joe. 'Uncle Joe was a gentleman's tailor who worked in the back room, sitting cross legged on the table and smoking a pipe with a chimney formed from a squeezed outer casing of a Swan Vestas matchbox to keep the cinders from falling on the cloth.'

Sunnybank Place is also the home of Alex and Muriel Slessor who have an unsurpassed knowledge of the area. In October 1976, an uproar was caused when all vehicular traffic was banned from the Tarry Briggie. It was Alex Slessor who presented a petition signed by ninety protesters, and the following January, Grampian Region Roads Department amended the banning order 'after hearing objectors say that it was a vital link to the town centre'.

Another familiar figure in the area was Hubert Carter, the senior sacrist at King's College, who came to live with his daughter Mrs Irene Sheret and her family in Sunnyside Road after his retirement in 1945. Mr Carter, whose story really belongs to Old Aberdeen, was a skilled musician who came to Aberdeen originally as the Gordon Highlanders' band sergeant. He had a memorable 92nd birthday party at the Gordon Highlander's Regimental HQ at St Luke's in Viewfield Place, the 2nd Gordon's being the old 92nd. He died in 1974 aged 94.

Mrs Sheret's husband had a shoemaker's business at 26 Powis Terrace, and was likely to have known Connie Bain, shop assistant at John Smith, the newsagent's, a couple of doors along at No 32. Her story is a surprising one. Connie, quiet and ladylike lived at No 55 Elmfield Avenue with Henry Bain, a barman, and his wife. She was born in 1904 to eighteen-year-old Mary Smeaton, a member of a respectable middle-class Edinburgh family, and Hubert Bowes-Lyon, grandson of the thirteenth Earl of Strathmore. The birth took place in secrecy and Connie was reared by a Mrs Collie who lived in the Spital, and later, by the Bains. She took their name, though there is an enigmatic note - 'Birth C. seen' - in the admission register of Sunnybank School where she received the final three years of her education. Connie was, not, however, an aristocratic by-blow. Three weeks after she was born, her parents were married and later had two sons. They saw Connie briefly in early childhood, but otherwise did not acknowledge her existence in spite of the fact that Hubert Bowes-Lyon never denied paternity and under Scots law, Connie had been legitimised by the marriage of her parents. At a time when the class divide was vast, they seemed unconcerned that her

Elmfield Avenue. Connie Bain lived at No 55, third block from the right, upper flat.

upbringing was left to a series of working class families unknown to them. Her mother apparently was unwilling to jeopardise her position in society by admitting to having had a child outside wedlock.

The Bains had been concerned for some time that Connie was being denied her true place in society, and feelings came to a head in April 1923, when Lady Elizabeth Bowes-Lyon (Queen Elizabeth, the Queen Mother), a second cousin of Connie, did she but know it, married the Duke of York. The Bains sought legal advice. The following June, at the Court of Session, Connie obtained a decree of legitimation which declared her to be Constance Mary Bowes-Lyon, the legitimate, and eldest child of Hubert Ernest Bowes-Lyon, grandson of the thirteenth Earl of Strathmore. Her days in Sunnybank were at an end. In 1933 Constance Bowes-Lyon married George Dow, a tobacco planter at Blantyre, Nyasaland.

Sunnybank suffered grievously during the worst air raid in Aberdeen's history. On the evening of 21 April 1943, in a low level attack by a formation of Dornier 217 heavy bombers, thirty-one tons of bombs were dropped over the northern half of the city. The railway at Kittybrewster was a prime target. Willie Weir's farmhouse in the Spital, and St Peter's Cemetery were hit and the north end of George Street out to Spilt-the-Wind was ablaze. Bedford Road was one of the streets that took the brunt of the raid. No 60, on the Sunnyside Road corner was completely demolished and four families lost their lives. No 58 next door was also badly damaged. Another

Left, No 58 Bedford Road after the bombing of 21 April 1943. The jagged wall is all that remains of No 60. Courtesy, Mrs L Galloway.

Elmbank Road. The post war block centre, which replaced No 6 and its neighbours.

family died in the debris when No 48 Bedford Road on the Bedford Place corner suffered a direct hit. Across the road a couple of the 1934 bungalows were reduced to rubble, and others badly damaged, with the loss of five lives. Nina Scott remembers well the sotter of Bedford Road after the bombing, folks' belongings, children's toys strewn all over the road, the back greens full of detritus for a long time after. Erskine Street, Bedford Place and Elmbank Terrace were all hit. No 6 Elmbank Road was destroyed by a landmine which killed fifteen people 'The shattered tenement stood for a very long time with the severed stumps of its three floors open to the elements,' Ian Bryce recalls.

'The blitz was unforgettable,' says Fred Crawford. 'It came so suddenly we had no time to get to our shelter which was in Erskine Street, in the garden of Ralph McKenzie's house. Instead, we cowered in our cellars where we were joined by a couple of servicemen who had been caught on the streets. Bombs exploded all around, at Causewayend Church, in Bedford Place, in Sunnyside Road next door to my cousin and Bedford Road, where the bungalow of my best friend - he still is - was destroyed. Much later my aunt arrived at our house, having been bombed out of her flat in Stafford Street.'

One enduring memory is of glass in the street. Arthur Tough remembers leaving a Boys' Brigade rally at the Music Hall, anxious to find out if anything was left of his home in Old Aberdeen, and finding the Spital full of glass. Ian Bryce's mother, Mary Duncan, cycled over to Sunnybank the next day to see how her father was. As she approached the Tarry Briggie she found the road covered in glass so she dismounted and started walking through it. A policeman stopped her and told her she could go no further. 'But I have to see if my father is all right,' - and she told him that he was Joe Duncan, Sunnybank Place.

'Joe Duncan the painter, Joe Duncan the joiner, or Joe Duncan retired?' asked the policeman. On learning it was Joe Duncan retired he had good news. 'He's all right, I saw him going to his plot this morning as usual.'

Rebuilding took place some years after the end of the war, and is easy to spot. No 6 Elmbank Road, and its neighbours were replaced by a building in the style of wartime army married quarters, now Nos 2-8 Elmbank Road. In Bedford Road, No 60 was replaced by a modern block, 127 137 Sunnyside Road, and No 48 by No 96 Bedford Place on the corner. The Bedford Road bungalows opposite were rebuilt, their roofs covered with attractive red pantiles, all that was available at the time. (No 34, the 'white' tenement in the photograph on page 77, looks newer than its neighbours. It had nothing to do with the war, but was badly affected by subsidence and rebuilt in the mid 1990s).

By the 1960s, the railway presence at Bedford Road was diminishing. The repair depot and the marshalling yards, closed in 1963 and 1966 respectively. In 1967 the motive power depot followed suit and the railyard closed to livestock and freight. The following year local coal merchants, Ellis & McHardy having decided to transfer their coal supply from sea to rail transport, bought ten acres of ground, including a siding, from British Rail, successors to the LNER, who had absorbed the old GNSR in 1922. Their new depot stretched along Bedford Road from Powis Terrace to Bedford Avenue covering not only the old marshalling yards where once there had been a mass of rails, but the site of the original Reith & Anderson mart and the mini industrial complex. Old cattle pens had to be removed before the new coal distribution centre could be set up and when it was, passers-by were intrigued by its 'Ostrich' boom stacker which travelled along a 200 yard stretch of rails and fed the coal discharged from the railway wagons into a chute which then conveyed it to tipper lorries. By 1970 Ellis & McHardy had opened a new head office, Leith House, on Bedford Road. At the peak of its operation, the plant was handling 40,000 of coal annually, but in the 1980s, a shrinking market for coal coupled with acquisition by a hitherto unknown Canadian company, Mackan, brought about the eclipse of the Ellis & McHardy we used to know. The old marshalling yard is now the Kittybrewster Retail Park.

Elmbank House was still there, opposite the yard, the sole survivor of

Elmbank House from Bedford Road. The elms remain.

102

The former coach house of Elmbank House has been attractively converted.

the three Big Hooses, its residents privately glad to see an end of the coal distribution centre and its attendant coal dust. For much of the first half of the twentieth century Elmbank was owned by Frank H Cartwright, a cabinetmaker, then by his trustees, and was occupied by a number of tenants. A subsequent owner, Mr Tommy Morrison ran it as a guest house. The long table where everyone sat at mealtimes was a feature of the house. During the ownership of his son, Mr William Morrison, two houses were built in the front, first No 17 Erskine Street in the early 1970s, and No 13a, in 1980. Elmbank, now both No 12 Bedford Road and No 15 Erskine Street was converted into seven flats at this time, with an extension at the rear. Here, in the little garden, a couple of elms remain. The octagonal kitchen garden became garages, though an original wall of Seaton brick remains here. The coach house, on higher ground behind the house was attractively developed as a separate house, No 16 Bedford Road.

By the mid 1990s Elmbank had deteriorated badly with the roof letting in water. A disrepair notice was issued, entitling the residents to substantial grant aid and the house was thoroughly overhauled and refurbished in 1997. Over this critical period they all got to know each other well for the first time, romance blossomed and two of the residents are now married. Ken Robertson's flat in the former servants' quarters still retains its original shutters and dados in lobby and bathroom. 'Elmbank,' he says, 'is still known locally as the postmaster's house. '

Sunnyside Gardens today, the site of Sunnyside Farm.

By the time the Land Association acquired the Spital Lands back in 1900, much of the ground suitable for feuing on the west side had already been given off. 'Consideration should be given as to whether some road-making should not be gone into at Sunnyside,' Walker & Duncan suggested the following year. Nothing happened and it was not until after the war that the directors of CALA focused their sights on Sunnyside Farm. The fields were still being grazed and yielding vegetables, while much of the remaining ground was given over to allotments. Here indeed was scope for housing. Willie Weir's lease was terminated in 1946. (He would not be so easily got rid of in the Spital where he owned the land). The builder Mr Donald C Stewart had acquired the land and that December, was granted planning approval for 'ninety-five dwelling-houses proposed to be erected on an area of ground at Old Aberdeen, part of the Spital Lands'. Mr Leo Durnin was the architect. A request for full planning permission some three years later was 'deferred', then on 6 March 1950 given the thumbs down altogether. During these years the Council was preparing a University Precinct Development Plan and it was felt that '(Stewart's) development would materially prejudice the carrying out of the proposals envisaged in the University Precinct Plan'.

The following year progress of a sort was made when the Town Council and the University agreed to divert and culvert 'that part of the Powis Burn which is adjacent to and within lands in the ownership of the University' -

where it flowed past the site of the Hermitage, almost reaching the spot where the Gibberie Wallie had been. There was a dispute as to who actually owned this stretch of the watercourse, Town or Gown, but both sides agreed that the covering-in of the burn was 'desirable in the public interest' though there were members of the public who were sad to see it vanish into a reinforced concrete pipe, linking up with the culverts already in existence at Bedford Road and College Bounds. Problems relating to the development at Sunnyside remained unresolved for a couple of years and it was not until 1953 that Stewart's trim development was up and running to an approved design. Sunnyside Avenue and Sunnyside Gardens formed the arms of a rather squint triangle with Sunnyside Road as the base. Sunnyside Farmhouse would have lain between Nos 12 and 14 Sunnyside Gardens. Sunnyside Avenue continues on, roughly parallel with Bedford Road, to meet Hermitage Avenue at right angles, midway along its length. Hermitage Avenue, named in memory of the long gone summerhouse on the Firhill or Hermitage Hill, links Bedford Road and the Firhill Road.

After its sand had been commercially exploited, the Firhill itself, by then a dip rather than a hill, became a parade ground for the university's Officers' Training Corps and Air Squadron. The Squadron had its mess here and Saturday evenings in the 1950s would find those old wartime colleagues, Professor R V Jones and Professor Edward Wright yarning at the bar. When the Roy Strathdee OTC building went up at the far end of Don Street, the student militia withdrew from the site, and their old headquarters declined into a rickle of huts. Fortunately the Firhill site was tidied up by the mid 1990s, and is now a student car park. None of this has defeated the sand which still refuses to go completely away.

The Firhill today. It makes an interesting comparison with the picture on page seven.

Chapter 8

Sunnybank School

The whole of the lights - the electricity being generated from the apparatus at the school - were lit, and seen from the outside, the place had an imposing appearance.
Opening of Sunnybank School, Aberdeen Daily Journal, 22 October, 1906.

Sunnybank Public School opened for business in August 17 1906, and that October, parents and friends attended the inauguration ceremony. As always on such occasions, the great and the good had forgathered on the platform. Among them were the newly appointed headmaster, Mr D B Lothian, Mr J A Ogg Allan architect to Aberdeen School Board - this was his seventh school - and the Board's chairman, the Reverend Gordon J Murray who pronounced Sunnybank 'quite the prettiest name in the Board's list of thirty-two schools'. One prominent member, Dr Mitchell of Old Aberdeen, was unable to be present. 'The ladies,' said the Reverend Murray jovially, 'will forgive his absence when I tell them that he was being married this afternoon in London while they were inspecting the School he was largely instrumental in erecting.'

Eight years previously, in December 1898, little Primrose School in the Spital had a tenth of its grant deducted on the instruction of Her Majesty's Inspectorate, for overcrowding and defective offices (toilets that didn't work). The geography of the Spital prevented Primrose School's expansion so Dr Mitchell decided to seek other remedies. It was widely known that Aberdeen Town Council was proposing to buy the Sunnybank estate, so Mitchell suggested that the School Board consult with the Council with a view to securing a site at Sunnybank for a new school. By 1900 very little had happened apart from in-fighting at the School Board. New schools at

Sunnybank School in 1906. 'A finely planned school with 17 of its 19 classrooms facing south'. Note the old trees to the right.

Old Aberdeen, Woodside, Causewayend, Kittybrewster and King Street were already overcrowded, but the decision was taken to enlarge Woodside and Old Aberdeen to the annoyance of Board members representing the Elmbank, and Spital areas. Mitchell intensified his campaign and by 1901 the Board had secured a two acre site for the new school on what had been the oval lawn of Sunnybank House at an annual feu duty of £70.

More time passed. Causewayend's supporters were now demanding their school be upgraded to a three-class per standard (year) school. In May 1903, however, a new School Board took over and Mitchell became convener of its School Buildings Committee. He argued instead, for a new two-class per standard school for Sunnybank. He won the day. Building work began in October 1904 and the school opened two years later, eight years after it was first mooted. Without for Mitchell's perseverance there would have been no Sunnybank School.

It was the largest of any elementary school in the city, standing so high that the windows of top floor where manual work and cookery and laundry were taught, offered views of the whole city and the coast from Girdleness to Cruden Bay. The playground was extensive, fully one and a half acres. 'The fine old trees on the ground have been kept where possible,' said the Reverend Gordon Murray, (which would have delighted the heart of Major

107

Mercer), and he added: 'there is a considerable fall or slope towards the south which has been terraced and laid out as a small garden, enhancing very much the amenity of the place.' Most classrooms were south facing, bright and sunny, saving the pocket of the overburdened ratepayer to some degree on heating bills as the Reverend Murray was pleased to stress. The domestic science classrooms had horse-hair chairs and carpets so that the girls could be taught how to beat the dust out of them. Everything was of the most modern - steam heating, mechanical ventilation and electric light generated on the premises. It was too costly to introduce a cable from the Corporation. The total expenditure, Murray revealed, was £17,500. He hoped that the new school would be a centre of light and learning for the whole district. A school holiday had already been given on September 28 to mark the inauguration of the great Marischal College frontage - and that gave the Reverend the opportunity to shoot off a little dart: The School's nearest neighbour, he said:

is King's College, and we have been hearing a great deal lately about the university. No doubt a university is an important factor in the life of the community but for the great mass of people in our land the elementary school is of far more consequence. Accordingly it has all along been the pride and boast of the School Board of Aberdeen to make our elementary schools second to none.

Then the electric lights were lit and everyone went outside to look at them and were much impressed.

There were 1169 places all told, 337 for infants and 832 for juniors and seniors. The infant department was straightway oversubscribed, when 183 boys and 167 girls enrolled, while the junior and senior departments were sixty-three pupils over-capacity within the first week. A class of fifty-eight pupils was removed to the Hall 'there being no classroom available'. Sunnybank had quickly become the 'in' place. Before long Old Aberdeen School had vacant places and the School Board issued a communiqué barring from Sunnybank those pupils from the 'Orchards', Pittodrie Place and University Road - 'who do not already have a place on the roll or an existing family connection with the school'. Regardless of such an embargo, Edith Farquhar (Mrs Clark) born in Orchard Street in 1902, and her two sisters went to Sunnybank establishing the family connection there. She found it, 'very beautiful, very nice.'

Apart from routine classes, a beginning was made with a school library. Eighty-five volumes, no less, were bought with grant of £5 given by the School Board but were only 'at the disposal of the two highest classes'. On Exhibition Days parents visited classrooms and saw the work done by the pupils throughout the session. As ever, measles, whooping cough and scarlet fever stalked the pupils. Occasionally, there was a death from diphtheria. HM Inspectorate duly pronounced the school to have 'a capable head and staff of decidedly good quality'. In August 1913 there were two half days, one for Timmer Market, one for the visit of Field Marshal Roberts to receive the freedom of the city. The usual days off were given at 'term' so that children could help with the flitting. This was as major an event in the city as well as in country districts as families, depending on their circumstances, sought better or roomier or cheaper accommodation. The crush on space at Sunnybank continued. One October the headmaster noted 'the prescribed syllabus of PE exercises must now be departed from for want of time and space to continue.'

Routine was disrupted during the First World War. In May 1914, Old Aberdeen Public School was taken over for military purposes so its pupils had their schooling at Sunnybank in the afternoon while Sunnybankers were taught from 8.30am till 1pm. Twelve-year-old Mary Duncan from Sunnybank Place suddenly found herself an victim of the anti-German feeling prevalent at that time. She went to school proudly wearing a sailor suit which had belonged to a Russian princess, the niece of the Tsar Nicholas II. Her father, the Grand Duke and his family had been guests of the Earl and Countess of Elgin at Knepworth House where Mary's aunt was housekeeper, hence the gift. Her classmates were horrified, mistaking the Tsarist double eagle embroidered on the dress for the German eagle. It had to be removed. Mary (the late Mrs James Bryce), remembered Harry Gordon from those days as 'an untidy boy who was always snivelling'. (This would have been before the future comedian and his family moved from No 11 Powis Place to Urquhart Road).

The 12-year old Mary Duncan in 1914, wearing the Russian sailor suit that caused anti-German feelings at Sunnybank. Courtesy, I B D Bryce.

Sunnybank, like other schools in the city, was affected by the appalling flu epidemics that were such a scourge after the Great War. It closed from October 11 for a month in 1918, and again between February and March 1919. Eventually normal routine resumed and the school's prowess at football came to the fore. On 20 May 1922 the Football Championship Shield was won by Sunnybank, and many triumphs were to follow. Had Willie Cooper been in that victorious team or was he too young then? A baker's son, Willie lived in Fraser Place and attended Sunnybank from the end of 1914 until 1924 and that June was awarded a prize for perfect attendance. After school he went on to play football for the Junior team, Mugiemoss. Sunnybank FC might have been the logical choice, but it hadn't come into existence then. In 1926 he signed for the Dons, and began a legendary career at Pittodrie which lasted until 1948.

By leaving in June 1924, Willie Cooper had avoided the upheaval that would take place at the start of the autumn term. Sunnybank's days as an elementary school were over. It had been upgraded to become one of new intermediate centres, the forerunners of the junior secondaries. Younger

Willie Cooper with Sandy in 1977.

scholars were notified which of the newly created primaries they now had to attend. Gordon Cardno of Hillhead Terrace in the Spital, a 'displaced' Sunnybank pupil remembers marching down College Bounds with his class in a crocodile, making their way to their new primary, Old Aberdeen School.

Sunnybank Intermediate School opened on 19 August 1924 with an enrolment of 219 boys and 260 girls. John Ritchie had succeeded David Lothian as head of Sunnybank in 1921, but he now he went off to take charge at Ashley Primary, while a new head, James Thomson, would remain at the helm for Sunnybank Intermediate's fifteen years of existence - and beyond. Stanley Rennie, who lived at No 25 King's Crescent attended Sunnybank Intermediate before going on to the Central, and recalls it as lighter, cleaner and more spacious than his primary, Causewayend School. 'It was in pleasant surroundings compared with the run-down conditions in Causewayend. The teachers seemed less authoritarian and more approachable, but the big attraction for me was in being allowed to cycle to school on my new £3 19s 9d Hercules bicycle. This was a degree of freedom which was not afforded to primary school children.'

Another pupil who came from Cassie-end Primary to Sunnybank was Alberto Morocco, whose father had sold ice cream from a barrow before buying a little shop in Causewayend, opposite the school. His teacher, Miss Green, became aware that the young lad had artistic ability and did her best

Alberto Morocco.

to encourage it. When the time came to leave school as a fourteen-year-old in 1932, she recommended that he be admitted to Gray's School of Art, a move his family warmly supported. There he remained for six years, influenced by two of his tutors, famous names in Scottish art, James Cowie, and Robert Sivell, the formidable Head of the School of Painting. After an interesting war Morocco was appointed Head of Painting at Duncan of Jordanstone School of Art in Dundee. More than that, he established himself as one of Scotland's finest and most popular portrait and landscape painters.

In the late 1930s, the able, well-liked and now sadly missed Chris Anderson, a player and subsequently a director of Aberdeen Football Club, and a Secretary of Robert Gordon's Institute of Technology, was a pupil at

Chris Anderson.

Sunnybank. Tommy Donaldson, a near contemporary of Anderson's at school recalls from those days, another Pittodrie player and director, Charles Forbes, though as maths teacher he was on the other side of the fence. His brother Harry P Forbes was the Sunnybank Road chemist and Miss Forbes, their sister, was school secretary.

In the 1930s Sunnybank Intermediate was experiencing a space crisis, just as it had as an elementary school. The council houses across the road from the school grew in number throughout the 1920s and 1930s, and the roll was increased even more dramatically by children from the homeless familes living in the former Jute Works in Froghall, and from the new scheme that was being built on the same site. In 1932 HM Inspectorate reported: 'This advanced division centre is conducted with good sense, vigour and skill. Numbers have grown and accommodation is

Early Days at Sunnybank School

Uniforms and best dresses as well in this photo of 1929-30. Nina Milton is in the back row at the far end. Courtesy, Mrs Nina Scott.

A Sunnybank School trip to Cambusbarron, Stirling in 1939. Courtesy, Margaret Gemmel

Everyone is in uniform in this photo of 1930. Courtesy, Dorothy Gerrard who is 2nd left back row.

Mr James Thomson, headmaster, centre, with pupils in 1932. Courtesy, Laura Galloway (Souter) centre row, 2nd right.

now taxed to the utmost. In view of a further increase in enrolment next session, the Education Authority have plans for erecting a permanent addition in the immediate future'. An so an extension to the school was in the pipeline - which in time would bring about the demolition of Sunnybank House. Two years passed and the inspector's report was still bemoaning the lack of new accommodation. By the end of the 1937-38 session, things were looking up. The report stated: 'This school, the largest of the advanced division centres, has over 900 pupils on its roll...These difficulties (of lack of space) have not been allowed to interfere with the development and efficiency of the school...' and added, 'new accommodation will soon be available', which must have been music to James Thomson's ears. Moreover Sunnybank was praised for its 'spirit of questioning and experiment, bold but never rash...'

Even more pupils were about to arrive in the area. In 1936, the upper Lands of Powis, the last remaining portion of the original Powis estate had been sold to Aberdeen Corporation for development as a housing scheme and a substantial increase in school places to accommodate the newcomers was essential. The situation was further complicated by the phasing out of intermediate centres at this time and their replacement by junior secondaries. Sunnybank Intermediate Centre was due to be transformed into Powis Junior Secondary School in 1939, located in a splendid new school recently completed in St Machar's Drive. Sunnybank's head, James Thomson was headmaster-designate. Sunnybank itself would now become a primary, and with the new Powis and Froghall schemes in its catchment area, the need for its spacious new extension becomes obvious.

Yet a further complication arose in the unwelcome shape of Adolf Hitler. Thomson was well aware that if war were declared, his fine new school in St Machar's Drive was in danger of being requisitioned for military use. It would be particularly vulnerable if still unoccupied. He was determined that the area should not be denied the secondary school it so urgently needed. On 1 June 1939, he addressed his staff 'on matters both valedictory and prospective'. He closed Sunnybank the following day to allow the flitting to Powis to take place, and reported: 'Most of the classroom materials had been transported and placed in position by noon. The afternoon was spent in removing heavy material, science equipment, general stores etc.' Legend has it that Thomson then marched his senior pupils out of Sunnybank School onto Bedford Road and up St Machar Drive, to take possession of the new school, which on 5 June opened as Powis Junior Secondary. To wait till the traditional opening time in the autumn term might be too late. Thus, in the 'bold but never rash' tradition of the school, he stole a march on the military.

Sunnybank, with John Sutherland as the new head, opened as a primary in August 1939. By now the promised extension, parallel wings towards the Spital end of Sunnybank Road, was nearing completion, as was a refurbishment of the older classrooms. Then - 'All schools closed owing to the outbreak of war with the German Reich,' wrote Mr Sutherland in his log - this was on 3 September - and when Sunnybank re-opened again soon after, there were further dilemmas. Work on the extension had stopped and the existing school buildings were taken over by the military authorities. Pupils were farmed out to Old Aberdeen and Causewayend Schools while St Machar's Church halls were pressed into service, as in days of yore. However, classrooms gradually became available again, and though many workmen were still in the building, most of the children were back by before the end of the month, except the infants who were still at Causewayend. That September all pupils were fitted with gas masks and since Sunnybank was designated an Air Raid Precautions Centre, teachers from Kittybrewster,

The Sunnybank ARP post. Winnie Maitland, Elmfield Avenue back row, first left. Mrs Hay, Sunnyside Walk. Margaret Gemmel, sixth left. Courtesy, Margaret Gemmel.

Old Aberdeen, Linksfield and Seaton all descended on the school for ARP instruction.

During the air raid of 21 April 1943, Sunnybank Primary suffered extensive damage to its south side. Nevertheless, in the days that followed, the school did what it could to help the local community, serving school

Killed by enemy
action 21st April
19 43

Kathleen A S Mitchell
aged 5 years. June
L Porter aged 9 years
Ernest M. Wallace
aged 10 years. Robert
Reid aged 10 years
John M Moir aged
9 years. Erected by
scholars and staff

*The memorial to the
Sunnybank children
who died in the air raid
of 21 April 1943*

dinners to the homeless. Sadly, five pupils were among those who had died in their homes during the raid. It was decided to erect a plaque in their memory. By 21 May, £15 2s had been collected and Mr James, of Gray's School of Art was commissioned to carry out the work. This poignant little memorial remains at Sunnybank School, quite near the entrance. It has the words, 'Killed by enemy action, 21st April 1943', and gives the children's names and ages. The Christ figure is shown with five children gathered round.

Sunnybank's new extension was now deemed adequate to accommodate the military, even if the plumbing hadn't gone in. Mr Jim Glennie who had enlisted in the Gordons was billeted there along with Camerons and HLI recruits, men from Glasgow, the North, even England, as well as local lads. In 1944, after a terrible New Year week-end at the old Froghall Jute Works, he recalls that they found Sunnybank 'real luxury, with central heating. We slept on three boards with three palliasses or mattresses - 'biscuit's in army slang - just six inches

Jim Glennie at the time he was billeted at Sunnybank. Courtesy, J Glennie.

off the floor. We didn't have showers, just a basinful of water which was scarce. The corporal kept an eye on us in case we used too much. Sometimes we marched to the Uptown Baths and had to jog all the way back. We had a row of dry toilets in the playground. The children were in the top half of the school and used to wave to us when we were doing our drill. We spent ten weeks there, training at the Black Dog and Collieston, before being posted south to Southend-on-Sea, then to Chalfont St Giles where the Gordons boys joined the 5/7th Battalion.'

After the war, the extension was at last brought into use. 'The large, lower playground was fenced off until 1946,' writes Fred Crawford. 'I recall it being opened at last, the great joy of the larger playground and the new classrooms which included a gymnasium. Another joy of the end of the war was getting paper to write on instead of slates. At last we were able to keep and even take home our work, instead of rubbing it out every day. Mr Sutherland the headmaster was a large remote man with a small head and a big body. The deputy was Mr Downie who taught us in P6 and P7. He was a fierce man in the good old spare the rod and spoil the child tradition. He retired in 1962.'

John Sutherland had retired 1950 'leaving the school in good heart'. Concerning the war years he wrote: 'There were many difficulties of accommodation and school arrangement. Owing to the splendid loyalty and co-operation of staff all complexities were successfully overcome.'

Mr Ian Sharp became headmaster in 1972 in succession to Mr John M Wright whose retirement came after a long period of absence following a car crash. Mr Sharp wrote: 'I had inherited a going concern, the wheels of which were turning very smoothly due to the effort of Mr W G Melville, deputy head, and staff. And he notes - 'school uniforms much in evidence'. We find Mr Sharp handling problems that every teacher will recognise. He ticks off a bully whose parents then descend on him. 'The father threatened to knock me through the wall.' Pupils bitten by large dogs roaming about in the playground, pupils with feet stuck in drains, 'a bit of a fracas in the playground', are all coped with in the course of the day's work. One day Mr Sharp writes philosophically in his log: 'at playtime on Thursday one of our weaker vessels scraped a legend on the wall of the boys' toilet. This type of vandalism angers me but I'm afraid it has existed since the dawn of civilisation.'

He is anxious to instil in his pupils his own love of the outdoors. There are outings to Hazlehead, Countesswells and Dinnet Moor though a visit to the beach to collect shells is unsuccessful. 'We had to return almost immediately due to a thick mist.' More successful is a trip in 1974: 'At 1.30pm Mr Simpson the janitor and I set out with five senior pupils for Holburn Tropicals to buy more fish for our aquarium.'

There is good liaison with Mr George Sinclair, headmaster of Powis, and Mr Ian Macdonald of Old Aberdeen. Sports are held at Powis Field and the whole school marches there. A half day holiday is given to celebrate the winning of the Aberdeen Schools' Football Association Primary League cup 'a very successful season with no defeats.' The school was maintaining its outstanding record in school football. In 1976 the Jimmy Knowles trophy, named in honour of the ex-champion boxer, was presented for the first time for excellence in sport. Jimmy Knowles, who lived in Froghall attended the prize-giving and presented the trophy in person.

Nursery teaching was already underway. In March 1973, a second nursery class had been set up, while in 1975, German was taught in Primary 7 on an experimental basis. The following year proposals to install special units for deaf children were under discussion. It was decided that the handwork room would be converted and work would start when money became available. In 1977 Sunnybank Primary was officially designated a nursery for deaf children. Meanwhile Mr Sharp had been appointed a Fellow of the Educational Institute of Scotland and his deputy, Mr Melville, now had the opportunity to return the compliment Mr Sharp paid him when he took over the school in 1972. When Mr Sharp was given leave of absence to attend an EIS conference, Mr Melville wrote in the log: 'An honour most richly deserved, the culmination of many years hard work. He has given of his time and energy in an unstinting fashion, serving on committees both nationally and locally to improve the lot of his teacher colleagues.'

Sunnybank continues as a positive, pro-active mainstream primary school. Mr Andrew May, head teacher since 1985 in succession to Mr Sharp has a staff of over 30 full-time and part-time teachers. The roll in 1997 was 312, with thirteen classes between Primary 1 and Primary 7. These days lack of space is no longer a problem and the building is shared with Sunnybank Community Centre.

Nursery provision now consists of three different units, twenty full-day children, with a further twenty part-timers attending in the morning, and another twenty in the afternoon. A third nursery has a mixture of children with normal hearing and up to four with hearing loss. In addition to its conventional role as a local primary, this continuing work with deaf children is one of several features which distinguish Sunnybank from other primaries. There is now an intensive tutorial structure for children with hearing problems, from three to twelve-year-olds. 'You wouldn't be able to pick out deaf children in the playground,' says Andrew May. 'At one time they were withdrawn but not now. They get special tuition, but they also integrate with the rest of the school.' Children with language difficulties from all over the North East are also taught at Sunnybank. They have their

Sunnybank pupils with Mr Andrew May in 1997.

own speech therapists, and when tuition is completed, they return to their own schools.

One development in recent years, in common with other city schools, has been the growth of computer work. It has proved a first class aid to reading, making it more fun. Outward bound activities, including ski-ing, continue as they did in earlier years. 'It may be hard to believe,' says Andrew May, 'but there are more girls playing football at primary level in Aberdeen these days than boys. Two of them are in the Sunnybank Primary School team - one of them in goal.' The school promotes a happy, healthy life style. From 12.40 pm until 1pm - and this is quite separate from PE - an exercise scheme called 'Kids in Condition' is underway. Attendance is voluntary but everyone takes part in these exercises designed to promote circulation and vitality. School dinners are prepared in the School's own kitchens and the lunch menu, offering three choices, is posted every day on the notice board. Twenty-five percent of pupils taking dinners spontaneously opt for fruit with their meal.

Given the number of post-graduate students from all over the world who are studying at Aberdeen University, Sunnybank, so close to King's College, (our 'nearest neighbour' as the Reverend Murray said at the opening ceremony in 1906), has become one of the most cosmopolitan schools in the city. Murray would never have dreamed that there would be children from China, Taiwan, the United States, Hungary, France and Peru on the register, as well as a good number of Asian children, many of whose parents have made their temporary homes in Powis, Froghall, and Linksfield, all within the School's catchment area. The fathers, in many cases, are studying for postgraduate degrees in the Social Sciences and in Forestry.

Andrew May rightly argues that children should be aware of the culture of the country in which they live and at Sunnybank all pupils learn about Scotland and its history. There are celebrations on St Andrew's Day with the head wearing the kilt and all the staff sporting tartan. The anniversary of that great poet of universal brotherhood, Robert Burns, is another red letter day in the calendar.

Chapter 9

Sunnybank Football Club

Event of the football year was Aberdeen Sunnybank's wonderful feat in winning the Scottish Junior Cup.

Fred Martin, Bon-Accord Annual, 1954.

Sunnybank for many people means Sunnybank FC the Junior football team, which traces its origins back to Sunnybank School. It was formed in 1936 by two local lads, Bill Fyfe from King's Crescent and A J Smith from Jute Street, and started off as a juvenile team, Sunnybank FPs which trained at Jute Street. Most of the players were former pupils of Sunnybank Intermediate, and of Cassie-end Primary before that, and they played in the City Boys' League. When war broke out the club disbanded. The Sunnybank team reformed in 1946-47 this time as Sunnybank FC, but soon amalgamated with another Junior club, Belmont FC, which had many ex-Sunnybank players in its ranks It was decided to retain the Sunnybank rather than the Belmont name. The new club became Sunnybank FC and the black and white hoops of the old juvenile team became the club colours. One of the benefactors of those early days was the club's first honorary president, John Deans, mine host of the Red Lion Inn in the Spital.

Over the years Sunnybank has had many fine players and has won numerous honours, the most famous being the Scottish Junior Cup at Hampden at the end of the 1953-54 season. The *Bon-Accord* reported:

'Little fancied 'Bank' surprised even their most fervent supporters with their defeats of Central League crack teams Baillieston and Petershill in the latter stages of the competition, and their grand showing against the Dundee team Lochee Harp beating them 2-1 in the Final.'

*Mr John Deans displays the Scottish Junior Cup
at the Red Lion in 1954, courtesy, Sandy Pirie.*

*Sunnybank FC 1953-54
Scottish Junior Cup Winners with Club Officials, courtesy, Sunnybank FC.*

Sunnybank FC
Archibald Cup & County Trophy 1947-48
Courtesy, Sunnybank FC.

Billy Stephen and Billy Chalmers were the scorers and Bobby Simpson the captain. They were the first Junior team in the city to win the Cup. 'The 'Bank' had a very good team at that time,' recalls Jim Thom, the club's Honorary President. 'We had the best left half in Junior football, a player from Jute Street, Wullie Garden, who went on to win a few Junior Scottish caps.' Teddy Scott from Ellon was Sunnybank's centre half for that glorious season, during the course of which he was signed by Aberdeen Football Club. (He's still there).

Sunnybank FC had drawn a crowd of over 10,000 to Linksfield Stadium when they beat Broxburn Athletic 2-1 in the quarter final of the Junior Cup. The semi-final at Pittodrie, when they defeated Baillieston 4-2, was watched by a crowd of 19,500. In those days, the 'Bank' played their home games at Linksfield which they shared with three other Junior teams. Having a ground of their own would be the realisation of a dream. In fact, back in October 1949 the Club had bought a piece of ground at Heathryfold for £365 from the Hays of Seaton, though unfortunately it was the subject of various planning embargoes imposed by the Town Planning Scheme of 1933. These had to be removed before the erection of club buildings could go ahead. In the years that followed, club members beavered away, getting the ground levelled and building walls, but the real catalyst was the winning of the Cup in 1954.

One who was there from the beginning, working away at developing the new ground, was Billy Chalmers who scored one of the winning goals that eventful Saturday in May 1954. He represented Sunnybank for about four years, and thoroughly enjoyed his playing days. The family is a footballing one, for his brother James played at Queen's Park as an amateur before going on to play for Aberdeen then Dunfermline Athletic. His mother, Mrs Agnes Chalmers, now in her nineties, still lives in Old Aberdeen. Billy keeps in touch with the players of his own era. 'Quite a few of us are still alive,' he jokes, and follows the current results from the newspapers.

'Between 1955 and 1957,' recalls Jim Thom, 'the Committee at that time did a power of work at week-ends, along with a local builder. We opened the park in 1957.' The supporters' club which ran the tea kiosk raised money for the dressing rooms. A social club was next on the list and in 1960 the supporters' club took over the Lounge - it became the Sunnybank Lounge - at the Dancing Cairns pub to help raise funds by running bingo. 'The social club cost £37,000,' says Jim Thom. 'A loan from the brewers did the trick, and we had it paid back by 1973. That was five years after the opening in 1968.' In 1974 they went ahead with an extension at a cost of £75,000, borrowed this time from the bank. No great risk was involved. The bank estimated the land Sunnybank FC owned was worth £2,000,000.

'Teams from down south look forward to their trips to Aberdeen to play us in Friendlies,' says Jim. 'They come year after year, some of the biggest names in the Junior game, Pollock FC from Glasgow and Glenrothes FC from Fife.' And well they might. Sunnybank today has a first rate ground, a modern pavilion, a superb social club - and a well-stocked trophy cabinet. As far as players are concerned, Jim Thom points out that these days there are difficulties at Junior level. Up-and-coming young players are snapped up straight from school by the senior teams. Sunnybank relies on ex-Highland League players for which they have to pay 'a fortune'. Nevertheless, in 1997 Sunnybank FC didn't do too badly. As League Champions they were awarded the Bon Accord and Evening Express Championship Cup.

Chapter 10

Froghall Past

And then the line of the march goes to the eastward of the road in a south-east direction till it comes to the back of the houses at Pickiltillum opposite to Froghall.
Report for ascertaining the Town's Outer Marches, 6 August, 1790.

Froghall lay at the southern tip of the Lands of Sunnyside. It was the most westerly of the Spital Lands and an early name for a part of it, Wester Peter, was a reference to the old parish of St Peter's. Logie's Plan of the early 1750s shows Froghall as an anonymous fairm toon west of the Spital Hills and south-east of Sunnyside Farm. It was named for the first time on Taylor's Plan of 1773 (on page 11), and was reached by a track which left the old Inverurie highway just beyond the settlement of Causewayend, at the present day junction of Canal Street and Elmbank Terrace. The track later became Froghall Lane and is now Froghall Terrace.

What was the derivation of the word Froghall? One popular idea, that it came from the numerous frogs which resided in the Jute Works ponds, should be taken with a pinch of salt. The ponds were created sometime after Froghall Farm had vanished. A more likely theory is that the name comes from the Gaelic *frog*: a hole full of water and 'hall', a corruption of the Scots howe or hollow and so, a hollow filled with water. An earlier alternative is provided by the *List of Pollable Persons* of 1696 which notes two tenant farmers in the Lands of Sunnyside, the larger, Andrew Aberdeen, 'in Sunisyde' itself, the smaller 'Robert Chalmer, in Stankyaird'. A stankyaird was a yaird, - a piece of ground - containing a stank, that is stagnant water or a pond. The word came into Scots from the Old French, *estanc*: a pond - *étang* in modern French. Stankyaird and Froghall therefore mean much the same thing, ground covered with stagnant water, and could well indicate the same place. Confirmation is provided by *The Powis Papers* where, in a valuation of teinds of 1711, testimony is given by 'Robert Chalmers, Tenent in Froghall'. (Chalmer and Chalmers is used interchangeably). By the early eighteenth century 'Stankyaird' seems to have been abandoned in favour of 'Froghall'.

Taylor's Plan shows wee dwellings at the junction of the Inverurie highway and the Froghall Lane track. This was likely to have been the croft of Pickiltillum which in the 1790 Riding of the Marches is described as 'opposite to Froghall'. Early in the September of that year, a group of gentlemen rode out, on the instructions of the Town Council, to 'visit and examine the whole of the (march)stones, both old and new'. Among them was the creator of Taylor's map in person, the cartographer and land surveyor, Captain George Taylor of Annfield. Riding of the Marches, originally 'redding' or putting in order, was not the fun ceremony it became in the latter half of the twentieth century. In earlier times this 'perambulation' ensured that there was clear passage on the King's Highway; by the eighteenth century it had become necessary to check that no local laird was encroaching on the town's land.

After leaving Kittybrewster, the inspection team followed the line of the march east then south-east, 'at the distance of about forty yards from the

March Stone No 59 sits on the pavement outside No 10 Elmbank Terrace. This was formerly the Sunnypark area. The wee shops of Elmbank Terrace are to the left.
Courtesy, John Souter.

road', the road in question being the old Inverurie highway at what is now Elmbank Terrace where they entered the Spital Lands, 'the inclosures belonging to Mr Moir of Scotstown'. They continued to follow the march 'till it come to the back of the houses at Pickiltillum opposite to Froghall'...where there is a key-stone'. This was one of the stones marking the boundary of St Peter's[*] parish, the original Spital parish. They decided to have a march stone, subsequently No 59, placed at Pickiltillum in addition to the extant key-stone, and sure enough in the 1868 ordnance survey the line of the march is shown running at the back of the little houses at the southern tip of Sunnypark, where Pickiltillum used to be. The modern replacement stands on the same site, across from the Froghall railway bridge near the junction of Elmbank Terrace and Froghall Terrace, that is, outside No 10 Elmbank Terrace, which is actually in Froghall. You can stand here and look east to the site of Froghall Farm, now occupied by Spencer Coatings Ltd. This Froghall section is where the Spital Lands and the city's Freedom Lands march together

This area grew in importance after the Aberdeenshire Canal was excavated here in the early nineteenth century. Froghall Canal Bridge, predecessor of the railway bridge or Tarry Briggie, was built at the junction of Canal Street, the Inverurie highway and Froghall Lane. John Milne in his *Aberdeen* of 1911 tells us that:

There were several locks on the part of the Canal bordering on Elmbank Terrace, and above the bridge there is, in a nursery, a small red-tiled house which was a cabin for the lockman who opened and closed the locks when barges passed up and down.

On 6 June 1812, the *Aberdeen Journal* was advertising 'to let lands of Froghall, Causewayend and a small enclosure at Sunnyside'. The lands of Froghall Farm seems to have been given over to market gardening for Wood's Plan of 1821 on page 128 shows 'Nursery, Mr Smith' between the Froghall buildings and the Canal, which is represented by the dark wavy line on the Plan. In the *Aberdeen Journal* of 16 July 1834 there was advertised:

the farm of Froghall occupied by James Smith, seedsman to let from next Martinmas for twenty years. Nine acres of ground, two houses, barn, stable and byre. Seen by applying to Mr Smith at his shop at 74 Union Street.

Froghall Cottage is noted for the first time in the Aberdeen post office

---

* The key symbolised St Peter. Christ said to Peter: 'And I will give unto thee the keys of the Kingdom of Heaven', (Mathew 16,19).

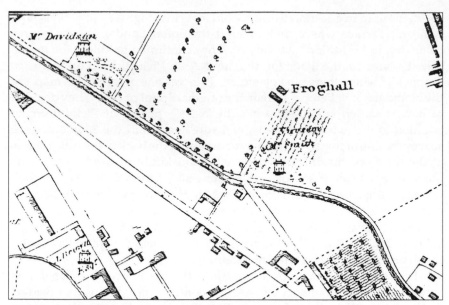

Wood's Plan of 1821 shows a group of biggings at Froghall and a small nursery belonging to 'Mr Smith'. The little house could represent Froghall Cottage. The dark wavy line is the Aberdeenshire Canal. Canal Road meets the Inverurie highway (Elmbank Terrace) and the track that became Froghall Terrace at the Canal bridge. The little cottages of Sunnypark are nearby.

directory of 1854 as on the 'north side of canal, half-a-mile above Mounthooly'. The anonymous Plan of the City of Aberdeen in 1862 shows Froghall Nursery on what would originally have been the farm's lands, and Froghall Cottage with its market garden, as two separate entities, on either side of Froghall Lane where there was already a handful of small buildings. Both extend as far east as the Froghall Farm buildings, and no further. North and south of the farm and east to the Spital lay open country though the easterly stretch was now transversed by an extension to Froghall Lane, which had involved the feat of engineering a road up a considerable brae to break through to the Spital near the novelist George MacDonald's digs at No 37. The two halves of the Lane did not join up in those days, stopping on either side of the fairm toon. During the 1860s, Froghall Nursery was extended considerably, covering the eastern half of Froghall on both sides of the Lane, from the Sunnybank House boundaries in the north, to Viewton Place in King's Crescent in the south.

The Froghall fairm toon itself comprised of a group of buildings round a courtyard dominated by a three-sided stone-built dung stance, nicely sited for carting muck to the nursery lands. In spite of the presence of the stance, the houses around the farm were by no means exclusively occupied

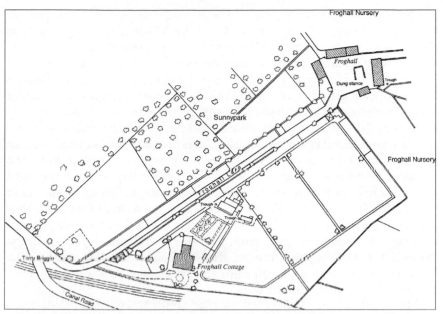

Froghall Farm, top, showing the houses round the three-sided dung stance. The Jute Works later covered this area and spread out on both sides. The market garden of Froghall Cottage, bottom, stretches north-east to Froghall Nursery. Jute Street was later extended through to exit in Froghall Lane/Terrace opposite the Jute Works.

by nurserymen. The 1851 census returns show Robert Wilson, bookseller in residence with his wife and family at Froghall Farmhouse. Perhaps that was the house shown on the 1868 ordnance survey with an exclusive carriage drive running parallel to Froghall Lane. By 1861 the farmhouse has gone over to multi-tenancy. Then there was a residence simply known as 'Froghall', occupied in 1851 by Robert Taylor, his wife and family. Taylor ran a rope and twine business in 'Froghall Lane, Spittal', for many years. Perhaps it was the same place as Froghall House, which the 1855-56 valuation roll shows to be owned by James Henderson, the architect. It was tenanted around this time by William Souttar clerk to the GNSR, with his wife and ten children, one of whom James, was to be the architect of the Salvation Army Citadel.

Until well on in the nineteenth century, only a handful of folk were living in the Froghall district, among them Mrs James McDonald, gardener, and Joseph Massie a shoemaker. Compared with Causewayend to the south, Froghall, at this time, was very sparsely populated rural area, and bar the sprinkling of houses round the farm and the few biggings in the Lane, was given over to two great nurseries. Froghall of course was one, the other was Sunnypark.

In the 1830s, George Martin had been tenant farmer 'at Sunnypark at Canal Bank, within the Spital Lands'. Like Major Mercer's grounds at Sunnybank, his parks enjoyed 'a warm southern aspect', hence the name. By 1841 Martin had gone and Sir Michael Bruce and his wife Dame Isabella Moir had leased Sunnypark to a new tenant, not a farmer but James Cocker, formerly head gardener at Castle Fraser. The year before, Cocker had a quarrel with his employer over picking fruit on the Sabbath. It was contrary to his religious principles. He would gather fruit on a Saturday night, no matter how late, but never on a Sunday. It is unclear whether he was given an ultimatum, either to pick fruit on a Sunday or go, or whether he left the godless Castle Fraser of his own accord. Whatever happened, he brought his family to Aberdeen where he found that the south-facing, sloping land at Sunnypark, adjoining Froghall Nursery and just outside the city boundary would be ideal for his purposes. Here he laid out a new nursery covering the west of Froghall from the Sunnybank House policies in the north down to Froghall Lane on the south-east and the bank of the Aberdeenshire Canal - the future Elmbank Terrace - on the south-west, with the policies of Elmfield to the west.

The 1851 census returns tell us that James Cocker had come from Forgue by way of Insch, and had a wife, three sons and a daughter. The houses of the old hamlet of Pickiltillum had been incorporated into Sunnypark and it was possibly one of these little houses that was later converted into a seed shop, an early Cocker's Garden Centre. The 1871 census returns show how well the Cockers had progressed. The family was now living at Canal Road, just across from the Sunnypark Nursery (sometimes confusingly referred to as Sunnybank) and James Cocker is employing sixteen men and twelve boys. One of his sons is a nurseryman assistant.

But by 1882 James Cocker was dead. His eldest son, also James who had earlier been taken into partnership, was currently at the helm, and his three sons, James, William and Alexander were also in the firm which now traded as James Cocker & Sons. Trees, greenhouse plants, herbaceous flowers, flowers for bouquets and pansies were grown at Sunnypark, where they must have provided a vivid contrast to the squalor of Froghall Lane, which by then had become notorious for its dunghills and ashpits. In 1889 *Scotland of Today* reported on Messrs Cocker's 'extensive and perfectly-appointed nurseries' at Sunnypark and Morningfield- the latter a new nursery - both of them 'in a splendid state of cultivation'. Apart from developments at Morningfield, the Cockers had also put a new nursery at Springhill under cultivation in 1902. This expansion in other parts of the city's periphery was not only due to the firm's success. The Cockers were gradually squeezed out of Sunnypark during the later nineteenth century, ironically by a plant, but not one grown locally. In *Mechanical Aberdeen*, Dr John S Reid writes:

Jute was of rising importance in the second half of the nineteenth century. It was easily dyed, it took bright colours, it mixed with flax, tow, wool, and silk and was largely used for upholstery, schoolbags, coat linings, and in the manufacture of blankets and caps. It was the carrying material of the world.

In February 1873, the prospectus of the Aberdeen Jute Company was published. John Miller, founder of the Sandilands Chemical Works was company chairman, and William Leslie, builder, architect and Lord Provost was among the firm's promoters. It seems likely that these astute business-men had noted a profitable changeover from linen to jute at the Dundee factories where they were establishing useful contacts. They had found a sizeable piece of ground in the Spital Lands that was suitable for their needs. It was rented out as a nursery, but to a firm that was rapidly expanding elsewhere in town. And so they had a word with the Spital laird, H W Knight Erskine. By 14 May of that year, the *Aberdeen Journal* was able to report:

We understand that the Aberdeen Jute Company have acquired about fourteen acres of ground at Sunnybank (Sunnypark) Nursery forming part of the Spital Estate for erecting their mill and power house factory. About three and a half acres of ground will be required at present, and the surplus land will continued to be occupied as nursery ground till it is needed for extension. The ground lies between Causewayend and the Spital and is thus close to parts of the town chiefly occupied by the working classes. In addition to a moderate rate of feu duty it possesses the advantage of being exempt from municipal taxation. Messrs Thomson Bros & Co of the Douglas Foundry, Dundee, the company's engineers are at present engaged in the preparation of detailed drawings (and) we may expect that specifications will soon be in the hands of the contractor with a view to tenders for the work.

In June 1873, the first ordinary meeting of Aberdeen Jute Company was held in the Royal Hotel, Bath Street, with John Miller presiding. He announced the good news, that 42,758 shares had been allocated among 921 members, raising a capital of £85,516, a massive sum in those days. But the bad news was that plans to commence work on building the factory had to be delayed. Locally, the buildings at Sunnypark could not be erected until the sloping nursery land had been levelled; internationally, a general depression was affecting the jute trade. But the directors did not dither. The old buildings at Froghall were demolished, the ground prepared, and the factory, begun in September 1873, was completed a few months later. Unfortunately, world trade was still depressed, and plans to employ between 400 and 500 hands to produce jute sacks, were delayed. At last, by the late summer of 1875 trade was showing signs of a revival and Mr James Aberdein, manager and secretary, went to Dundee, to finalise arrangements for the supply of the raw material. The Company had already provided him with that handsome new house in Elmbank Terrace, whence a short walk along Froghall Lane would have taken him to the factory. The opening of Aberdeen Jute Works 'at Sunnypark' - sometimes the address was simply 'Froghall' - eventually took place on September 28 and spinning began.

World markets improved and the weaving department got underway in March 1876. That year the directors decided that it was more economical to import jute direct from Calcutta and the Dundee links were broken. No time was lost in placing orders. In August 1876, the *SS Asiana* out of Calcutta berthed at Regent Quay with 7000 bales of jute aboard; on 10 April 1878, the barque *Guinevere* brought another cargo of jute from Calcutta in a voyage that took four months. While import arrangements may have been good, industrial relations were not. In April 1878, fifty girls stopped work when they heard their wages were to be reduced but returned after better terms were agreed. The following February, 370 workers went on strike when another pay cut was proposed. James Ducat, who had replaced James Aberdein, was at the sharp end of wage bargaining and survived as manager for nearly forty years.

The welfare of the Jute Works girls was given priority by the sisters of St Margaret's Convent, recently established in the Spital. A 'Home for Working Class Girls at Bayview, Spittal', was commissioned by the Trustees of St Margaret's in 1881, and until it was ready, the sisters provided the girls with temporary quarters at No 17 Jute Street. The morning shift was worked between 6am and 8am when the girls returned for breakfast. They then worked at the factory until 8pm. After that they returned to No 17 Jute Street and sewed. The Home, St Martha's, eventually opened in 1887. Stone steps at the rear gave access to Froghall, as still they do, and the girls would have been able to get to the Works from St Martha's in a matter of minutes.

By the 1890s 13,000 bales of raw jute were being handled annually at Froghall and the Post Office Map of 1880 opposite shows how the Jute Works dominated Froghall. They covered what was the southern part of Sunnypark Nursery where it fronted onto Froghall Lane, though the northern half at this time was still occupied by Cockers, and the little house of Sunnypark was still there. The Froghall Farm buildings had vanished and part of the Froghall Nursery had been obliterated by the larger of the two Jute Factory ponds used in the manufacturing process. It sat in solitary splendour at this time, but the second pond was soon to follow. The stanks were returning to Froghall! The long market garden belonging to the Froghall Cottages remained intact and the city boundary is marked by the dark broken line running below and continuing eastwards south of the Bay

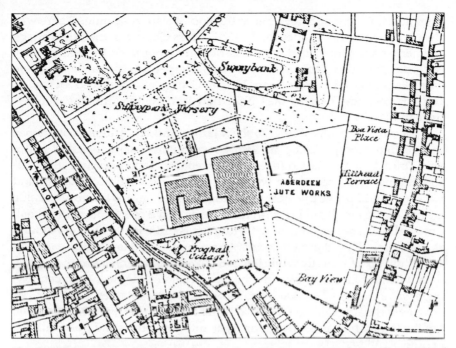

The Post Office Map of 1880 showing the Jute Works covering the southern part of Sunnypark Nursery. The first and larger of the two ponds is to the right of the Works. Froghall Nursery which was on this site has vanished. The Froghall Cottage market garden is intact, but Jute Street, which stops at the city boudary is poised to go through. The proposed extension of Canal Road (broken lines between Froghall Cottage and Bay View) running north did notmaterialise. Bay View formed the kernel of St Margaret's Convent.

View cottages which would soon form the kernel of St Margaret's Convent. St Martha's Home would be built in the empty feu just north of Bay View. The map also indicates that Canal Street, would, at some point in the future, continue on to run parallel to Jute Street, then to cut across it at right angles to give access to the Jute Works (shown by broken lines,) between the east block and the 'stank'. At this time, Jute Street itself, laid out in 1874 by its owner, Daniel Macandrew, came to a stop at the city boundary.

The mighty Canal Street extension never took place. When Froghall became part of the city in 1883, it was Jute Street that was extended a little further north to exit in Froghall Lane, opposite the Jute Factory. In doing so it loped off much of the eastern end of the Froghall Cottages' market garden, but since this entire area was now owned by Daniel Macandrew, no one was going to argue. At one time there were five families within the walled enclosure of Froghall Cottages, which was comprised of a lodge near the gates and three cottages together at the end of a short avenue. There was always a gardener in residence. In 1851, a Mrs Cheyne owned the cottage and her tenant, John Christie, was market gardener there for many years. According to the 1871 census returns Hugh Harper was the gardener, while John Skakle a jeweller from Banff, his son George who was also a jeweller, and a brother employed by the GNSR, had been living within the complex since the 1860s.

The valuation rolls of 1875-76 show James Stalker, gardener with house and garden, George Collie, as well as a printer, a salmon fisher and a blacksmith living at the Cottages. Other tenants, labourers and stonecutters among them, came and went, but the easily confused Skakles and Stalkers would prove the most enduring families. In 1891, George Skakle is head of the family, living with his wife and five of a family at Froghall Cottage but his father, John, now a widower, is still with them, still working as a jeweller. The other two tenants Alex Douglas and James Sim each had a wife and six of a family while James Stalker, gardener, was at the Lodge, with wife and family of two. By the early years of the twentieth century, there was a change. The Skakles had gone and James Stalker, gardener, not only owned all the Cottages, acquired after the death of Daniel Macandrew, but the family had also louped the dyke into Jute Street and gone into the granite business.

Access to the Cottages was by the gates at the west end of Froghall Lane which for centuries was the only artery that ran through these lands. But the late nineteenth century saw a little flurry of road development. Froghall Lane was widened when the Jute Works were built and increased traffic,

The Froghall Cottages lodge with the tenement of the Ancient Shepherds beyond.

generated by the granite yards nearby in Jute Street, made this a busy section. The eastern leg of the Lane, at the Spital end, retained its country lane atmosphere for some years, but was eventually brought into line and some ground and a small building beside George Macdonald's old digs at the junction with the Spital were taken over to permit widening at that end. Meanwhile, a curiously-shaped new road was laid out by the Spital laird, H W Knight Erskine, beginning and ending in Froghall Lane. In May 1898, the Town Council granted permission for this new road: 'commencing at a point in Froghall Lane 74 yards east of Jute Street, and thence running southwards eastwards and northwards to Froghall Lane at a point 94 yards distant from the point of commencement,'

It was christened Froghall Road. It might more appropriately have been named Froghall Circle, though that term was not used in Aberdeen until the 1930s. The street directory did its best to pin it down, locating it on the 'south side of Froghall Lane near end of Jute Works'. The new road formed a great loop on the western slope of the Spital Hill, with an upper level and a lower one as befitted a road built on a hillside. It provided the infrastructure, if one can put it so grandly, for firms such as Rennie &

The lower section of Froghall Road, right around 1921. James Forbes' yard is extreme right. The huge Froghall granite works of Charles McDonald Ltd are to the left, with the small, square yard of George M Stalker Ltd below. Jute Street is extreme left. Top, the Jute Works with lum still intact, stretch into the distance. Courtesy, Aberdeen City Library and Cultural Services.

Angus, builders, which until that time had been considered part of Froghall Lane, though they sat some distance back from it, across rough ground. The Ernan Granite Yard of James Forbes & Co now found itself sitting partly in the Lane, partly on the new road. The Froghall Granite Works of Forbes' neighbour, Charles McDonald, took up much of the west side of Froghall Road, extending through from Jute Street. The photograph on page 135 shows both yards side by side with Froghall Road between them.

Near the beginning of this chapter we encountered march stone No 59, which stands outside No 10 Elmbank Terrace and whose predecessor, an ancient key-stone, stood at Pickiltillum which is roughly the same place. The gentlemen of 1790 who were inspecting the city's march stones noted another key-stone a little to the east, in the middle of an arable field 'at present in bear' (barley), where the march took a slight dip south. Here they decided to place another new march stone, No 60, which is shown on the 1868 ordnance survey in a field just north-east of Froghall Cottage. This field was, in time, covered over by the Froghall Granite Works and stone No 60 found itself just outside the south-east corner of the yard where it backed on to Froghall Road.

A handful of industries were in existence when Froghall Road appeared in their midst, and houses now began to go up. Nos 23, 25 and 27 at the foot of the road are the oldest while nearer the Spital end of Froghall Road, on the upper part, Ferndale built in 1912 and Laurel Bank, in 1911, still

March Stone No 60, extreme left, in Froghall Road, June, 1976.

Nos 10-18 Froghall Road.

display the original granite date slabs. Opposite, Nos 10, 12, 14 16, and the later No 18, as shown above, were built and owned by a stonemason, John Lumsden Melvin, conductor of Grandholm Mills Band, an elder at Causewayend Church and foreman to the builder, Joseph Shirras. Mr Melvin was very handily placed for his work. From about 1910 until 1930, Joseph Shirras had his yard at the south end of Froghall Road before he moved to Sunnybank.

As for Froghall Lane, in August 1903, it was promoted to Terrace. The suggestion was put forward by the Loyal Order of Ancient Shepherds, and the Town Council was pleased to agree. The Ancient Shepherds planned to build four houses, including a ground floor shop on the south side of Froghall Lane at its junction with Jute Street, and were anxious that their proposed dwellings should have a more imposing address. (Their little development emerged as a one storey shop and double tenement, Nos 47-49 Froghall Terrace). Just as Froghall Road might more appropriately have been named Froghall Circle, Froghall Lane might more suitable have been renamed Froghall Road, had that name not already been taken. It was never a terrace - a row of houses of similar design - but a thoroughfare, with a handful of houses at the Spital end, granite yards backing on the south side of the dip, the Jute Works on the north side, the Ancient Shepherds' new tenements at the Jute Street junction, and near the Tarry Briggie, the Froghall Cottages within their walled enclave.

Across at Sunnypark, as the Jute Works had expanded, the nursery of James Cocker & Sons had shrunk greatly, though three greenhouses at the back of the Works were still in operation during the early years of the twentieth century, and the cottage of Sunnypark still survived. Cocker's gave up Sunnypark altogether in 1911, moving west to consolidate at Morningfield and Springhill.

By then horticulture of a similar if humbler nature was underway a stone's throw from Sunnypark. Not long after the City of Aberdeen Land Association acquired the Spital Lands in 1900, about thirty plotties were laid out on waste ground on the western slopes of the Spital Hill, between Froghall Lane and the rear of Boa Vista Place. They were a Mecca for locals. Here men from Jute Street, Powis Place, the Spital and Canal Street, paid an annual rent of around £1 and grew flowers and vegetables. Mrs Molly Stephen, née Steinson, who lived in Jute Street as a girl, remembers a neighbour, Mr Steel, one of the allotment holders, a dapper figure with his white moustache and a flower always in his lapel. Mrs Elizabeth Bandeen, John Melvin's daughter, recalls a Mr Hutcheon who came round the doors selling fruit and flowers. Some folk at the plotties kept a few hens. Local bairns like Norah Morrison would stop to feed the family hens - the grain was often bought from Gavin & Gill in John Street - before taking the path through the plots, the old right of way, and a short cut to the newly built Sunnybank School. When Joe Shirras flitted from Froghall to Sunnybank, this was the path that his foreman John Melvin took to the new yard.

For the first thirty years of the twentieth century, the bulky mass of the Jute Works continued to dominate Froghall, its workers at that time producing harn, used as a backing for carpets. They got a week's holiday without pay, and as the gates were locked, they had no option but to take it. Holidays were later increased to two weeks, but only one with pay.

Local people of the older generation retain their memories of the Jute Works. Norah Morrison remembers standing at the Tarry Briggie with other bairns, throwing snowballs at the workers as they came past. It was in the fields surrounding the Jute Works that Izzy Masson grazed her cows, then herded them across the bridge and into her dairy at the top of Fraser Place for milking. Mrs Dorothy Gerrard looking down from her childhood home in Hillhead Terrace recalls the two ponds, one hot, the other cold, a great source of fascination. Molly Stephen skated there in winter; children swam in them in summer. Gordon Cardno, a golfer in his youth, used to practice teeing off in his back garden in Hillhead Terrace, sometimes slicing balls into the ponds. 'They must have found dozens of balls when they filled them in.'

In the early 1930s, there was a world slump in jute, and unlike its trade rival, Richards & Co at Broadford, the Aberdeen Jute Company did not weather the storm. In 1932 the Jute Works went out of business.

Chapter 11

Froghall Present

Froghall housing scheme tenants are up in arms about their neighbourhood which they claim is a 'forgotten area'.

Evening Express, 16 June, 1970.

The failure of the Jute Works was an ill wind. The site was exactly what Aberdeen Town Council was looking for. On 31 August 1933, the press announced 'Jute Works bought by Corporation'. The buildings and the site of over fourteen acres at Sunnypark had been acquired at reduced price of £6000. Workmen's dwellings, said the Press, similar to those in Torry, would be built to provide homes for between 200 and 300 families 'removed from a sum clearance area'. At this time there was an urgent need, not to say a legal obligation, to house families left homeless by the city's slum clearance programme. This was emphasised that October, when a deputation from the Unemployed Section of the Aberdeen Trades and Labour Council reminded councillors that many such families were now living in tents and caravans at Haudagain and Canal Road and urgently required rehousing.

During the previous decade the Council provided around 330 dwellings specifically for these families - in fact only a fraction of the council houses they had built during that period - but it was not nearly enough to cope with the need. But now there was a carrot. The Government, as part of a national housing drive, was offering subsidies purely for 'slum clearance or relief of overcrowding'. And so the Aberdeen Jute Works Scheme was born. The City Architect, Mr A B Gardner, submitted plans for 246 dwellings of the three-storied tenement type, 186 three-apartment plus

139

sixty of the four-apartment type in brick and rough cast (ie wet harl). Traditional granite structure was waived in favour of modest cost - £74,153 2s 4d for the lot - and speed in construction. By December 1934 the Council, working under the provisions of the Housing (Scotland) Act 1930, and with the approval of the Department of Health for Scotland, was ready to accept lowest tenders. For the record, the brick work went to S B Russell, the carpenter work to R & J Reid Ltd, the plumber work to William Burnett, and the slater and rough cast work to John Durnin.

Work began on 7 January 1935 and it was soon noticed that the Jute Works ponds were causing problems. Mr Gardner and the City Engineer, Mr Thomas F Henderson, set off on a site visit. They discovered that the area was water-logged, the result of a broken culvert. The development of that part of the site, they concluded, could not go ahead. Seventy-two houses (and their accompanying subsidy), would be lost. One might have expected that the soggy ground would have been noticed during a preliminary survey. It was not, and that indicates the speed with which the Jute Works Scheme was set up. At the time Councillor T Scott Sutherland - and here speaks the millionaire architect - suggested that in view of the high cost involved in acquiring and developing central sites, why not reconstruct the old culvert, drain the scheme and utilise all the ground? A sensible idea, but not one that was taken up, and to this day, the site of the ponds has never been completely built over. Instead, a partial remedy was found. More space for housing was created by demolishing the west block of the Jute Works and the great lum. Everybody living in the area at that time remembers it coming down on 18 May 1935. As a result only fifty-four houses were lost and they were rescheduled for Torry, while that October a second development of forty-two additional four-apartment houses was approved.

Plans for the road layout could now be finalised. One new street, Froghall Avenue, would commence in Elmbank Terrace approximately fifty yards west of the railway bridge, run north-eastwards, then eastwards, and end in a turning circle. Sunnybank Place was to be extended to meet it. A second street was to commence on Froghall Terrace, seventy yards east of Jute Street and run north-westwards to join Froghall Avenue. This emerged, not quite as envisaged, as the cul-de-sac of Froghall Place. Street No 3 was planned as a cul-de-sac commencing in Froghall Terrace approximately 25 yards west of Jute Street running north-westwards terminating in a turning circle. This became Froghall Gardens and it was built over the demolished west block of the Jute Works along with No 38 Froghall Terrace. At the end of the day, the total was 132 three-apartment and 102 four-apartment houses. Work finished on 19 September 1936. Rents were fixed at 8/- per week for the three-apartment, and 9/- per week for the four-

Froghall Gardens. The boxer Jimmy Knowles lived in the centre block.

apartment houses. For those who couldn't afford to pay, rent rebates were available under the 1935 Housing (Scotland) Act.

By now the Aberdeen Jute Works Scheme had been renamed the Froghall Scheme; the name of Sunnypark was completely lost. Considering it was so hastily put together, what emerged was a spacious, leafy scheme in the Garden City style. Tenants from condemned property, cramped and lacking sanitation, were overwhelmed at the spaciousness at their disposal, though ideas put forward by councillors to improve the scheme by utilising the old Jute Works ponds as swimming and paddling pools, a favourite with Fraser Mac - Councillor Fraser Macintosh - or as an ornamental stretch of water, came to naught. But Froghall had a lot going for it. This was no vast, peripheral scheme, entailing costly bus fares into town. It was closely knit, making for neighbourliness. A few minutes' walk in one direction took residents to Causewayend and the bargain stores of George Street; in the other, to the little shops of the Spital.

While the new council houses were going up beside what was left of the old Jute Works, these buildings underwent a major conversion, and along with Torry Battery and the Castlehill Barracks, re-emerged as 'transfer housing colonies', clearing houses, 'where tenants who proved satisfactory were eligible for better accommodation'. Conditions at the Jute Works were bad. Families lived in big cubicles, separated by partitions. There were no windows and the atmosphere, a result of the use of gas all day for lighting, heating and cooking, was fetid. The floor was concrete, and when it rained there was ceaseless drumming on the corrugated iron roofs. Wash basins sat in the yard outside and children ran up and down all the time. There were complaints that dead cats, dogs and even a horse had been found in the ponds. Their decaying carcasses were blamed for causing illness among the children. Molly Stephen recalls a friend being worried in case it was her father's horse - he was with Wordie's - but it was some other unfortunate beast. Yet in spite of their poor surroundings most of the tenants were fine, cheerful folk, as Norah Morrison found when she went there to get her fortune told.

Pressure, was put on the Council to improve conditions but to little avail. On 18 February 1935, for example, we find councillors discussing the motion. 'that considering the unhealthy conditions prevailing in the houses at the Jute Works, immediate steps should be taken for the removal of the tenants to one or other of the new housing schemes.' This was merely remitted to the Finance Committee for a report. Priority was given to the re-housing of 'medical cases', but little progress was made until John Birkbeck arrived on the scene, striding along in his plus-fours. We met him in *Round About Mounthooly* at a later point in his career when he was minister at John Knox, Gerrard Street, during the 1950s and 1960s. During the war he had served with the Scottish Commandos, and had been awarded the Military

The Rev John Birkbeck.
Courtesy Mrs M Birkbeck.

Cross, but even before that his life had been an eventful one. Greenock-born, he had spent his childhood in an Anglican orphanage in Capetown, running away when he was twelve, not to the circus but to the copper mines of Northern Rhodesia where he found a job as a 'grease boy'. Later in South Africa he worked as a newspaper copy boy then in London as overseas editor with the Press Association. In the early 1930s he decided to train for the ministry. He saved hard, had private tuition to fill the gaps in his formal education and was admitted to Aberdeen University where he went on to have a distinguished academic and athletic career. By 1936 he was a divinity student and assistant minister at Causewayend Church.

One day in Jute Street, he had come upon a large drunken Irishman beating his wife. He made the man stop. A crowd gathered round to see what would happen next, but Birkbeck who represented Aberdeen University at boxing, rugby and cricket was not easily overawed. The bully went off, shamed, and Birkbeck later visited the family at the Jute Works. He was appalled at what he saw. He instigated a Sunday night service in the huge communal wash-house and in January 1937 organised a memorable dance and cabaret show, again in the wash-house, with street musicians and the unemployed providing the music. One of the highlights of the evening was a draw which he had set up with the help of Peggy Simpson, soon to become Mrs Birkbeck. Local shopkeepers and firms had contributed the prizes, and there was something for everyone. And then, as the local press reported:

A little ceremony which was not without its touching side was performed. A young divinity student, Mr Birkbeck, has been doing missionary work among the Jute Works dwellers, giving a word of encouragement here and a word of comfort there. He has won the esteem of the people and to show it they clubbed together, giving coppers out of their meagrely filled purses, and presented him with a fountain pen and pencil set.

The proceeds of concert that evening raised 13/6, which was sent, anonymously to Provost Watt's Infirmary Fund.

Birkbeck meanwhile had sent an independent report to the Department of Health for Scotland, and the Department was also petitioned by the tenants themselves. Officials visited the Jute Works in February 1937 and found that out of the forty-six families there, only four men had work. At this time standard rent for a 'house' of two rooms was 5/3 weekly, but some tenants were paying 7/9 and 11/- a week, an accumulation of rent arrears and gas bills. The Department pronounced the accommodation 'ultra substandard' and suggested that the Town Council advise the public that the Jute Works housing colony was a temporary expedient, and would be closed down and tenants relocated as soon as possible. On a practical note, the Department recommended the installation of hip and spray baths in a section of the wash-house, and the filling-in of the ponds. However the Jute Works still had a role to play as emergency accommodation. When, for example, a fire gutted a property in James Street in April 1938, those rendered homeless were immediately housed in the old Works.

During the war, the buildings were requisitioned by the War Department and provided a very unpopular billet for servicemen. As Jim Glennie recalled: 'It was a terrible place. We slept in bunks in three tiers and although there were showering facilities, (presumably in the famous wash-house), we were allowed very little water.' Towards the end of the war the

143

Jute Works were occupied by the enemy in the shape of Italian prisoners of war who became familiar figures in the Froghall and Spital areas. No one seems to remember exactly where they worked or what they did, but they would have been involved in road mending or agricultural work. Elizabeth Weston (née Hutton), born and brought up at No 18 Froghall Road, the home of her grandfather, the stonemason John Melvin, remembers the one that tried to get away. 'He escaped from the Jute Works and came up the side of Ernan Cottage in Froghall Terrace, and into our garden at No 18. My mother got a shock to find him in the kitchen. When she appeared he dashed out the back door and down to the granite yard below on the 'low road' - the bottom half of Froghall Road. After that there was a great commotion - soldiers or guards were chasing him - I believe he was quickly

From left, the last tenement in Jute Street at its junction with Froghall Terrace, Causewayend Church, Froghall council houses and right foreground, the Jute Works.

recaptured.' The blitz of April 1943, is another unforgettable memory. 'We stood in Froghall Road and watched the clock on Causewayend Church ringing as it burned.'

Elizabeth Weston's home at No 18 was built later than the neighbouring Nos 10-16 and had a garage. 'Next to No 18 was a vacant feu owned by Mr James Forbes who had the granite yards immediately below our house, on the low road. We rented this feu and when I was small it was part of our garden where my grandfather grew vegetables. Next to the garden was an old blacksmith's shop where I well remember the smith, who I think was a Mr Smith, pumping the bellows for his fire, heating metals until were red hot and plunging them into water to sizzle and cool before he hammered them on the anvil. After the smithy, the road curved round and there were

St Martha's playground lies derelict today (cf 'The Spital' page 193). St Martha's, No 19 the Spital, looms above. The steps descending to Froghall Road (not visible) are to the extreme right.

no more houses on that side.' Her aunt, Elizabeth Bandeen remembers that the yard of James Leith & Son, Contractors, and the old Shirras yard, beside the little group of houses, Nos 23-27. St Margaret's Convent and St Martha's Home backed on to Froghall Road and as a child Mrs Weston was greatly intrigued by the sisters and their charges. Opposite No 18 was a plot rented by Mr Birnie of No 12 where he grew vegetables. It was this plot which was concreted over in 1955 to provide a playground for the girls of St Martha's.

Nearby, at the steep, Spital, end of Froghall Terrace, local women still shudder to recall the difficulties of negotiating it in winter when it could become a sheet of ice. If you had a baby in a pram as well, it was a desperate place. But

The treacherous brae. Froghall Terrace viewed from the Spital. Froghall Road is on the left.

Stanley Rennie of King's Crescent, looking back to his boyhood, had a different use for prams, or at least their wheels. 'Froghall Terrace in those days,' he recalls, 'had the minimum of vehicular traffic, largely because of the steep brae running down to the Jute Works. For those reasons it was a magnet for children with their own 'transport' be it bicycle, 'kairtie' (a 5ft wooden plank with a pair of old pram wheels at each end and steerable), or sledging on snowy days. Boot and shoe soles underwent excessive wear when used for braking! The only major obstacles to this unbridled joy were

A latter day view of the Froghall plotties. Courtesy, G R & M Winram.

workers from the Jute Works and the numerous granite yards as they streamed home at midday or teatime.'

Across on the other side of Froghall Terrace were the plotties, which by wartime numbered about forty. In later years, their character changed. They were used not so much for growing plants as for housing lofts of racing pigeons guarded by dogs in kennels. They eventually deteriorated into an untidy rickle of buildings, a weed-ridden eyesore. Many locals were relieved when, in July 1979, CALA announced plans to develop thirty-five two-bedroomed houses there, with carport underneath, designed by Mr P White, architect. In due course, the attractively landscaped Froghall View, a 'Private Road', appeared on the site. In spite of protests, the ancient right of way was obliterated.

In 1970, disquiet that had been simmering in the Froghall housing

The plotties were replaced by Froghall View.

scheme, surfaced in the local press. There were complaints that it was a forgotten area, that houses were in poor condition, that the place had a bad reputation, that the Council repeatedly ignored complaints. Locals decided on action, and the Froghall Tenants' Association, with Mr Frank Yeomans as the first chairman, was formed, with funds of 2/7. A list of improvements sought by tenants was drawn up, and a community newspaper established. Councillors listened more sympathetically, impressed by the sense of self-help and neighbourliness. All this happened before community centres became commonplace, or before statutory provision was made for community councils. Froghall was part of a pioneering arts and community workshop movement that was taking place in council schemes in various parts of Scotland. Later, a local firm provided premises in Causewayend for the Tenants' Association. It was demolished during the road widening programme at Mounthooly, but was subsequently replaced by a custom-built centre which sits discreetly behind some bushes in Powis Place.

Self-help had come to the area even before the days of the Tenants' Association. Mr Billy Kerr, a Froghall resident and a slaughterman to trade, had done some boxing when he was younger, and his son Tony, recalls how he started up a boxing club, the Froghall Pals, in what spare time he had, to keep boys off the streets, to give them something to do. The club met in a shed to train, the old bakehouse storeroom at the rear of No 39 the Spital,

The Spital 'gym' where the Froghall Pals worked out. It was originally a baker's store.

The 1970 Commonwealth games. From left to right, Adam Smith, John Gillan, Tony Kerr and Tommy Begg. Courtesy, John Gillan.

where there is access from Froghall Terrace. 'Kids would come from all over the place, not just Froghall.' Tony Kerr recalls. 'My father would sometimes have to give them their bus fares home.'

'Billy Kerr was a dedicated man and a second father to me,' says John Gillan, another ex-Froghall boy, whose boxing career lasted from 1959-76. Both Tony and John were star pupils of Billy Kerr's. They later joined Tommy Begg's Aberdeen Amateur Boxing Club where they trained under Adam Smith. Both boxed for Scotland. John Gillan represented his country fifty times, three times at the European games. He took his first title at sixteen as a fly-weight, and won the Scottish title six times between 1970 and 1976. It was in 1970 when he was twenty-two that he won the silver medal in the Edinburgh Commonwealth Games, boxing as a light-weight. Tony Kerr had done well too, reaching the quarter finals, and there was a glorious homecoming for both of them after the Games. The whole of Froghall turned out to greet them and Froghall Avenue was festooned in bunting.

Recalling Tommy Begg who was his manager from the time he was fourteen until Begg's death in 1972, John Gillan says, 'Tommy hardly reached five feet yet could push me to my limit. He was always thinking up new exercises, and wouldn't stand any nonsense - but his bark was worse than his bite.' John left Froghall at twenty-five when he got married but still remembers the good community atmosphere. He and Tony Kerr are still friends and both men run their own businesses.

Froghall had another great boxer of an earlier generation, Jimmy Knowles, who lived at No 3 Froghall Gardens with his wife Hilda. Born in 1914, and fighting as a bantam-weight (not over 8st 6lbs), he was one of the few to beat the legendary Benny Lynch. He won on points in 1933 and went on to become Scottish bantam-weight champion. He gave up the ring after injury and later worked as a meat cutter with E C Matheson & Son. Jimmy Knowles died in November 1976 at the age of sixty-two following a heart attack. Only a few months earlier he had presented the trophy named in his honour, for all round sporting excellence, at Sunnybank School.

The Froghall housing scheme remains a pleasant-looking, friendly place as you walk through it on summer's day. Many gardens are well-tended, with people taking a pride in their homes. There is an mix of inhabitants, for members of the Moslem community have been provided with homes there while the men pursue postgraduate studies at Aberdeen University. Unfortunately, the scheme continues to be bedevilled by problems as it has been from the start. There is a relatively high proportion of single parent families, and of families with financial and social difficulties. Many residents are angered too, by the proliferation of drug dealers in their community, and want them cleared out. Time to create a better image for the estate.

Unlike the housing scheme, old Froghall including much of Froghall Terrace and Froghall Road, rarely makes the headlines. In Froghall Road, John Melvin's old vegetable patch has been built over and Woodrope Ltd, who make ropes, twine and nets are there now. Further down the hill there is a little nucleus of light industry including Mitre Glass Fibre, Victoria Light Engineering, Long Technology, and others. That part of the low road, including the area occupied by Forbes' Granite Yard until the mid sixties has been taken over by Chandlers International (Aberdeen) Ltd.

At the opposite side of Froghall, the Cottages, Nos 51-57 Froghall Terrace, still sit in their walled enclosure of dressed granite trimmings and brickwork. The gates are flanked by pillars, and there is a granite plaque announcing 'Froghall Cottages'. Apart from the lodge just beside the gates, there were at one time three cottages, but these have since been converted to form two roomier homes. Inside the gates there is a little avenue of pollarded limes, and Molly Stephen who lives in the lodge with her husband, Charles, remembers that when they first came, the trees which had not been pruned back at that time, made the avenue very dark, though there was a lovely mass of wild hyacinths in springtime. Attached to the wall beside the avenue is an ancient ring, perhaps a relic of Canal days.

Her long garden gives a glimmering of what the old market garden would have been like before Jute Street was built across it. The path is paved with slabs of contrasting granite. Molly's father, James Steinson, was a lind polisher with G M Stalker in Jute Street, where the family used to live, and

Mrs Molly Stephen in her garden at the Froghall Cottages. The slabs of the path are in different types of granite.

as is so often the case, in the homes and gardens of former granite workers, one finds mementoes of the old industry. There is one other here, a milk bottle holder hewn out of pink granite with holes for quart, pint and half pint bottles. She recalls her father saying that the young apprentices would be told by the older men - if you make a mistake, bury it and start again, the boss will never know. One wonders how many partly worked granite slabs lie beneath the King's Crescent, Jute Street, or the King Street areas, or wherever there was a concentration of granite yards! Molly Stephen remembers that in the old days, the rent was paid to the Stalkers who owned the Cottages, and had been gardeners there before they became granite merchants. The Jute Works were across the road from the Cottages and she retains a vivid picture of wash-house doors opening to let the steam out. Mr Tough was the caretaker, and he kept the wash-house spotless.

The Jute Works, or part of them, are still there, having evaded attempts at complete demolition over the years. The well known paint manufacturing firm, Isaac Spencer & Co, purchased the three acre site, all that was left of the original fourteen acres, after their premises at Albert Quay were destroyed by fire in 1960. Isaac Spencer's origins go back to the late nineteenth century and the production of cod liver oil, but within a short time, the firm had diversified into the manufacture of paints and allied products, a side line which soon became a main line. Many of Aberdeen's leading industrialists have served on the Board, including members of the Lewis and Irvin families and Charles Alexander, while the best known managing director was the former Don, Archie Glen. The firm, now Spencer Coatings Ltd, specialises in a wide range of heavy duty anti-corrosive industrial paints. In January 1995 planing permission was granted for 148 flats on the site, so in the future we may see houses there.

The area where the ponds used to be, which was unsuitable for housing became a GPO workshop and store. Staff inevitably referred to it as 'the Jute Works'.

Masons and polishers at the polishing mill at Charles McDonald's Froghall Granite Works, Jute Street in the 1880s. McDonald sits with his hands clasped. The usual granite yard dog is third left from McDonald. Note the overhead crane with crab, rope and chain. The Jute Works are in the background. Courtesy, Aberdeen City Library and Cultural Services.

Chapter 12

The Froghall Granite Masters

Lord Provost Rust was in his younger days, a first-class craftsman who could wield the mall and puncheon with the best of them.

William Diack, The Granite Industry in Aberdeen, 1949.

Froghall, or speaking more strictly, Jute Street, was, like King's Crescent, a thriving centre of the granite trade in its heyday. Jute Street had been laid out by the builder Daniel Macandrew in 1874 as an access for the Jute Factory at the time of its creation and Aberdeen Town Council's Street Committee recommended that it be so named 'in accordance with the wishes of Mr Macandrew'. It ran north-westwards from King's Crescent originally coming to a halt at the south wall of the Froghall Cottages' enclosure. As well as building his innovative concrete villas at the Jute Street-King's Crescent corner, Macandrew feued off 177 feet of building stances on the north-west side of Jute Street, intended for more humble dwellings. A row of tenements duly appeared, bearing the date 1878, while others were built soon after 1880 on the opposite side of the road. Plans to continue Canal Street, northwards then north-eastwards across Jute Street to exit opposite the Jute Works failed to materialise, and so it was to the empty ground where Canal Street was meant to run, just outside the city boundary, that Charles McDonald relocated his firm in 1881 and renamed it the Froghall Granite Works. But it was, and is still known by those who used to work there, as Charlie McDonald's.

McDonald was the first granite merchant to move into this area. He had been born in Dyce in 1849 into a granite-working family - his father and two brothers were masons to trade - and after serving his time, emigrated to Barré, Vermont, a great Mecca of North East granite masons, whose skills were in great demand in America. 'Being a skilled workman and a man of exceptionally fine taste, Mr McDonald prospered in America even above many of his fellows', recorded his obituarist. On his return to Aberdeen in 1877, he set up a small yard in Gerrard Street, then moved to Nelson Street as the business grew. He established substantially larger premises in the Jute Street/Froghall area in 1881 whither the stone-cutting firm of Arthur Taylor, his Nelson Street neighbour, followed him two years later. The pattern would be the same as in King's Crescent. When one granite merchant found a good spot, others gregariously joined him. But while MacDonald's Froghall Granite Works, at what became Nos 46-50 Jute Street, was outwith the city boundary saving the need to pay rates, at least for a couple of years, Taylor, at No 43 Jute Street, within the city boundary, enjoyed no such initial advantage.

A third yard, George Thom's Albion Granite Works began to operate in 1885 at Nos 65-67 Jute Street, opposite McDonald's. Thom's first yard had been in Canal Road, but he had his eye on a suitable site, not yet feued out for housing, just along from his tenement home at No 59 Jute Street. Thom and his family now flitted 'over the shop' to Albion Cottage at the back of the yard. By 1890 the St Machar Granite Works of George M Stalker also found a home in Jute Street, immediately next door to Charlie McDonald's, though the Stalker yard was much smaller. The last granite yard to settle in the area was the Ernan Granite Works of James Forbes. It was on the opposite side of Froghall Road from McDonald's - the layout of the Forbes, McDonald and Stalker yards is shown on page 135. Forbes too had moved around before settling in Froghall. From 1884 he was briefly in Charles Street, then at No 21 Mounthooly, at the old mini industrial complex which is now the cul-de-sac of Canal Place.

By the time that James Forbes came to Froghall in 1892, Charlie McDonald, at forty-three, was on his death bed. He had been an innovative granite master, a man ahead of his time, as far as both technology and working conditions were concerned. Most granite firms specialised in monumental masonry, but McDonald, who employed around 150 men, undertook both monumental and architectural work. *Mechanical Aberdeen* reports the yard to be well-mechanised, specialising in preparing imported granite from Norway and Sweden, though a greystone quarry near Scalloway in Shetland opened by the firm had proved unprofitable. His trade, apart from the English market, was, as his obituarist in the *In Memoriam* of 1892 noted, 'with the Australian colonies where his products were greatly in demand'. One of his most important orders, at a cost of several thousand pounds, was for a massive front for a Melbourne bank. The anonymous scribe did not however, disguise his disapproval of McDonald's humanitarianism:

154

Charles McDonald's letterhead. The branch office was in Melbourne.
Courtesy, Andrew Cheyne.

About eighteen months ago he erected at considerable cost, a building for his stonecutters that was and still is, an entirely new departure... It was a large wooden structure with slated roof accommodating about 120 workmen and while so constructed as to allow abundant air space, it afforded complete shelter for the workmen in all kinds of weather.

To mark the opening of this building, McDonald also announced an improvement in his men's weekly working hours, from fifty-one to forty-nine for the same wages. This caused consternation within the employers' association, the Aberdeen Granite Association. McDonald was urged by his colleague to toe the line and return to the old hours. 'He resolutely declined to do so, and as a result', reported *In Memoriam*, 'his name was struck off the roll of membership'. He later won the day and was readmitted to the Association, while his men 'continued to enjoy the concession he had made'. The obituary concludes with a further whiff of reproof.

between himself and his men there existed, not the bonds of service but the links of affection. Though holding advanced 'Labour' views, he was not accustomed publicly to parade them, but as indicated his concessions were many and liberal. He made over a cottage at Culter as a convalescent home for sick children.... He was large-hearted, open-handed, in sympathy with everything that was good and true. He gave ungrudgingly of his means to every worthy object - he was perhaps charitable to a fault.

The business continued after McDonald's death and by 1900, the machinery in use, some of it invented by McDonald himself, was being driven by a 200 hp steam engine. Shortly before the First World War the firm amalgamated with Rust & Alexander, whose principal, James Rust -

McDonald's yard looking towards Jute Street. 'Dogs' are being fitted to 'dogholes' for lifting the huge granite blocks. Courtesy, Aberdeen City Library and Cultural Services.

Alexander was by then long gone - subsequently became managing director. The name, Charles McDonald Ltd, continued in use, as did the Froghall premises.

Rust, son of a Danestone grieve, was as William Diack related in *The Granite Industry in Aberdeen:*

in his younger days, a first-class craftsman who could wield the mall and puncheon, and fashion a delicate scroll or an elaborately-carved Runic cross with the best of them.

He was also one of the most able movers and shakers that Aberdeen Town Council has known. He had served his mason's apprenticeship with Alexander Milne's Imperial Granite Works in St Clair Street, while his civic apprenticeship was on the old Parish Council. In 1914 he was returned unopposed as councillor for Rosemount. Five years later he became convener of the Housing Committee at a time when the Council's ardour for slum clearance was not yet paralleled by an equal enthusiasm for the provision of new housing. Rust took the bull by the horns and launched Aberdeen's first modern housing scheme at Torry. He became city treasurer in 1920 and during the decade that followed he acquired the estates of

Hilton and Kincorth for council housing, the former in 1925, for £22,000, the latter three years later for £45,000. His first *coup* as city treasurer was the purchase of the magnificent estate of Hazlehead for £40,000 restoring a part of the lost Freedom Lands to the people of Aberdeen. In 1928, he bought the Music Hall for £34,000, for the city, from the liquidators of the Aberdeen Music Hall Company. To him we owe the fact that the original ARI building at Foresterhill is in granite. To quote William Diack again:

It was in a large measure through his influence that the threatened blemish on the architectural fame of Aberdeen - a brick Infirmary on the outskirts of the Granite City - was averted. The directors of the Royal Infirmary and the architects of the proposed buildings were flirting with the idea of erecting the new hospital of brick - all in the interests of a short-sighted economy - but the vigorous protests against the threatened blot on modern Aberdeen architecture was made by a patriotic body of citizens. And it is giving away no secret to that it was largely through the influence of Mr Rust that the fine range of buildings at Foresterhill were built of the grey granite of Aberdeenshire.

He became Lord Provost in 1929 in succession to Sir Andrew Lewis. Two years later Aberdeen University honoured him with a well-earned LLD. At the time of his death in 1945, he was still managing director of Charles McDonald Ltd. How did he manage to run the Froghall Granite Works, carry out so much pioneering civic work and undertake the ceaseless demands of a Lord Provostship?

'He was never at the yard,' recalls his daughter, Miss Margaret Rust, who before retirement was a solicitor in the Town Clerk's Department, and in charge of the city's archives. Charlie McDonald's was in good hands, however, run by her brother, James Rust Jnr, and later by James' son, Dugald Rust. Miss Rust remembers from childhood, the ceaseless noise of the tools grinding on granite as

James Rust, Lord Provost and granite master.

she walked along Jute Street. There is a story of a clock that used to sit on the mantelpiece of the ground floor flat of No 73, opposite McDonald's. It had never gone, its workings all shook up by reverberations from the yard. Eventually it was given away by its exasperated owner, and once removed from the granite zone, worked perfectly.

Andrew Cheyne came to work as draughtsman at McDonald's in 1945 after five years in a German prisoner-of-war camp. He had served an engineering apprenticeship at John M Henderson's in King Street, but by the time of his release from captivity, was suffering from dermatitis. Because of the hazards of red lead poisoning, Henderson's were unable to re-employ him. He had been an outstanding evening class student of technical drawing at Robert Gordon's Technical College and the Head, Dr Alex West, showed his drawings to James Rust Jnr, who having looked through them, asked the sur-prised Cheyne, 'When can you start?' He was taken on as a draughtsman, assistant to the renowned R Connon Garden, architect, and manager of McDonald's who, having spent a lifetime with the firm, retired before the year was out. The firm at that time was employing eighty men, and Cheyne found himself working non-stop, keeping the masons busy with designs for memorials, and at the same time translating archi-

*James Rust Jnr with clerical staff.
Courtesy, Andrew Cheyne.*

tects' plans into full-sized, highly detailed working drawings for a whole range of buildings, shop fronts, banks and building societies.

The full-sized drawing for a memorial would be done on tracing paper and pasted onto the stone to allow the mason to cut round the lines. He was amazed at what people asked to go on their gravestones, and in his day, has produced a 1965 Ford Prefect for an car enthusiast, sheep and pigs for a farmer, even eggs for an egg producer. Working drawings for the architectural side of the business were also done in the yard. This latterly included a life-size model in cardboard for the steps leading to the Post Office and the upper level of the St Nicholas Centre. They took up so much room that they had to be laid out in Froghall Terrace for inspection, and that meant waiting for a dry day.

Draughtsmanship apart, Andrew Cheyne, an authority on all the techniques of granite cutting and polishing, and has many a tale to tell about the industry. Doug Mennie, he recalls, could cut a memorial book in granite using a diamond saw in eight and a half hours, to such a high standard that it could go straight for hand polishing. Once, when circumstances dictated,

Mr and Mrs Cheyne.

he cut two books within that same period. Then there was the new Van Dyne polishing process in which McDonald's were interested. William McKay's already had it, and knowing that it was McKay's' practice to lay out newly completed memorials in a row for inspection, Andrew strolled into their Holland Street yard at an appropriate time to do a bit of industrial spying. He was bending down examining the fruits of the new process when he felt a hand on his collar and he was firmly ejected from the yard. He remembers too, an amazing 'scam' that went on for a time in a neighbouring Froghall yard. Machinery would be mysteriously switched on about 5am, whine away, then be switched off before the workforce arrived at 8am. It was soon discovered that stolen stones were being worked in the yard, supplying a market for cheap headstones.

Charlie McDonald's closed down in 1979, and the business was taken over by John Fyfe. Cheyne joined the John Fyfe staff but stayed on for a year at Froghall, overseeing the decommissioning of the yard. This was a heartbreaking time, watching the machinery he had installed over the years being pulled out and scrapped. These days the hallmark of his trade is clear to see outside his home - a piece of Correnie granite with his name in gold lettering.

A housing development, McDonald Court, Froghall Terrace, is now on the site of McDonald's yard. March Stone No 60, which sat against the wall of the yard in Froghall Road, was destroyed when McDonald Court

March Stone No 60, foreground outside No 74 Jute Street.

McDonald Court, site of Charles McDonald's Froghall Granite Works.

was being built. Its replacement was sited to the south, in the garden of No 74 Jute Street. McDonald Court, nearer the original boundary line and attractively landscaped with rowan and chestnut trees would perhaps now make a more appropriate setting .

Arthur Taylor, whose firm arrived in Jute Street in 1883, came from Morayshire and served his apprenticeship in William Keith's King Street yard. It was Keith who built the amazing Scots baronial Rubislawden House in 1881 which later became the Gordon House Hotel and is now a home for the elderly. Taylor himself was a brilliant granite cutter and sculptor of figures. Like Charlie McDonald he was an innovator. At a time when granite was cut laboriously by manual labour, Taylor is credited with being the first manufacturer to use pneumatic tools. These were introduced from the United States and demonstrated in Aberdeen at Kittybrewster Station in October 1895. The GNSR used the Westinghouse braking system, and the power was provided courtesy of their compressed air cylinders. Arthur Taylor initially used an engine and belt as a source of power, so 'whether he was actually the first to install a proper compressed air plant is not quite so certain', writes William Diack. Whatever the facts, Taylor was quick off his mark. In October, 1897, he was awarded the contract to manufacture the statue of Hygieia, goddess of health, to mark the presentation of the Duthie Park by Miss Elizabeth Duthie to the people of Aberdeen. He had not only submitted the lowest tender of £415, but, at 6

Lions for the base of the Duthie Park's Hygieia statue being carved in Taylor's workshop. Note the pneumatic tools. James Philip is in the foreground. Courtesy, Aberdeen City Library and Cultural Services.

ft 6 ins, plans for the tallest goddess as well. This was to be a historic occasion, the first time that pneumatic tools were used on granite in Britain. Hygieia stands near the Polmuir Road gates, atop an elegantly fluted, ornately carved 30ft high Corinthian column. Although it is difficult to see, she is assisting a snake (apparently symbolising health) to have a drink out of a cup. The plinth is guarded by four pink granite lions, and the whole magnificent ensemble is Category 'B'-listed. In commemoration of the occasion, Taylor later presented the two pneumatic 'Hygieia' hammers to Aberdeen Mechanical Society.

Another of Taylor's masterpieces, created after the Boer War, was similar in composition to 'Hygieia', a fluted

The Lions today.

161

Oak Villa, left, with granite pillars, Arthur Taylor's house in Ashgrove Road. Another granite merchant, John O Rettie, lived in Abbey Green, the villa on the far right.

column, Ionic this time, with a figure on top and four lions at the base. But the subject was very different. The figure was a rifleman and the statute was dedicated to the memory of the men of the Cape Mounted Rifles. William Diack described it as 'one of the finest military memorials ever produced in an Aberdeen granite yard'.

Arthur Taylor had no turning shop so it may be that the columns for these statues were turned in the Bower & Florence yard, just round the corner in King's Crescent. Arthur Taylor himself lived at Oak Villa in Ashgrove Road which boasts a fine pair of pillars - that trademark again - and he would no doubt have ordered them from one of his colleagues.

Aberdeen's statue of Edward VII, instigated by Colonel Innes of Learney of Militia Barracks fame and designed by the sculptor Alfred Drury and the architect A Marshall Mackenzie was created in Taylor's yard. By January 1912, the chosen block of Kemnay granite had arrived in the yard, and Drury's full-sized model was *en route* from London though with respect to Drury, cutting a statue out of granite is a very different matter from making a plaster model. There is a famous photograph of James Philip, one of Taylor's top craftsmen, getting the King into shape with a hand puncheon. Philip's many fine pieces included work on Lord Cowdray's coat-of-arms for Dunecht House along with Thomas Pirie, and the memorial to those who perished when the *Titanic* sank on her maiden voyage in 1912. Alas, the time was not far distant when he and his colleagues would be fully

Knickerbocker glory. James Philip carving Edward VII with a hand puncheon. Difficulties over a choice of a site for the statue were eventually resolved when it was placed at the Union Street-Union Terrace junction.

Below, Thomas Pirie, Philip's colleague, working on Lord Cowdray's coat-of-arms. for Dunecht House with a pneumatic tool.
Both photographs, courtesy, Aberdeen City Library and Cultural Services.

occupied carving numerous memorials to the fallen of the First World War. He must have taken great pride in carving from Kemnay granite, Aberdeen's War Memorial Lion, to a design by William Macmillian. It was unveiled at the Art Gallery-Cowdray Hall complex at Schoolhill in 1925. Working with Philip on the Lion was George Cooper Clark another of Taylor's top granite cutters. Clark, incidentally lived at No 6 Orchard Street, which was built by George Thom of the Albion Granite Works. Clark's widow, Edith has a photograph of Philip taking dimensions from Macmillan's plaster model while her husband stands behind,

The War Memorial Lion. Philip in the foreground takes dimensions while George Cooper Clark works on the lion's body. Courtesy, Edith Clark.

working on the body of the Lion.

Arthur Taylor, who had been a leading member of Aberdeen Granite Association died in 1930, and was succeeded by his son, Arthur Taylor Jnr, who had served with the Artist Rifles in the First World War, and was a keen hillwalker and a member of the Deeside Field Club. Ian McLaren of Bower & Florence remembers him well. 'Arthur Taylor was quite a character. He was a bachelor, always well-dressed, well-groomed and polite. He lived in apartments in the Caledonian Hotel after the house in Ashgrove Road was sold. If one met him of a morning in King's Crescent he would wave his walking stick and call, 'Good morning - how are things in town?' This was rather curious, because he had just come from town! But he was a very charming gentleman.' Arthur Taylor Jnr died in 1955 and the firm closed down. At that time there were still over forty granite yards in Aberdeen and skilled craftsmen like George Cooper Clark had no difficulty in finding work elsewhere. He went to Edward's yard in Pittodrie Street and later to Crichton's in Regent Walk. The site of Arthur Taylor's yard is now covered by flats, Nos 35-45 Jute Street.

George M Stalker came on the scene in 1890, setting up his St Machar Granite yard next door to Charlie McDonald's at Nos 32-36 Jute Street. Like most granite merchants of his era, Stalker had worked his way to the top of the trade, serving his apprenticeship with Peter Bisset's building firm, then going into partnership with the King Street granite merchant, Alexander Wilson, who had been in the business since the 1870s. On Wilson's death in 1890 Stalker, then in his early thirties, went solo. He had once lived in Jute Street, next to the Albion yard, and knew the area well. When George Thom retired, Stalker took over his Albion yard, and used it for storage. He and his brother, who joined him in the business, were landlords of the tenements at Nos 69-79 Jute Street, and the tenants of Froghall Cottages also paid their rent to the Stalkers until well within living memory. It seems likely they were members of the Stalker family who had lived at the Cottages for years, eventually owning them.

The firm were strictly monumental masons and polishers and George M Stalker was one of the first to go on granite selling trips throughout the UK. His son, also George, joined the firm and proved to be both a skilled designer and craftsman. He died in 1931, aged only forty-nine, predeceasing his father. George M Stalker, who had lived for many years at No 534 King Street, followed him five years later, dying in harness at the age of eighty. His grandson, Mr Alan Stalker, who served his time in the yard before going abroad was the third generation to join the firm. Stalker's, like its founder, was one of the longer lived of the Aberdeen granite yards, surviving until 1980 when like Charlie McDonald's, it too was acquired by John Fyfe. Stalker's site is now covered with housing and the boundary

Stalker's old store yard which was once the Albion Granite Yard.

with Charlie McDonald's has been obliterated.

The final yard in this group was the Ernan Granite Works of James Forbes who had come to Aberdeen from the Inverernan area of Strathdon, hence the name. This was Forbes country, and Duncan Forbes, a retired shipmaster living in the city had earlier named his lovely house in the South Stocket - now Beechgrove Terrace - Ernan Lodge, though there was no connection between the two men. In 1892 James Forbes feued an extensive piece of ground from Henry William Knight Erskine, part of the Spital Lands, in Froghall Lane. Owing to a misinterpretation of the feu charter,

Ernan Cottage.

Forbes thought he was required to build a house there, hence the two-flatted Ernan Cottage, perched beside the yard. He lived there for a time and later moved to No 8 Erskine Street, which, with its neighbour No 10, forms a matching pair. The façades of both houses have distinctive slabs of pink granite. Yet again, the mark of the granite merchant. (They are the middle block of houses shown on page 75).

The Ernan yard had an unusual asset, an artesian well which in the early days was used to provide power for the machinery. A notebook in the possession of the Forbes family gives notes of its dimensions, along with many other details on the running of the yard, including gravestones ordered, and their costings. As with so many granite firms, three generations were involved. James, the founder, was succeeded at the helm by his son, Frank, an excellent draughtsman, and the family have a wonderfully intricate sketch of his, not for a granite memorial but a wrought iron gate. Frank in turn was followed by his son, William. During these years, James Forbes & Son specialised in headstones of Celtic design, and had many orders from Wales where one of their travellers was based. The end came in 1966 when William Forbes fell ill. The Rusts across at Charlie McDonald's took over all outstanding work, and the yard closed. Fortunately Mr Forbes enjoyed a long retirement, dying in 1996. At his King's Gate home there are many mementoes of the yard, including a fine block of polished pink granite, which Mrs Mary Forbes has ingeniously converted into a sundial, granite balls and other artefacts and small knickknacks such as rings, made by the

TELEPHONE N° 21445.

JAMES FORBES & SON *Limited*

GRANITE MERCHANTS

ARCHITECTURAL & MONUMENTAL SCULPTORS

ERNAN GRANITE WORKS · 28/34 FROGHALL ROAD,

ABERDEEN

The letterhead of James Forbes' Ernan Granite Works. Courtesy, Rachel A Forbes.

The workforce of Forbes' Granite Yard. Frank Forbes, with boater is extreme right. Miss Steele, secretary, sits centre, with the yard's dog to her right. Courtesy, Rachel A Forbes.

men in their spare time, from granite cores. The old Froghall yard is now the premises of Chandlers International, Aberdeen Ltd. The artesian well is still there.

Jute Street is now silent. The original tenements, built to house the jute and the granite workers, remain intact, and the sites of the old yards are identifiable only insofar as they are covered with modern housing. But one yard does remain, though no longer connected with the granite trade. George Thom's Albion yard, later Stalker's store, is still there, and has been home to a variety of firms over the years.

Part 2

Spital Lands East

Lodges, St Peter's Cemetery, King Street.

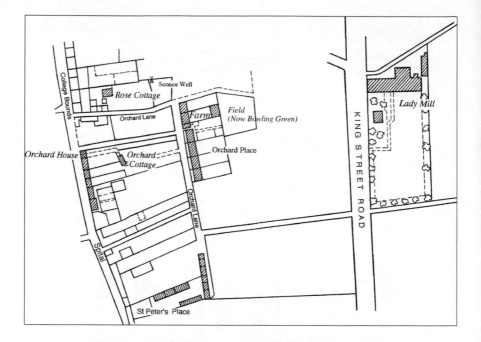

This conjectural plan shows how the 'Orchard' area would have looked in the 1880s. Nos 1a and 1b have been added to the original houses of Orchard Place and the field that later became the Northern Bowling Club has appeared to the rear. The little cottages near the foot of St Peter's Place have not yet been demolished to make way for the upper part of Orchard Street, which does not exist. Orchard Walk and Orchard Place, some years in the future, are still known as Orchard Lane. Note the track, now obliterated, which goes down to the Lady Mill, then on to the brick kilns at Seaton.

Chapter 13

The 'Orchards':
House, Cottage, Place and Lane

'...an Orchard planted with upwards of a hundred various Fruit Trees,'
Aberdeen Journal, 21 November, 1810.

In Part Two we put the east side of the Spital Lands under the microscope. Their character was very different from the Lands of the west side. They included the southern part of Old Aberdeen with its early nineteenth century charm as well as the lost lands verging on the Links, given over for many years to a sewerage farm, a dung stance, and a knacker's yard. The map of the Spital Estate of 1883 identifies the east side clearly, as we would expect; we start just south of Love Lane, marching with the freedom and royalty boundary of the city, crossing the King Street Road to the Rifle Range, taking the cart-road to the Gallow Slacks, following the freedom and royalty boundary north until it is intersected by the Powis Burn, turning back south-eastwards to follow the burn upstream to the Lady Mill... well perhaps this isn't so clear after all. We better have a look at the east Spital Lands in modern terms.

Love Lane is now St Peter Street, and we follow it eastwards, crossing King Street to reach No 392 just before Merkland Road East. We continue eastwards between the remains of the Gallowhills gasholder (which was in Aberdeen) and Pittodrie Stadium (in the Spital Lands). This gap was the old cart-road to the Gallow Slacks - boggy, low-lying ground. Golf Road is then followed to just south of Regent Road, where we now turn to run diagonally westwards, passing between the back of the Chris Anderson Stadium (in the Spital Lands) and Linksfield Academy (outwith) to reach the King Street Mill pub. We cross King Street to University Road whose south side was within the Spital Lands, going as far as that entrance to the Butchart Centre which is nearest College Bounds. The old line then went behind the gardens of Nos 48-20 College Bounds - today we can walk alongside them using the right of way through the Butchart car park - to meet Orchard Walk at its junction with Orchard Place. We then go westwards along Orchard Walk whose south side was also within the Spital Lands, to its junction with College Bounds at No 10. We head southwards along the Spital for a short distance and reach the west side of the Lands by climbing up towards the Primrosehill Centre.

If this seems crazy, that is only because of today's topography of culverts and built-up areas. The route just described followed what were once obvious, natural boundaries, the Banstickle Burn at the St Peter Street end, then the course of the Powis Burn which is fully culverted now, but which flowed in open cut, as least in part, until relatively recent times. After 1804 or thereby, the east Spital Lands were divided into inner and outer sections when King Street was laid out. It was the Northern Turnpike, which, after passing the burgh boundary at Love Lane-St Peter Street became known as the King Street Road until it reached the Bridge of Don; and so it remained for many years. We can start by looking at the inner part of these lands, circumscribed by University Road, College Bounds-Spital, Orchard Street, and the King Street Road. St Peter's Cemetery is also a part of these inner lands.

When the Aberdeen-born builder John Clark, returned from London at the beginning of the nineteenth century, he decided to build a new house for

A detail from Taylor's Plan, 1773, showing just north of the 'Play House', the extended rig bordered by trees which probably formed the curtilage of Orchard House. Note the 'Church Yard' sitting on a mound. This was the old Spital Kirkyard, the 'germ' of St Peter's Cemetery. The road around them was the East Back Gate, parts of which became Orchard Lane, the first of that name, later Orchard Walk and Place, and Merkland Place.

himself hard by the roadside where the Spital ended and College Bounds began. It was a little to the north of the old Spital Play House, then well within the living memory, and it towered above its humbler companions. It must have looked particularly spectacular to the traveller heading north, a striking contrast to the lowly thatched cottages of the Spital which he had just passed. The frontage was of honey-coloured hand-tooled blocks of dressed granite, but the house's most unusual feature was the fine mansard roof, uncommon in the North East at that time. When the old roof was taken off a few years ago prior to re-roofing, there were no tell-tale marks indicating an earlier roof of more conventional design, so we can assume that it was original. John Clark was showing off his skills and a new London fashion. The Plan of Captain Taylor (1773), opposite, indicates a virtually continuous line of dwellings where Clark later built his house, and there is structural evidence, including a cellar with a cobbled floor two and a half feet below ground, that he had followed the common practice of erecting this new house on the foundations of an older one.

Gordon's Plan (1661), shows that the houses on this part of the King's Highway, north of the 'Ruins of the Spittall Kirk' had little orchards in their long, narrow back rigs. Taylor's Plan a century later shows these rigs, running to the East Back Gate or Road, beyond which Moirs' cornfields stretched. They had been amalgamated to form larger units, more square in

Orchard House. The little door, right, once led to the common close.

shape. The one immediately north of the Play House, formed the extensive curtilage of Clark's new dwelling. By 1810, perhaps in financial difficulties after his outlays, Clark was offering it for sale, under the name of Orchard House. The description in the *Aberdeen Journal* of 21 November, confirms an obvious assumption, that the name was taken from the large orchard in the garden. It would prove catching, attaching itself to thoroughfares great and small in the area. For starters, the East Back Gate became Orchard Lane.

The advertisement, setting out the many assets of the house, is worth quoting in full:

Orchard House etc South end of Old Aberdeen.
To be sold by private bargain. A complete family house, with attached and detached offices, consisting of Breakfast and Dining Parlours, Drawing Room, five Bed Rooms, two Dressing Rooms, sundry Closets, excellent Kitchen (with brick oven) Scullery, in which is a Pump well of spring water, and also soft water, under ground Cellar etc; a Coach House and Stabling for three horses, Wash House, Brew house, with two fixed Coppers; a Laundry with drying-room, Ironing Store, and Mangle: a good garden well-cropped; an Orchard planted with upwards of a hundred various Fruit Trees, just in bearing, Forest Trees Etc. Also a Summer House, with Terrace commanding an extensive view of the sea, and surrounding country, with a small enclosed field adjoining. The House was built, and Ground planted within the last ten years, by the Proprietor, John Clark Esq who will show the premises any day from ten till two o'clock. Letters (post paid) will be duly answered.

'Built...within the last ten years' confirms the date of Orchard House is early nineteenth century; a date stone of 1770 on the façade is misleading. Clark had no luck, or perhaps the price he sought was not forthcoming. On 5 November 1817, an advertisement appeared in the *Aberdeen Journal* stressing the house's pleasant and extensive premises between New and Old Aberdeen, 'well-adapted for the residence of a genteel family being in the neighbourhood of Public Schools where every branch of learning is taught'. Moreover, 'the garden and grounds are very extensive and there being a large supply of water from a Pump house in the Offices, the Property might be converted into almost any kind of manufactory.' The notion, that Orchard House and grounds would do equally well as a genteel residence or as a factory was no doubt intended to increase its marketability.

Orchard House was advertised again on 25 February 1818 at £1000 and again on 11 March. To improve the chances of a sale, the property was now offered in three separate lots, if desired. Included in Lot One at £250 are the 'Unfinished House' - the first reference to what became Orchard Cottage - as well as a summer house in the grounds. The second lot included Orchard House itself, the offices and grounds at £600. The third lot, at £160, is most interesting: 'Inclosed field extending from the street to the Sconce Well'. The 1868 ordnance survey shows the well and its field to be outwith the curtilage of Orchard House, standing, in today's terms, near the junction of Orchard Walk and Orchard Place. Orchard Walk - part of Orchard Lane in those days - was the street from which the 'inclosed field' extended to the Sconce Well which sat in its north-west corner.

The sale was being handled by the solicitor James McCook, and by

George Jaffrey, builder, either that same George Jaffray, responsible for the Old Aberdeen Town House, the Hermitage and other distinctive Aulton buildings, or perhaps a son. They had limited success. By February 1819, a Mr James Hutcheon is in residence at Orchard House and planning:

> to take in and educate a few young boarders. Professor of Divinity Dr Mearns, or Mr Paul, Professor of Natural Philosophy at King's College will supply particulars as to the character and ability of Mr Hutcheon.

Hutcheon's scheme appears to have been abortive. On 23 December, Orchard House was again advertised for sale or lease. The embryonic Orchard Cottage had not made much progress, strengthening one's suspicions that Clark had overreached himself. 'There is on the premises the shell of a house, detached, which can be completed at a moderate expense and made a pleasant and comfortable dwelling'. So stated an advertisement of 3 August 1825.

In 1834 Orchard House, then tenanted by a Mrs Cardwell and 'the house behind Orchard House' which must have been the Cottage, finished at last and tenanted by a Mr McKenzie, were both offered for let. To be accurate, the Cottage was not quite 'behind Orchard House' for that would have impeded the 'extensive view of the sea, and surrounding country', but a little to the south-east, built hard against the walls of the back rigs of the

Orchard Cottage as it used to be.

175

two neighbouring Spital houses. It was a plain dwelling, facing east, of two storeys, built of granite rubble, harled over. There were windows on either side of the front door, and three on the first floor and little side pavilions, at least one of which may have been original. For a gardener's cottage, for that is assumed to have been John Clark's purpose in attempting to build it, it appears remarkably spacious by the standards of the time. Entry to the Cottage was by a common close on the south side of Orchard House. The little door leading from the House is still there. Access was also possible from Orchard Lane.

The older maps indicate that the orchard 'with upwards of a hundred various Fruit Trees' was at the rear of the House, rather than in front of the Cottage, and indeed it was bearing fruit before the Cottage made its appearance. A market garden was planted out in the long stretch between the Cottage and Orchard Lane, and it also ran north behind the rigs of neighbouring houses, covering the ground as far as the Orchard Walk section of Orchard Lane. Another market garden lay immediately to the south of the House. Writs in the Aberdeen City archives relating to these neighbouring properties, later Nos 174-184 Spital, (now demolished and replaced by the Spital Walk development), indicate that the back rigs of these houses were amalgamated and leased out by their owners for purposes of cultivation. Interestingly, a feu charter relating to a part of this ground was granted in 1749, by George Moir of Scotstown and Spital to Malcolm McCook, a Spital shoemaker, and the father of James McCook, Advocate, whom we now find attempting to dispose of the neighbouring property.

On 8 March 1837, events caught up with John Clark, or perhaps by this time, his son. 'Orchard House, Old Aberdeen lately owned by Mr Clark and now to the Common Court of Old Aberdeen in virtue of a decree of Declarator of Irritancy' was offered for sale in the *Aberdeen Journal*. This indicates that the feu duty was outstanding, may have been for some time, confirming one's suspicions of financial embarrassment. The irritancy could have been simply purged by making the necessary payment. It wasn't, and the due legal processes were invoked. Orchard Cottage may have been sold off at this time, the Sconce Well and field too, for a well was an asset in an Aulton always sair hauden doon by lack of water. Orchard House remained in ownership of the Convener Court of Old Aberdeen until the 1860s, though there was no shortage of tenants in those years.

In the 1840s, there was a wedding and a bankruptcy at Orchard House. In September 1840 Alexander McPherson, plumber and brassfounder of Leith, was married there to Margaret, daughter of James Cassie, merchant, Aberdeen, while on 29 November 1843 the *Aberdeen Journal* reported that 'Mr Gordon Black, lately a merchant in Aberdeen now residing at Orchard

176

House, Old Aberdeen has executed a Trust Deed for behoof, of his creditors'. The House, which was never formally divided, was now shared by two, sometimes three families, a situation by no means unknown in Aberdeen until relatively recent times. Alexander Falconer, assistant session clerk, was a tenant in 1840s, followed in the 1850s by a tailor, Peter Mathieson. Throughout this period William Stephen, shipmaster, also lived in Orchard House and as an old salt would have enjoyed that 'extensive view of the sea' from the terrace. The Old Aberdeen Police Assessment Rolls of this period - policing in the old sense of cleansing, paving, sewerage, lighting and water supply - indicate that tenants were assessed as well as proprietors, and Stephen paid one of the highest rates in the area, clearly a man of substance. For policing purposes, Orchard House was included as part of the Spital, while the earliest valuation roll of 1855-56 notes Orchard House merely as No 1 College Bounds, (later renumbered as No 2). The address was sometimes 'Old Aberdeen' sometimes 'Spital', you could take your pick. Confusion may have been caused by the fact that College Bounds started just before rather than after the natural break of the present Orchard Walk.

More confusion followed in 1860 when the boundaries of Old Aberdeen were fixed as a preliminary to its becoming a police burgh with revenue raising powers, aimed at the improvement of policing standards. A part of the boundary ran along 'the garden of Orchard House, along the south boundary of said garden to the street'. This definition encompassed the all-important garden well, but there was doubt as to whether Orchard Cottage was included or not - there seems to have been uncertainly as to where the south boundary of the Orchard House garden truly lay. Captain Stephen, who by this time had moved out of the House and bought the Cottage, was clearly unwilling to pay any more 'cess' than he needed to, arguing that Orchard Cottage was outwith the Old Aberdeen boundary. The dispute rumbled on inconclusively for some time.

By 1865 Orchard House had a single tenant, a teacher, David Ross, and soon after it was bought by Alexander Hay, whose family were to remain there for over a hundred years. Hay, though he appears in the street directories as 'late merchant' owned public house premises at No 64 Regent Quay, the National Bar as it later became. He seems to have tried his hand as a property tycoon. In the 1870s, the valuation rolls indicate a gaggle of mysterious houses, Orchard Court, College Bounds, in the vicinity of Orchard House, owned by Alexander Hay. Their rateable value is low and they are tenanted by carters, combworkers, dyers and labourers. Ten years on, there are many vacancies, and eventually Orchard Court vanishes. It may have been these low buildings immediately south of Orchard House, shown on contemporary maps - there is a gap there now. Hay also factored property in Regent Quay and a case was brought against him in 1881 concerning some irregularity over rent he collected there. He died the following August, but his widow and family stayed on.

John Leighton from Fettercairn had owned Orchard Cottage before Captain Stephen moved across. He appears in the first Old Aberdeen street directory of 1840-41 as 'builder and lodgings, Orchard Lane', but the Cottage, in whose completion he possibly had a hand, is not mentioned by name at that time, probably because it didn't have one. Leighton may have bought the 'small house attached' at the sale of 1837, and named it a few years later. Among his student lodgers of this period were Alexander Barrie, brother of the playwright, and Alexander Whyte who graduated in divinity and later became an eminent theologian. The lodgers were not exclusively students. James Ritchie, shipowner, had digs there in the early 1850s, and may have given a favourable report to Captain Stephen.

Even before the Captain took up residence at Orchard Cottage, Leighton, now 'late builder', had moved to Orchard Place, a small but charming new terrace of houses facing Orchard Cottage from across Orchard Lane, looking up its long market garden. 'Place' at this time was used in the same original sense as in Mackie Place or Skene Place, to identify 'upmarket' residences. The valuation rolls from 1855-56 for the next twenty years or so, show that Leighton owned Nos 1, 2 and $2^{1}2$. He had probably built them with his retirement in mind with tenants rather than lodgers as his chief source of income. Gellatly's Map of 1855, surveyed a year or two earlier, shows the present No 1 and 2 Orchard Place standing alone, while the five houses forming the original terrace are all present on the anonymous Plan of 1862. The feu charters held by today's residents show the land to have been originally feued out by Dame Isabella and Sir Michael Bruce.

The Orchard Place houses were all built with the long back rigs traditional to the Spital and Old Aberdeen, and the Plan of 1862 shows orchards in the rigs of Nos 1 and 2, quite separate from the Orchard House orchard on the other side of the Lane. Mrs Doreen Bruce of No 2 Orchard Place still has an orchard in her back garden today. No 1 is a distinctive, narrow, white house, gable-end to the road, and Mrs Nancy McKidd of Orchard Walk, who lived there in the 1970s, recalls it as roomier than one might suspect, with a cellar and an upper floor. She was told by former residents that it was originally a byre or steading, and Doreen Bruce has heard that it used to be a smithy. Certainly, the valuation rolls of 1855-56 show Leighton's tenants to have included Charles Mathieson, a blacksmith, while William Stirling a carter tenanted the neighbouring cottage.

In the later nineteenth century, the residents of Orchard Place ranged from the exotic to the ordinary. Charles Souter, 'verminist and rat catcher' tenant at No 1 was succeeded by James Turner, mason and slater. Lodgers

The original houses at Orchard Place as they are today.

included a mariner, carter, mechanic, labourer, engine driver and clerk. George Milne, who had also lived in Orchard Cottage, was owner occupier of No 3 for many years. No 4 from the 1870s for the next thirty years was owned by Alexander Thom, a butler who resided in Helensburgh. His tenants in the early days were Miss Thom, presumably a daughter or sister, who took in lodgers, and James Smith, colporteur, who sold religious tracts. Miss Elenora Milne owned 'No 5 Orchard Place, College Bounds' and she too took in lodgers.

Access to Orchard Place could be gained either via the common close at the south side of Orchard House, assuming it had not been blocked off, then down the Orchard Cottage garden path while another more private path ran from the rear of Orchard House on its north side. Both these paths ended in little gates opposite Orchard Place. This little terrace could also be reached from Orchard Lane, which we can follow, starting it where it leaves College Bounds, the section now called Orchard Walk. Here on the left hand side (just outwith the Spital Lands, I have to confess), were a group of buildings, little more than huts, including a weaving shed and a Free Kirk Sunday School, which survived into modern times, though with different uses. Next to them, a little back from the road, was Rose Cottage, which was standing in the 1830s and sounds like the house advertised in the *Aberdeen Journal* of 14 July 1835:

Wild gardens in Orchard Walk. The site of Rose Cottage.

To let house at 10 Orchard Lane occupied by Mrs Lyall ...A large garden with fruit bushes and berry bushes and a byre.

George Gordon, the King's Crescent historian who used to live in College Bounds, recalls Rose Cottage, (not to be confused with the one at the top of Merkland Road), as a plain, single storey cottage, with windows on either side of the door, and a long, well-stocked garden. It was owned for many years by James Reid 'late farmer' and like the houses of Orchard Place had a variety of occupants over the years. In the 1840s, George Grub, the College Bounds shoemaker, in the 1850s, the Reverend John Forbes session-clerk and rector of the (Old Aberdeen) Grammar School - the two jobs went together - and a tax man, Robert Hall, of the Inland Revenue. In the 1850s and 1860s, George McKenzie, commercial traveller, was followed by his son William. There was something of a to-do early in 1853 when Elizabeth McRobbie stole a willow basket from Rose Cottage. On 16 February she was sentenced at Aberdeen Sheriff Court to nine months imprisonment, a harsh sentence, but it was her third offence. By 1885 Rose Cottage owned by Mrs Elizabeth Cromar of 12 College Bounds nearby, was tenanted by a retired accountant, James R McConnachie.

Orchard Lane passed by the long garden of Rose House and the Sconce Well and its field, then widened out in a great sweep, before turning to run

The Sconce Well's field would have been around here.

in front of the Orchard Place houses, which would later give their name to this section of the Lane. Some yards after passing the Place, the Lane divided. One track turned again, sharply eastwards this time to reach the King Street Road opposite the Lady Mill. The track then continued straight from the Mill, eastwards through the fields to the Links, on a similar alignment to the present Linksfield Road, turning north to the brick kilns at Seaton, where locals could buy a cart load of bricks. Before the King Street Road intercepted it around 1804 this part of Orchard Lane had run direct to the Links. The other track continued to run southwards, past a group of farm biggings, (later to be swept away by the creation of Orchard Street), gaving access to St Peter's Place, a close behind the Spital which was being laid out by the 1860s. The main track continued on to run behind the Spital Kirkyard - later it was obliterated by the laying out of St Peter's Cemetery - then on to what is now Merkland Place, before curving up towards the Spital, on the stretch that is now the upper part of Merkland Road. This is the rectangular shape seen on Taylor's Plan on page 172.

There was another access to the houses of Orchard Place from the Spital, via Susie's Close or Susie's Roadie, which starts today beside the mosque, the former savings bank, at No 164. It exited near the Orchard Place houses, and was even better placed to link with that section of the Lane which ran down to the King Street Road.

By the 1880s, Nos 1 and 2 Orchard Place were owned by Thomas Forbes

The intriguing No 1 Orchard Place. Was it a byre, a dairy, a smithy - or all three?

cattle dealer, adding credence to the story that No 1 had once been a byre. A few years later two further houses were added at the north end. No 1a was owned by James McDonald, a Gallowgate baker and No 1b, Alexandria Cottage, by Alexander Alexander, a dairyman. According to the relevant valuation rolls, he had also acquired the next two houses, No 1 and No 2 and $2^1 2$. And something interesting had happened. A new park had been broken out behind these houses, all of which, apart from No 1a were part of the Alexander Alexander domain. Mrs Doreen Bruce who has lived at No 2 since the early 1960s, learnt from Mrs Jaffray at No 1b that her grandfather used to farm there. No1a was named Northfield Cottage, taking its name, one might guess, from the new field at the bottom of its garden. Orchard Lane, now put out a side-track which gave access down the side of this new field.

By 1883, eight feus had been given off on the east side of Orchard Place, bringing Henry William Knight Erskine an annual sum of £21 8s 1d. The area was still predominantly a rural one, offering Henry William plenty of space to indulge his favourite ploy - laying out new streets.

Chapter 14

The 'Orchards':
Street and Road

The Committee had before them plans lodged by Messrs Smith & Kelly of the following new streets to be laid put upon the Lands of Spital, viz: (1) a new street between Orchard Street and University Road...

Aberdeen Town Council Minutes, 6 December, 1897.

By 1890, Henry William Knight Erskine was well advanced in his plans to create new streets on the west side of the Spital. He now turned to the east side, to the largely rural area we were looking at in the last chapter. That July his architects, Smith & Kelly were given permission to lay out a new street to be called Orchard Street on vacant ground on the west side of King Street, coming as far west as the line of the Orchard Place houses to the north, and the foot of St Peter's Place, which gave access to the Spital, on the south. Here Orchard Street came to an unsatisfactory termination. As a thorough fare it was useless. Access to the Spital was barred by the long back rigs of the Spital houses, which, with the exception of a couple of wee closes, formed a terrace all the way down to College Bounds.

By 1892 Orchard Lane was enjoying mixed fortunes. The section that gave access to the old farm cottages at the foot of St Peter's Place, was, like most of these biggings, obliterated by Orchard Street. Only a fragment remains today, the lower part of St Peter's Place. Back up on College Bounds, the Lane's west to east section which went past Rose Cottage and continued on to the Sconce Well's field and beyond, was renamed Orchard Walk, while the section running past the Orchard Place houses took the name of the houses, Orchard Place. The section that ran down to the King Street Road and the Lady Mill was obliterated by the gardens of the new tenements which now appeared in the gap between the original Orchard Place houses and Orchard Street. In the late 1890s, Nos 6, 8 and 10 went up. They were matched after a fashion by the curiously numbered No 11, 7 and 9 on the west side, which flanked Susie's Close. None of these six late Victorian tenements bore any resemblance to the original Orchard Place group. The architectural philosophy of being 'sympathetic' was nearly a century in the future. One of the principal architects of this little development was William Ruxton while builders included local carpenter James Green, George Godsman of Mannofield, James Willox of Gilcomston and the granite merchant John Crichton who had difficulty with his one of his tenements which the town planners found encroaching too heavily on Susie's Close.

In Orchard Street itself, granting feu charters gathered speed towards the end of the 1890s when it became clear that the street would eventually relinquish its status as cul-de-sac in favour of thoroughfare. Ground on the north side was the subject of a feu charter which Henry William Knight Erskine granted in 1897 in favour of the Aberdeen Building Co Ltd, who did much work in the area. Shortly afterwards the Building Company granted a feu charter in favour of Andrew Arthur, Joiner, Aberdeen, who built No 18 and the neighbouring tenement. Part of this well-built property still remains family hands.

In December 1897, another new street planned by the Knight Erskine team, Orchard Road, to run 'on the Lands of Spital' between Orchard Street and University Road, was given the go-ahead. By the turn of the century it had attracted only one customer, the tall, gaunt tenement, No 4, built for John McRobb, overseer, and stood back-to-back with another McRobb property, the distinctive No 10 Orchard Street, which was designed by the distinguished architect James Souttar of Salvation Army Citadel fame and has a curvilinear gable and a pink granite shield bearing the date 1899 to show that it was something by-ordinar. These features also relieve a plain exterior. Sewers were yet to be dug in Orchard Street and Souttar had, for the time being, to drain the building into a covered cesspool.

Moving down the north side of Orchard Street towards King Street, No 6 was built by George Thom, the Albion granite man. It was initially tenanted by a stonecutter, probably one of his own men, a salmon fisher and two blacksmiths. Jean Simpson recalls that throughout the life of the granite yards, Orchard Street and Road were popular with stone masons. In 1899 the architects Milne & Pirie, built a neat villa for William Scorgie, boiler-maker at No 4. He shared the house with his son William Jnr, a solicitor. They owned much property in the area, and the firm of Scorgie & Davidson naturally carried out the legal work. A third generation of this family was Frank Scorgie, a Director of Education for Aberdeen in the post-war era. No

From right, No 4 Orchard Street, for many years home of the Scorgie and Erskine families, No 6 home of the mason George Cooper Clark and his wife Edith, and the distinctive No 10 with its pink granite shield and curvilinear gable.

4 Orchard Street later became the home, for many years until 1996, of a family coincidentally called Erskine, who were intrigued to find the feu charter had been originally granted by one Henry William Knight Erskine. On the south side, George Godsman, who was also building houses in Don Street in the late 1890s, was responsible for the attractive row of privately owned two-flatted houses between King Street and St Peter's Place.

By this time, Sunnybank Road, linking the Spital with Bedford Road via Bedford Place, was being laid out and the Council decided that the time was ripe to extend Orchard Street to the Spital, creating a cross country link between King Street and Bedford Road, opening an east to west axis where south to north had been the norm. The carpenter, James Green, who had been involved in removing the old Spital houses on the line of the extended road, was granted planning permission in 1899 to build seven new houses and shops on this continuation, on the south side of the road, Nos 47-65, with Ruxton as architect. Three years later Green got the go-ahead for six houses on the north side to a design by the well known architect, R G Wilson.

Shops began to appear on this new, upper part of Orchard Street. The Northern Co-operative grocery premises which had opened at the Spital-Orchard Street corner in 1903 (later occupied by Wilburn), soon flitted round the corner to the north side of Orchard Street. The grocery, bakery,

185

and butchery departments ran from Nos 28 - 32. On the south side were two shops, No 47, next door to St Peter's Place, and No 51 with a door in between. 'They were owned by my father's aunts,' recalls Mrs Edith Clark, 'the Misses Jamieson, Maggie and Katy from Shetland. They ran a drapery business at No 51, selling wool and specialising in Shetland knitting. They stretched babies' shawls on a frame in the backshop.' 'Their work was of the finest quality,' recalls Mrs Anne Cocker of roses fame.' Jean Simpson remembers that for a small charge Miss Jamieson would press and stretch a baby's shawl. Golf socks were on sale at 6^12d and the sisters also made up the uniforms for the inmates of the Poorhouse in a very hard material. Quite a change from babies' shawls, where the wool underwent a whitening , softening process. No 47 was a licensed grocer where Mrs Clark helped out for a time looking after the till, which was not a favourite task.

The grocery business was subsequently acquired by Mr George Milne. Mr George Elphinstone, born in St Peter's Place during the First World War, remembers a little ledge outside the shop where local lads would sit in the

Looking east down Orchard Street. The Misses Jamieson's drapery is now a general store while George Milne's licensed grocer's has become a house. The difference in alignment between the upper and lower sections of the street is clear.

summer time. When his mother was having folk in for tea he would be sent in for half a pound of Abernethy biscuits. If the biscuits were overweight Mr Milne would split an Abernethy in two, to get the weight just right. It was here that Mrs Cocker, then Anne Rennie, a local girl, educated at

Sunnybank School and the Central, worked as bookkeeper during the war years, and Alec Cocker's old Austin which used to draw up outside during their courting days, was a familiar sight in the street. Anne was a part-time ambulance driver; 'I ruined my eyesight driving in the blackout.'

The drapery business vanished many years ago and today, a general store occupies that site. Across the road the Co-op buildings continued to be busy over the years. George Gordon remembers Orchard Place packed with shoppers' cars. These branches were closed following the opening of the superstore at Berryden, and for a time Jimmy Gatt, the furniture restorer, had premises there. The buildings are gone now, replaced by new flats.

On the other side of the St Peter's Place divide, Pennie, the butcher, was at No 43 which is now a house. Mathieson, the painter, was across at No 26 on the Orchard Street-Place corner, now occupied by an antique shop, while on the Orchard Road corner George Elphinstone recalls the wee grocer's shop run by Mr Crichton. He was succeeded by his nephew, David Harman, who sold fish as well.

Edith Clark, born in 1902, lived in Orchard Street all her life until 1997, apart from a short spell in Forest Avenue. She returned to Orchard Street after her marriage to George Cooper Clark, one of Arthur Taylor's top granite cutters. She remembers the street when there were no trees. Mrs Clark's father, James John Farquhar, was a photographer who started off as a portrait artist with a studio at the Victoria Bridge, and later went over to commercial work. In the early days he was photographer to Craiginches Prison, taking shots of the prisoners with arms crossed and their hands on shoulders. Carefully positioned mirrors allowed him to take profiles. At night he would take pictures of floodlit city buildings. Mr Farquhar had the first car in Orchard Street, a Rover. 'It was 'air-conditioned' - freezing cold,' Edith Clark recalls. J J Farquhar managed the photographic business of Fred Hardie for ten years, among whose stock was a substantial number of George Washington Wilson glass negatives, purchased at auction in 1908. Unfortunately J J Farquhar died 1935, a few months after acquiring Hardie's business, and Edith's mother sold the business to a young photographer, Archie Strachan. It was he who later gifted the negatives to Aberdeen University where they now form the George Washington Wilson Collection.

Other Orchard Street residents included Tommy Cox, the well known Old Aberdeen grocer, and Mr Falconer whom Jean Simpson recalls spending more time in his little a shed at Willie Weir's farm in Merkland Place than at home. He had it comfortably furnished with lino on the floor and an easy chair, and kept ferrets and rabbits there, presumably well apart.

No 4 Orchard Road, right, in stark contrast to the terraced houses of the 1930s.

We left Orchard Road with its gaunt tenement, No 4, standing in solitary splendour. George Elphinstone as a lad played football on the rough ground beyond the house and opposite, he recalls, were plots. Beyond them again was the 'Northfield', behind the Orchard Place houses, though that was a few years before George Elphinstone's time. By 1914 the field had been extended and transformed into the Northern Bowling Green. This private club was established in King's Crescent by 1893, but twenty-one years later moved to Orchard Road. George Tait, brought up in College Bounds recalls that, 'as boys we visited a garage in the area where Steve McCall, one of Scotland's top boxers (he once fought Len Harvey) put on a show for us. What a thrill we got when he shadow boxed to the tip of our noses. Beyond his garage was one of the three pieces of ground where we showed off what football skills we had. One of the boys who played with us was Jack Booth who later became one of the best golfers in the district and won competitions all round the area. I'm sure that he represented Scotland in the home countries internationals. The Northern Bowling Green was opposite 'our' pitch and with hindsight (now that I have reached the bowling stage), I suppose the racket we made would not have been appreciated by the Northern Bowlers'.

Jean Simpson recalls Orchard Road in the 1920s and 1930s as a street with a great deal of rough ground and loose granite lying around, and consisting mostly of back gates and back gardens belonging to the King Street houses between Orchard Street and University Road. It was not until

Lord Provost Tommy Mitchell, right, enjoys an 'end' at the Northern Bowling Club in the late 1930s. The green was once a farmer's field.

the early thirties, that the bowling green and the lonely tenement at No 4 had some company when the terraced bungalows that stand on both sides of Orchard Road were built, with a selling price of £350. By 1925 the Bowling Green's title had been altered to 'Northern Bowling Club'. Today membership stands at 200, with a thriving ladies' section. Its greens provide a calm oasis, and in summer there is a splendid floral display in front of the pavilion, which sits at the south end. You can catch a glimpse of it as you walk along University Road.

Jean Simpson with her aunt Mary and cousin Maimmie, outside the Northern Bowling Green in 1923. Courtesy, Jean Simpson. ▶

189

University Road itself is something of a curiosity. It was laid out early, in the time of Dame Isabella and Sir Michael Bruce, their only 'major' road, much of the south side forming part of the northern boundary of their Spital Lands. Its original purpose was to link the Lady Mill, built in 1832 on the east side of King Street, with Old Aberdeen and the Spital. It was in existence when Old Aberdeen defined its boundaries in 1860, though the 1868 ordnance survey shows that no houses had yet been built - but what odds. At that time a thoroughfare was considered as a means of getting from A to B. The Fiddler's Well still stood on the south-east corner of the road, opposite the Mill, but the Powis Burn was already culverted. It went underground on leaving the Powis Estate at College Bounds and re-emerged on the far side of King Street, beside the Lady Mill. (Even these days, the Burn has been known to burst from its culvert at the College Bounds-University Road junction, repelling Grampian Transport buses). There had been no progress towards housing by 1883 when Henry William Knight Erskine, Dame Isabella's first cousin once removed, was attempting to sell the Spital Lands. The Particulars of Sale advertised, 'A fine block of building land on south side of the University Road, overlooking King's College.' This encapsulated HW's philosophy; a road on the Spital Lands means houses which means feu duty for me.

At last, by 1899, one group of buildings had gone up, late nineteenth century tenemental in style, a little different from the rest of University Road houses which duly appeared, though gaps remained until modern times. George Gordon recalls Jimmy Coutts who had a little dairy near the College Bounds end, just one of a number of little wooden huts in an area of allotment gardens, with a muddy path leading through to Orchard Walk. Jimmy Coutts had no horse and cart, but sold milk over the counter, while his loons with their urns did the door-to-door deliveries. Mrs Jean Bishop, worked at Coutts's Dairy and returned every day to her home in College Bounds with a jug of skimmed milk. The car park of the Butchart Recreation Centre now covers the site of the wee dairy, but the muddy path has been replaced by a right of way which leads through to Orchard Walk at its junction with Orchard Place. The Butchart Centre, which now shares the site with the University's Physical Education Department, was named after the University's redoubtable and long-serving secretary, Colonel H J Butchart. It was built in 1966 at a cost of £130,000 and though it is possibly the ugliest of Aberdeen University's modern buildings, the facilities were hailed as magnificent at the time of its inception.

And now to discover the fate of the older 'Orchards'. We left Rose Cottage in the last chapter, its long garden dominating the left hand side of Orchard Walk or Lane as it then was, as you entered from College Bounds.

The tenements with gablets, centre, are the oldest in University Road.

The Butchart Recreation Centre, University Road.

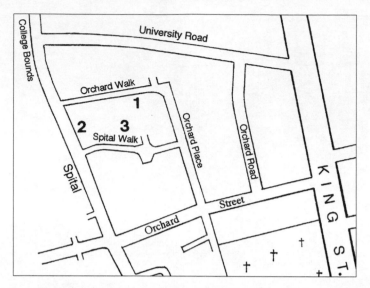

The Orchard area. 1 Site of St Theresa's: 2 Orchard House: 3 Orchard Cottage.

By the 1930s the Cottage was a hundred years old and the home of the Tester family. 'In 1939, just about the time the war broke out, the older members of the family moved to live at Oldmeldrum,' recalls George Gordon. 'After the war, the occupant was a cheerful country-bred fellow, Dod Allan. A family man, I knew him very well.' Harold Bishop, Jean's son, also remembers the Tester family and opposite, 'Hannah Bud' - Mrs Wallace, a recluse, and her daughter Bunty. The Balfour family lived nearby and Mr Balfour used to cut his hair with 'an old fashioned machine' in a lane at the back of house.

Edith Clark remembers her father-in-law telling her that the area between the Spital and Orchard Place used to be filled with market gardens and allotments. The old valuation rolls record until relatively recent times, numerous rigs, tails (small rigs) and garden allotments. These were still very much in evidence on either side of Orchard Cottage before the war. James McKenzie cultivated the plots on the Orchard Walk-Orchard Place area, up to the boundary of the Orchard Cottage garden. George Elphinstone who used to work as a chimney sweep would leave his soot for him. Mr McKenzie and his wife lived at No 32 College Bounds, 'nice folk,' recalls George Gordon. James McKenzie had to give up his allotments in the 1930s when St Theresa's Roman Catholic was built on this land. The McKenzies then took over the running of the general merchant's corner shop at No 12 College Bounds at the corner of Orchard Walk, just inside the Spital Lands. It had once been Divorty's. The McKenzies were succeeded in the shop by

Mrs Robb who lived with her husband at Crown Cottage, whose fate we followed in Chapter Five. This little shop is now part of a house. Margaret Henderson whose grandparents lived in Orchard Cottage recalls the little chapel of St Theresa's being built and went there from time to time to worship, and Doreen Bruce retains a vivid picture of clumps of daffodils growing outside, and nuns coming to gather them.

Orchard Cottage had remained in the possession of Captain Stephen, then his widow, and it was subsequently acquired by the Hay family of

The general merchant's store at No 12 is now part of the house at No10. The tall building beyond is Orchard House.

Photographed from No2 Orchard Place with St Theresa's Chapel in the background are from left, David, Alison and Linda Bruce, with Betty Leiper behind.
Courtesy, Doreen Bruce.

Orchard House who rented it out. Margaret Henderson, writing to *Leopard Magazine*, in June 1986 from London, recalled that her grandparents James Henderson and Mary Singer, married in 1865, had moved to Orchard Cottage from Don Street about 1880. They had nine children, and the boys are remembered as wild loons who kept a monkey in the willow tree there. The family stayed at Orchard Cottage until 1944 when Miss Henderson's eldest aunt died. Miss Henderson continues: 'I went to Orchard Cottage at the beginning of 1918 by which time part of the very large garden had been given to a market gardener who grew flowers and vegetables, but we still had to walk down long paths between the white rose bushes to get into Orchard Place. After the death of my aunt, the Cottage was bought from the Hays of Orchard House by Mrs Minty, daughter of Cabby Gray, 52 High Street, Old Aberdeen, a close friend of the Hendersons. She modernised it then gave it to a niece'. Miss Henderson concluded her letter; I have so many happy memories of Orchard Cottage, tea parties in the garden and the tent we had on the green, often used by the children when the house was full. Many people loved to visit the Cottage'.

Miss Henderson 's letter of June 1986 had been prompted by concern over the old family home, by that time at the centre of a controversial housing development. The Cottage was now owned by Aberdeen University, and until the early 1980s, its kitchen staff continued to cultivate the long garden, growing lettuce, parsley and herbs. The well was still there, of course, and as it had no well-head one had to be careful not to fall in. But after a tenant moved out in 1982, no replacement was sought, no new lease was drawn up. Orchard Cottage was offered for sale, and gardening ceased. This was the era when Aberdeen University, forced to retrench, had to put its property acquisition campaign into reverse. In the ensuing years, Cottage and garden became the subject of a series of planning applications resolutely opposed by residents who considered the high, concentrated style of housing proffered by developers as totally unsympathetic to the area. 'We are anxious to see the house sold to an individual family, not to speculators whose main interest is financial gain,' was the general feeling. One application, by Crown Park, became the subject of a public inquiry in January 1985 with the Secretary of State upholding the residents' objections. This triggered off the establishment of the Old Aberdeen Residents' Heritage Society in June 1985, which provided locals with a strong, official framework within which to operate. A quick opening goal was scored by having Orchard Cottage listed as a building of historical interest.

St Theresa's Chapel, redundant after the building of the Catholic Chaplaincy Centre in the Old Aberdeen High Street, had been acquired by the University and used first by the Music Department then, in the early 1980s, as a picture store; a collection of motley huts replaced the daffodils. After the picture store was moved to No 111 High Street, the University joined St Theresa's to the Orchard Cottage 'lot' providing the opportunity for an even larger housing development. Orchard Cottage, its windows, boarded up, its long garden overgrown with weeds was targeted by

Orchard Cottage left, and The Orchard development.

vandals while the battle continued to wage. The Heritage Society in a letter to the press on 24 October 1989, noted: '...over the years, many people have expressed the desire to buy Orchard Cottage for use as a family home, but have been consistently thwarted by the University's refusal to sell the house and garden separately from the adjacent St Theresa's Chapel.' One admirable suggestion, to build single storey sheltered housing on the St Theresa's site with Orchard Cottage as a warden's house and the long garden retained for residents' use, rather like the Mitchell Hospital in the Chanonry, was not taken up. Eventually by late 1991, an application by Bon Accord Homes, who had listened to the views put forward by the Residents, received planning permission. A mix of twenty homes, two-bedroomed flats and two, three and four bedroom townhouses, went up, forming a court, including Orchard Cottage, minus its long garden, and now No1 The Orchard.

By this time, Rose Cottage on Orchard Walk was long gone. The land was owned by Harrow, the florists, and by the 1960s the site was levelled and the present terraced houses, built by Laing, were quickly sold. This was the first development in the area since the war, and the houses, many with wild gardens, are attractive. The Sconce Well's field is there somewhere, under concrete, at the junction with the rear of the Butchart Centre. Orchard Walk, now much narrower, continues on past the side of Northern Bowling Club to Orchard Road, once an area of garages and corrugated iron sheds where folk used to keep hens. In recent times four houses, facing Orchard Road, have been slipped into a triangle between the back of University Road, the Butchart Centre and Orchard Walk.

Orchard House had a less traumatic career. The Hay family remained in residence and George Gordon remembers the Mrs Hay of the pre-war era, 'stately, middle-aged, and of pleasant countenance.' A daughter, Mrs Rattray, a widow who took in student lodgers was living there when Aberdeen University bought the house during their drive to acquire property in the 1960s. The University undertook to maintain the property while Mrs Rattray remained as occupier. After her death Orchard House stood empty for some fifteen months until April 1983 when Dr Norman Fisher of the Department of Cultural History and his wife, who teaches art at Robert Gordon's College, acquired it. Orchard House was by then in a thoroughly rundown state. 'The woodworm,' recalls Norman Fisher, 'was striking.' He embarked on a restoration that lasted some nine years, until September 1992. Dr Fisher received a Scottish Office grant towards restoration and found the Department's experts reassuringly 'fierce' about the correctness of the restoration. Their attention to detail was impressive, not only wet harl, naturally, but 'the correct mixture of lime and cement.' Much rebuilding was carried out. The new roof went on at this time, and windows, copying the originals, were made with panes of horticultural

The outer wall of the common close at Orchard House. It retains ghostly vestiges of old entrances.

196

glass which simulated the slight irregularity of old glass. As with all old houses there are a number of mysteries; a kitchen press on the north east side of the house was once a door leading out to some of the 'detached offices'. A little square building at the back of the house, removed in the 1920s to make way for a bathroom, has left enigmatic clues - a chimney, granite rubble and brick fragments of wall - indicating that the brew house 'with two coppers' may once have been located there. There are the remains too, of the common close that once gave access to Orchard Cottage. The surviving bricks, Dr Fisher thinks, came from Seaton, though Dr Leslie Macfarlane suggests they may have arrived as ballast from Holland. The House still has a large and leafy garden.

Finally to Orchard Place, whose original houses though modernised retain their charm. At No 5a, Wilma and Arthur Abel, who as a young couple had two rooms there before the house was converted, now have a pleasant and comfortable self-contained upper flat, and the whole 'long rig' garden behind, complete with pond and summer house. Of the tenements

Nos 6, 8, 10, two suffered war damage and only No 10 survives. Nos 6-8 have been replaced by a little court of pre-cast houses, entered through an arch. Across the way, Susie's Close, renamed Orchard Lane in 1902 since that name was by then available, exits between Nos 7 and 9 Orchard Place. It even has a house of its own, No 2, at the rear of No 7 Orchard Place.

The Abel's lovely 'long rig' garden at No 5a Orchard Road.
Courtesy, Wilma and Arthur Abel.

'a little court of pre-cast houses.'

Well, perhaps not quite finally. The last word must illustrate the uncanny hold that St Theresa's Chapel, demolished as part of the Orchard Cottage redevelopment, retains beyond the grave. It still maintains an 'outward and visible sign', two of them in fact, one in Orchard Street, the other at Orchard Walk. Indeed when one signpost was damaged long after the Chapel had gone, the then Grampian Roads Department carefully restored it, and replaced it on site.

Chapter 15

St Peter's Place

'It was in one of these houses that a chimney sweep who played the bass
fiddle lived...'

The Spital, Chapter 14.

Readers may recall that memorable row of old Spital cottages, just north of
the Merkland Road junction, which were replaced by a council development in the early 1970s. At least three common closes were in existence
there in the old days, leading from the Spital, between the houses, through
the long back rigs, to Merkland Place, the southern extension of 'old'
Orchard Lane. Best remembered was Willie Weir's set-up; he owned Nos
84-94 the Spital, but his farm was through the back, in Merkland Place.
These closes vanished of course, along with the old houses, but three other
Spital closes are still with us, though the common close at Orchard House
survives only in vestigial form. The others are narrow Susie's Close -
nowadays 'new' Orchard Lane - which linked up, like the others, with the
'old' Lane, and our biggest and best surviving close, St Peter's Place at No
134 the Spital, beside the Red Lion, which links the Spital with Orchard
Street. Its link with 'old' Orchard Lane was broken when Orchard Street's
upper section was laid out. However if you stand in Orchard Place, which
is a section of the 'old' Orchard Lane, and look due south, it becomes clear
that St Peter's Place was a continuation of the 'old' Lane, which would have
continued on past the foot of the Spital Kirkyard before St Peter's Cemetery
was built. The close is shown in the plan on page 170.

The 1868 Ordnance Survey shows only one house in existence on the
north side of the close, but at right angles to it, at the bottom, sat four little
biggings. Only the most southerly, 'the farm', now No 4 St Peter's Place,

St Peter's Place, a remnant of 'old' Orchard Lane. St Peter's Cemetery lies behind the wall at the back. The house to the left on Orchard Street was once Pennie, the butcher's. The gable of the old farm is visible behind the tall tenement.

There is a touch of Footdee about St Peter's Place. The tall houses of the Spital are behind, the rear of the Red Lion to the left.

would survive those Orchard Street roadworks. The two other houses which complete St Peter's Place went up soon after 1868. They were possibly even *in situ* by the time the OS map was published for the stonework of all three, the two cottages, Nos 1- 2, and the tenement at No 3 is very similar. The houses were probably built for Mrs Ann Presslie, poultry and gamedealer, and for a time, landlord of the nearby Red Lion Inn. By 1871, Mrs Presslie had sold the houses to Father John Comper, 'Incumbent of St Margaret's Mission Church in connection with the Episcopal Church in Scotland for behoof of said mission' - according to title deeds in the city archives. At that time Father Comper was bent on establishing a convent for the sisters of St Margaret, who were temporarily based in a house in the Gallowgate. It seems that St Peter's Place spent its early days as a convent - truly an ecclesiastical close! In 1876 Comper sold the site back to Mrs Presslie for the Bay View cottages had come on the market by then, their hilltop site offering a more spectacular location for a convent and chapel.

The 1883-84 valuation rolls show Mrs Presslie still there as proprietor, living in the tenement, which housed five families altogether. The cottages each had three tenants, with a labourer at the farm. There was also a fair amount of ground, byres and a stable. By 1901 the ownership of St Peter's Place had passed to the trustees of the late John Booth - I have a feeling Mrs Presslie went to New York, but I may be wrong - and two blacksmiths, a flax dresser and a hackle maker were in residence by then. William Balfour, a carter, was at No 4, with the byres and stable handily placed for his work.

George Elphinstone was born at No 4, the farm, during the First World War and has lived in St Peter's Place for much of his life. No 4 had a garden

George's mother, Mrs Helen Elphinstone and family outside No 4, the old farm, with a willow arch behind. Courtesy, George Elphinstone.

when he was a child and his father, Charles Elphinstone, planted willows which in time formed archways. Hens were kept as well. Mr Elphinstone ran a coal store in the yard, and kept his horse in the stable. Local folk came to buy coal by the stone, $\frac{1}{2}$ stone and bucket, and cinders as well. Firewood was on sale too, bunched by a bundling machine and secured with soft wire.

The business closed down after a fire, though the family stayed on. The stable lay empty and one of George Elphinstone's early memories - he was five or six at the time - was of a gypsy couple with a small child who asked if they could have somewhere to stay for the night. The stable was the only place available, and in the morning they brewed young George a cup of tea, so delicious that he still remembers it. There was also a big mission hall in the yard. His Aunt Elizabeth was married there and he still talks of all the biscuits and sandwiches they ate. He recalls too, the excitement of seeing the pistol packin' son of Mr Green, the Sunnybank carter, come riding down Orchard Street in his cowboy outfit, Stetson and all. That was quite a sight. He was riding one of the special horses that the Greens used to enter for the Seaton Park races.

It was about this time, in the 1920s, that the Tosh brothers, who lived in Orchard Place, took over the yard, got it going again, and ran the coal and firewood business for a time. They sold to Jimmy Tucker, and he was succeeded in the business by James Geddes, who had the contract for providing firewood for the schools. Dorothy Gerrard remembers going across to buy firewood from him during the General Strike when no coal was being delivered.

By the time George was twenty-one, the buildings had been con-

George, left and brother Bill during their days as coal merchants.
Courtesy, George Elphinstone.

demned, and the family moved to Scatterburn then to Northfield. When James Geddes gave up after the war, George and his elder brother Bill thought that they would now have a go at the old business, returning to the homestead and trading as 'Elphinstone Brothers, coal and firewood merchants'. In time they too gave up as more and more homes went over to central heating and the demand for coal and firewood slackened off. George subsequently worked as a chimney sweep and for the Links and Parks.

In the late 1950s, the Elphinstone brothers refurbished and modernised the houses of St Peter's Place, Bill taking the top house, No 1, while George and his wife, a Torry quine, converted No 2 which carries through to the ground floor of No 3, the tenement building which was re-roofed as part of the modernisation. You enter No 2 via the kitchen, then go down a step to

the cosy sitting room, where an old kitchen range lurks hidden behind the wall. In the adjoining room next door - we are now through to No 3 - Mrs Elphinstone has a marvellous collection of dolls and dolls' houses from all over the world. George Elphinstone was well known as a bass fiddle player in his younger day, and the bass fiddle resides here too. George's niece has the middle floor of No 3 now, and a student, the top floor. After brother Bill's death, No 1 was sold and a family from England live there.

Mr and Mrs George Elphinstone.

St Peter's Place has a 'feel' of the country and a touch of Footdee with its privacy and strong stone character. George Elphinstone has transformed the upper part of the yard, laying out a neat garden. Sheds have been taken down, though their ghostly outlines remain against the wall. Stable and mission hall are long gone and a row of garages was built here in the late 1960s.

George Elphinstone in his garden at St Peter's Place.

In the 1970s, Mr Vic Sinclair, hearing there was space available in the lower part of the yard took that over for his scrap metal business. His son now runs the firm at what must be Aberdeen's tidiest scrapyard. No 4, the old farm, is still going strong as Mr Sinclair's store .

Vic Sinclair, right and his assistant Larry Clark at No 4, the old farm.

Chapter 16

St Peter's Cemetery and its Residents

It has long been extensively used as a Burying Place by both Protestants and Catholics.

Particulars of Sale, the Spital Estate, 1883.

Our next port of call is St Peter's Cemetery. It extends north along King Street from Merkland Road almost as far as Orchard Street, and stretches back to the Spital. Here it had its beginnings as the Spital Kirkyard, the 'Church Yard' sitting on a mound marked onTaylor's Plan on page 172. This is the kernel of the present day cemetery. The old entrance with its stone arch is located just behind the Spital, at St Peter's Gate. It bears the Moir coat of arms, 'three negroes heads coupé with a ribband or scarfe about ye brow, knit behind', registered by Dr William Moir in the 1670s (But what about these earrings)! This Spital gate is now kept locked and access is by King Street and it is a fair tramp through the modern cemetery to the old kirkyard to have a look at the Moir burial ground. Their mausoleum sits at the east end of the mound, whose rectangular shape suggests that it was the site of the Chapel of St Peter's or the Spital Kirk, around which the parish of St Peter's developed. (See *The Spital* pages 121, 135).

The old kirkyard had not been part of the package when the Moirs of Scotstown acquired the Spital Lands in 1604. It had been granted to King's College by the Crown some thirty years before, during the post-Reformation shake-up of church lands. It must have irked the Moirs that such an ancient and hallowed piece of ground should lie at the very heart of their lands and yet be outwith their control. By the eighteenth century the Moirs were leasing the kirkyard. The Kings College Book of Land Rentals shows, for example, the following entry for 1791:

Mr Moir of Scotston for Spital Churchyard...........8/4.

By 1824 a massive building programme was getting underway at King's. Much of the west front of the College was demolished and rebuilt as we know it today, at a cost of £7000. £2000 came from the Privy Purse, which left the impoverished College to find some £5000. It is likely that at this time the kirkyard was sold to the Moirs to help raise funds. The College authorities may well have been glad to be rid of it. In the past, St Machar's Kirk Session had complained of ecclesiastical irregularities and loss of revenue through the College's laxness in permitting illicit (and free) burials to take place at the 'Spittalkirk' in opposition to the cathedral. For their part, Dame Isabella Moir, seventh laird, and her husband, Sir Michael Bruce, could now integrate the Spital Kirkyard with their land to the east, and inaugurate the whole area as a new public cemetery, run on a commercial basis. The Moirs, as owners rather than tenants, were also now at liberty to build a family mausoleum on the sacred mound and reserve it for the use of themselves and their heirs. Alexander the sixth laird, who had paid the 8/4 annually, had died in 1824 and was the first Moir to be commemorated in the mausoleum which dates from the 1840s, much the same time as the palatial Scotstown House was built for Dame Isabella and Sir Michael at the Bridge of Don.

The mausoleum did not get a great deal of custom from the lairds. Only Alexander Moir and Dame Isabella and Sir Michael are buried there, though a host of minor Moirs are commemorated by wall tablets. Isabella's successor, Mary Anne Moir, and her husband, Colonel Henry Knight Erskine are both are buried in Chapel of Garioch kirkyard, near the Colonel's Pittodrie estate. They are the sole occupants of a roofless, ivy-covered pile and are commemorated by a simple plaque and a text from Revelations: 'God shall wipe away all tears from their eyes.' Of their son Henry William there is no sign either in Chapel of Garioch or the Spital Kirkyards, although he was laird both of Pittodrie and the Spital Lands.

Although there are a few old headstones in the Spital Kirkyard, and many graves that are unmarked, most of those that are identifiable date from the 1820s. One such was that of 'Ann Ross, Sometime Housekeeper to Alexander Moir Esquire of Scotstoun,' who was buried there in 1824, the same year as her master. The lettering on her gravestone is handsomely chiselled. Another early resident was John Burness, a cousin of Robert Burns. Born at the family farm of Bogjurgan near Drumlithie in 1771, he

'here lies Ann Ross...'   The Burness 'milestone'.

worked as a shepherd and a baker, and in spite of a limited education, he became a successful poet and playwright, admired by his cousin. His most popular work, the poem *Thrummy Cap*, Burns declared to be 'the best ghaist story in the Scottish language that I am acquainted with.' Unfortunately alcohol and an ill-advised marriage took their toll, and to keep the wolf from the door he became a packman, hawking his books round the North East. On a fateful January day in 1826 he set off from Stonehaven to walk to Aberdeen, but never arrived. He perished near Portlethen church, caught in a blizzard. His body was later dug out of the snow and buried in the Spital graveyard. A memorial, resembling a bulky milestone, and looking curiously out-of-place was erected in 1912 to his memory, near the mausoleum, where he is thought to have been buried.

Robert Burns also has a connection with a modern memorial set against the outer wall of the mausoleum. It commemorates John Skinner 1744-1816, Bishop of Aberdeen and his son and successor of the same name. The elder Skinner was the son of the Reverend John Skinner of Longside, author of 'the best Scotch Song ever Scotland saw - Tullochgorum's my delight,' so said Robert Burns. Praise indeed. Bishop John Skinner, who lived at Berrybank, was one of the local *literati* who welcomed Burns to Aberdeen in 1787. Three years earlier in a historic ceremony in an upper room in Longacre, off Broad Street, Skinner had consecrated the American bishop, Samuel Seabury, and thus made possible the introduction of the Episcopa-

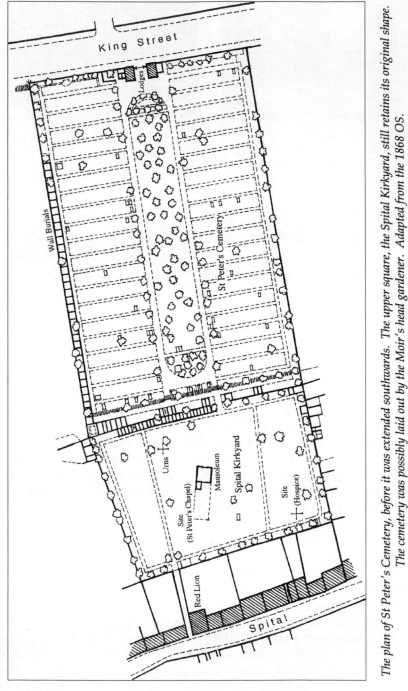

The plan of St Peter's Cemetery, before it was extended southwards. The upper square, the Spital Kirkyard, still retains its original shape. The cemetery was possibly laid out by the Moir's head gardener. Adapted from the 1868 OS.

lian religion to the United States. No mention is made of this on his memorial.

Skilled craftsman and engineers were also among the early residents of the old kirkyard. Peter Gill, watchmaker, who 'departed life 26th Jany 1850 aged 93'. Earlier lettering on his recumbent stone dates from 1828. Another well-cut recumbent stone commemorates, among others Alexander Day, 'Overseer, Spring Garden Works' who died in 1837; an upright headstone in a more flowing style is to the memory of James Smith, 'Overseer, Aberdeen Canal' who died in 1841, and his family.

In the 1860s the Red Lion Inn had crossed from what would become Firhill Place to the Spital-St Peter's Gate corner, the old Churchyard Wynd, and was now even better placed to offer refreshment to mourners. This was a time of antiquarian activity within the old kirkyard. The 1868 ordnance survey map notes 'Urns found here' on a mound a little to the north-east of the Moir Mausoleum. The Sites and Monuments Record shows that two urns were uncovered here in 1865, and were classed as 'Early British Type'. Unfortunately they are no longer extant but they were likely to have been Bronze Age cremation urns - which could indicate a pre-Christian burial site. Since pagan sites were consecrated and used by Christians, this may explain why Bishop Matthew Kyninmund chose such an outlandish place to establish his hospice back in the twelfth century when the Spital story began. The 1976 OS notes 'two Cinerary Urns found here 1884 and 1894' at the same site, but archaeological opinion is that the urns are referred to are those found in 1865.

The new commercial graveyard kept within the north-south boundaries of the Spital Kirkyard but broke through the centre portion of the former East Back Gate, which by this time had fallen out of use, and carried on east to the King Street Road, where a dignified entrance was created. Great iron gates in trellis pattern were cast, bearing an appropriately sepulchral part of the Moir arms, 'a mort head upon two leg bones saltyre ways' and the motto, *Non sibi sed cunctis:* Not for self but for all. Piers of dressed granite support the gates which were flanked by two sturdy, rubble-built lodges, complete with chimney pots. These appear to date from 1824-25 when the new venture was getting underway,

and were initially built as a house for the superintendent. That was Alexander Clark between the 1840s and 1860s, then Alex Morrison, who by the 1880s was settled more comfortably at Ivy Cottage nearby on the King Street Road. The south lodge was now in use as the cemetery office, the north, as the store. The 'clerk to St Peter's Churchyard and keeper of the Trades' mort-cloths' over many years was Ninian Kynoch, grocer and spirit-dealer, who lived round in the Spital, close to the kirkyard.

On passing through the impressive King Street portals, the early visitor would have been greeted by a fine vista, a long, narrow, heavily-wooded oval, reaching back to the Spital Kirkyard, and flanked by two equally long rectangular sections, planted with a variety of young trees, and awaiting further customers - only about forty gravestones had been erected by the mid-1860s. This modern cemetery was at a lower level than the old Spital Kirkyard and was separated from it by banking and a wall where the old East Back Road had once run.

On 22 June 1870, the *Aberdeen Journal* reported:

The proprietor has made improvements to St Peter's Cemetery, Spital. Seats have been provided and grass neatly cut. The public are now allowed admission on Sundays afternoons and evenings and it is hoped they will not abuse this privilege.

By this time Dame Isabella and Sir Michael were at rest in the mausoleum and it was the new lairds, Mary Anne Moir and her husband - though he would die that November - who were responsible for the improvements. A further section was added at King Street, to the south, and in 1883 the cemetery was extended to its present size, by the creation of two further sections on a higher level, again to the south, as far as Merkland Road which recently been laid out. An old lane that curved between the Spital and the King Street Road, which had earlier barred further development, was now redundant and was consumed by the new section.

That same year of 1883 the Spital Estate was offered for sale, (unsuccessfully as it transpired) and St Peter's Cemetery was described enthusiastically in the Particulars of Sale as:

recently extended and forming a practically unlimited area for development. It has long been appreciated and extensively used as a Burying Place by both Protestants and Catholics.

It had become a star performer, with a net annual revenue of £570, almost a quarter of the Estate's total annual revenue. When George J Walker of the surveyors Walker & Duncan, made a further valuation in 1894, the cemetery was still going like a fair. Total lairs now numbered 7566 of which

5645 were sold. Of the 1921 unsold, 1426 were new lairs while only 495 old lairs remained to be taken up. It was, however, no longer 'a practically unlimited area for development'. Between 1888 and 1892, 790 lairs had been sold. 'At this average,' reported Walker, 'ten years will sell the whole lot, but as the lowest priced lairs are about sold out, the sales will extend to a longer period. The annual revenues from St Peter's averaging over a five year period were now working out at £721 14s 4d.

When the last laird, Henry William Knight Erskine, sold the Spital Estate to the City of Aberdeen Land Association in 1900, St Peter's Cemetery was not included. There were few vacant lairs left by this time, and the cemetery was of no interest to a company set up to develop land. It

Mr Simpson L Mitchell's receipt for the purchase of his lair. It cost him £5 10s in 1901. Courtesy, Mrs J Yule (nee Mitchell)

remained in Henry William's ownership for the rest of his life. The Sunday opening of the cemetery remained in force and like many other families Dorothy Gerrard and her parents used to visit it of a Sunday afternoon. Gordon Cardno's grandfather, Mr Williamson, looked after the cemetery and older Spital residents can recall him cutting the grass with a scythe. Lairholders would pay him individually for work done. After H W Knight Erskine's death in the early 1930s, the Spital and St Peter's Cemetery Co Ltd acquired the cemetery. This company subsequently went into liquidation but the cemetery was continued as a going concern by the liquidator. In 1953 it was acquired by Aberdeen Corporation acting on a decision made two years earlier. The 'Town' now 'assumed responsibility for future care and maintenance, upkeep of lairs, headstones and railings and the collection of annual sums, payable by certain lairholders'.

So much of St Peter's lies hidden behind its great wall, that on entering the cemetery for the first time, the visitor is likely to be overwhelmed by the

Top left, urns in serried ranks. The designs at the base of the obelisk, left, commemorating Matthew Croll the baker, are in contrasting grey and white granite. Right, this handsome pillared portico with curved pediment commemorates Alexander G Brown, timber merchant and family. A fine essay in black, white and grey granite. Bottom left, a weeping angelic child mourns the three infant sons of Tom and Jessie Gaunt. Right, Henry Bain chose a mournful damsel in memory of his wife, Christina Barclay, who died in 1917.

sheer density of tombs, graves and sepulchres, by armies of draped urns, rugged crosses, petite obelisks, pillars, columns, mournful damsels and winged figures. This is a remarkable showplace of the monumental masons' skill, and the range of granites used is impressive; the contrasting greys and whites of Rubislaw, Sclattie and Kemnay, the cold pink of Peterhead, the rich edible-looking rosé of Corennie, the speckled pink of Hill o Fare, the black ebony Bon Accord from Sweden, and a rare sighting, the rosé gris from the Isle of Mull.

Unlike St Clement's graveyard in Fittie, where a fair number of those commemorated departed life in some far off land, the majority of those laid to rest in St Peter's were hame-drauchtit folk. There is pride in place: 'Archibald Farquhar, Residenter in Gilcomston'- even in relation to fatal accidents; the unfortunate John Leaper, was 'accidentally killed at Rubislaw Quarry' while the equally unfortunate James Alexander was 'killed on the railway near Fyvie.' There is also pride in inscribing the deceased's trade or profession; commercial traveller, flax dresser, pony dealer, market gardener, jeweller, gunmaker, furniture dealer, hairdresser, mason, cabinetmaker, dyer, upholsterer, gas inspector, missionary, auctioneer, minister, advocate, clothier, ironmoulder, saw trimmer, farmer, farrier, stationer. butcher, printer, slater, ship's plater, bookseller, doctor, pattern maker, sculptor, shore porter, even down to fine detail; 'sergeant manager of pensions of the late 92nd' - the 2nd Gordon Highlanders.

William Craib was 'Inspector of Works, Great North of Scotland Railway', Alexander Lumsden Davie, secretary to G. W. Wilson & Co Ltd, (GWW himself rests in Nellfield); James McHardy, who died in 1890 at 45 was 'late manager to Hall Russell & Co'; John MacPherson Stuart, was 'late manager of Stoneywood Works' and had a splendid Celtic cross. One gravestone commemorates a remarkable servant of Aberdeen University. John Booth who died in 1937 aged eighty-three was, for fifty-one years, the sole attendant in Medicine, Surgery and Midwifery. Asked once how things were going under Professor Sir Ashley Mackintosh's successor, 'Boothie's' reply was somewhat

Boothie's grave.

213

dismissive of modern technology: 'Ach, I dinna ken what things are comin tae. What wi the Perfesser, and this chielie Mac, twa stenographers and the dictaphone - michtie me, me and Ashley managed it a' wersels.'

Here lie Andrew Gage, cloth lapper, Broadford, William Fraser, carter, Old Aberdeen, Alexander Keith, house carpenter, Joseph Wishart, organ builder, James Scullion, gut merchant, Robert Davidson, cycle agent, James Walker, seedsman, Absolom Deane, master mariner, who died in 1828 at seventy-one and must have spent a lifetime before the mast. Alfred Caye, coach bodymaker, has an ornate masonic tomb and John Hardie, photographer who died in 1892 at 49, a handsome gravestone, surmounted by a large urn. One of the finest memorials in the graveyard, a pedimented 'triptych' in pink and grey granite marks the resting place of 'James Scott, plasterer', whose the firm for many years had its showroom at the west end of Union Street, with the yard behind in Justice Mill Lane. Matthew Croll, the Gallowgate baker, Peter McRobbie, the Sunnyside farmer and Marshall Watt the house painter, all well known, all rub shoulders in death. Near the Watt headstone, a trio of tradesmen, John Smith, blacksmith, Charles Panton, bootmaker and George Geddes, builder, stand in a friendly little row. Another of Watt's neighbours is the far-travelled Troup family commemorated by a well-head style memorial in pink, grey and black granite. James Troup of Aberdeen was HM consul-general at Yokohama, Japan. His son was killed in action in the Orange River Colony in 1900. Two of the most striking headstones are those of William Coutts, boilermaker, who dazzles in death, while a simple, modern stone marks the family burying ground of William Skinner, cattle dealer. The last interment here was in 1994.

Here are lairds and merchant; James Allan of Pitmuxton whose family gave their name to Allan Street, and the Davidsons, Charles and William, paper manufacturers of Mugiemoss, who have a handsome wall-mounted memorial. An appropriately large and important headstone marks the last resting place of our old friend from Elmbank Terrace, James Hay Bisset. He is designated as 'of Burnside and Ruthrieston'. No mention that he, nor for that matter, 'John Leighton, Orchard Cottage' were builders to trade. Ebenezer Bain, on the other hand is described simply as builder, though more specifically he was a house carpenter, and had been deacon and boxmaster of the Seven Incorporated Trades. Of his epic work on this famous and once powerful local institution, written some twenty years before his death in 1895, there is no mention.

A wall tablet with fine scroll work unequivocally commemorates one of the masters of the trade, 'Adam Mitchell of Heathcot, Builder in Aberdeen, who died 29th January 1877 aged 54 years.' Born in Kennethmont, the son of a prosperous tenant farmer who fell on hard times, the young

Adam Mitchell's wall tablet.

Mitchell received only a rudimentary education and worked as a herd loon. However he secured an apprenticeship at the granite yard of Macdonald and Leslie in Constitution Street, and cut his stonemason's teeth on the Duke of Gordon, now in Golden Square, and Scotland's oldest granite statue. Ambitious, intelligent and determined, he set up on his own as a builder and secured contracts for the new Aberdeen Grammar School in Esslemont Avenue, the Palace Hotel, the great villas of Albyn Place, the Denburn Valley Railway and the bridges of the Alford Railway. John Fyfe was supplying stone from the family quarry at the Tyrebagger for the Alford contract, but Mitchell, having cast an expert eye over the Hill of Kemnay suggested that stone 'might be got out of it' and money saved on cartage. He was right, and the famous Kemnay quarry came into existence. Mitchell was a public man too, serving as a Police Commissioner, then on Aberdeen Town Council from 1871, first as Master of Shoreworks, then as baillie until his death six years later. He owned the estate of Heathcot between Ardoe and Blairs on Lower Deeside. Heathcot House later became the earliest Deeside Hydropathic.

Mitchell's tablet is on the wall dividing cemetery from Kirkyard, and at right angles, is the north wall of St Peter's. At the kirkyard end is the tomb of James Sim, merchant, of Cornhill, an elegant, understated essay in grey, white and pink granite. Nearby is the family burying ground where Henry Cooper, the linsey woolsey man from Elmbank and Homewood finally came to rest. The wall-mounted shield is the strangest monument in St Peter's. A headless 'torso' has a rope round the neck. What can that signify? Henry was not in the hemp business. Drapery over the shoulders is more understandable. He did manufacture cloth, though of an inferior kind. Below the neck, hands are clasped in a sort of masonic handshake. Very odd.

Henry Cooper's strange shield.

Hurrying past Henry's tomb, we soon come on some other old friends; Thomas Hogarth of Elmfield, his daughter and her husband, 'Henry Arthur Crane, late Captain 72nd Duke of Albany's Own Highlanders.' Curious that Crane chose to be designated in this way, for he was a major and adjutant of the Gordon Highlanders Volunteers for over twenty years. Clearly he, or his wife who survived him, regarded the old Duke of Albany's, a regular regiment, as a cut above the Volunteers in spite of the fact that by 1913, the year of Crane's death, it no longer existed, having been absorbed by the Seaforths in 1881. The Seaforths amalgamated with the Queen's Own Cameron Highlanders in 1961 to become the Queen's Own Highlanders who in turn amalgamated with a well known north-east regiment in 1996. The Gordons got him in the end.

Moving now towards the King Street end of the north wall, we come to the family burying ground of the distinguished artist, Sir George Reid PRSA LLD, whose home, St Luke's at Kepplestone, now houses the Gordon Highlanders Museum. Reid, born in

Sir George Reid's memorial features the laureate's wreath to which the torches of life are bound.

216

1841, left Aberdeen Grammar School at twelve to take up an apprenticeship with Keith & Gibb the lithographers, then studied in Edinburgh. His early work can be seen in Samuel Smiles *Life of a Scotch Naturalist* of 1876, and he provided the portraits for William Alexander's *Johnny Gibb of Gushetneuk*. He is best known for his excellent portraits of the North East's most eminent men. He lived much of the time in Edinburgh, but died in 1913 in Somerset where he had gone for the sake of his health. His father and his wife, both of whom died at St Luke's, are also commemorated here.

Two massive trees guard the entrances to the Spital Kirkyard, viewed from the cemetery. On the extreme right is the grave of the granite merchant, Arthur Taylor, whose lady has lost her hand. Just behind, a part of James Scott's handsome memorial can be glimpsed.

Many of the granite merchants themselves are buried in St Peter's; William Keith, James R R Kennedy whose tomb is overseen by a stern stone lady, complete with mourning bouquet; and William Garden whose grave is surmounted by a small, determined Joan of Arc figure with her head in trees. Nearby Charles McDonald has favoured a petite draped figure, a mite too small for its plinth. The tomb of McDonald's Jute Street neigh-

Memorials to a bourrachie of granite merchants. Top left, is Arthur Taylor's handless lady. Right, the magnificently wrought cross on the tomb of George Stalker. Bottom left, Robert Gibb's gravestone has a finely detailed cornice surmounted by anthemion leaves. Right, James R R Kennedy's stony lady.

bours, Arthur Taylor, father and son who died in 1930 and 1955 respectively is adorned by the same lady as Thomas Whalen who died in 1902. She is in not nearly such a good condition as her twin, and has lost her right hand. George Stalker, son of the founder of the third Jute Street firm, and his family are commemorated by a particularly fine granite cross. The gravestone of Robert Gibb of the Excelsior Granite Works who died in 1907 has a fine cornice, and the original art nouveau lettering has been admirably copied to record a family death in 1967.

At the Merkland Road end of the cemetery, one stumbles across the tomb of Edward the Confessor, the eleventh century King of the English. What a surprise. How did he get in there? On closer inspection the recumbent tombstone is seen to bear insignia similar to Edward's, that of his great-niece, St Margaret of Scotland. No it is not St Margaret's grave either, but that of another old friend, the Reverend John Comper, founder of St Margaret's-in-the-Gallowgate and St Margaret's Convent in the Spital. The tomb and the slender, lofty calvary above it were designed by Sir Ninian Comper, Father Comper's renowned architect son. Behind the Comper tomb is the burial ground of the sisters of St Margaret's Convent in the Spital, whose names are recorded on a slab of white granite.

Left, Father Comper's recumbent stone is watched over by a graceful calvary. Behind is the memorial to the sisters of St Margaret's Convent in the Spital. Right, a poignant cross dedicated to St Peter's orphans. They were cared for at Priest Gordon's school and orphanage in Constitution Street, later the Shiprow Tavern and whose future at time of writing is uncertain.

Still at Merkland end, but much nearer King Street, is the grave of 'James Forrest Donald JP Teacher of Dancing' who died in 1934 at 64. A little scroll below reads: 'To our beloved master and benefactor from the staff of James F Donald (Aberdeen Cinemas) Ltd.' Here then lies the founder of the Donald dynasty, who established the North Silver Street Dancing Academy, a chain of popular cinemas, and saved the failing His Majesty's Theatre for Aberdeen by purchasing it in 1932. 'He was a keen business man with courage and enterprise', recorded the Bon-Accord. So many attended that funeral that when the hearse stopped at the cemetery gates, mourners were still turning into King Street from Castle Street.

Perhaps it has something to do with the flanking columns, but is there a touch of the cinema organ about James F Donald's headstone? The little scroll below is a tribute from his staff.

Finally from her home in the Spital, Jean Simpson can still recall hearing buglers sounding the Last Post when military funerals were taking place. St Peter's War Memorial, standing at the King Street entrance, is one of the finest in the city. Erected by the Commonwealth War Graves Commission, it takes the form of the beautifully proportioned octagonal Cross of Sacrifice, against whose shaft and arms of white Kemnay granite, the great downward-pointing bronze sword stands out. The wording of the memorial is contained on the plinth which is formed by octagonal slabs. The three facing the entrance act as headstones for those mentioned by name below:

To the Honoured Memory of fifty one sailors and soldiers who gave their lives for their country during the Great War 1914-1918 and who lie buried in this cemetery - of whom these three have no separate headstone: Private JR Summer, Gordon Highlanders, 15th February, 1916, Able Seaman A Stewart, Royal Naval Division, 18th July 1917, S Black, Trimmer, RNR, *HMS Brilliant* 13th April, 1916.

Their names liveth for evermore.

The St Peter's Cemetery War Memorial.

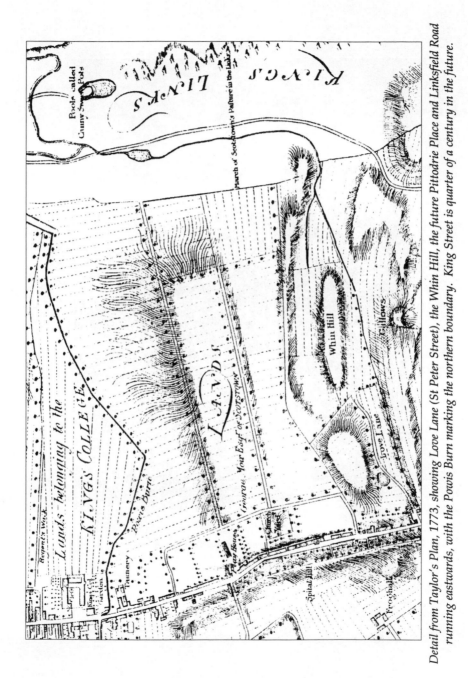

Detail from Taylor's Plan, 1773, showing Love Lane (St Peter Street), the Whin Hill, the future Pittodrie Place and Linksfield Road running eastwards, with the Powis Burn marking the northern boundary. King Street is quarter of a century in the future.

Chapter 17

Around the King Street Road
Dung, Sewage, Manure - and the Mill

Dung carts and sewage, a poorhouse, a churchyard - with a hideous barrack and powder magazine - these form some of the attractions planted by way of adornment to the road.

Professor W D Geddes, Local Aspects of the Fine Arts, 1874.

Our journey through the east side of the Spital Lands now takes us to the outer reaches beyond the East Back Gate, the old Orchard Lane, with its pleasant groves of fruit trees, to a vast expanse of sandy, benty braes, stretching to the Links and the sea. George Moir, fifth laird of the Spital Lands and an keen 'improver' was the first to make something of this unpromising territory. He was praised for his efforts by the writer and traveller Francis Douglas who commented in his *General Description of the East Coast of Scotland* of 1782 that Moir :

has gained a great deal of ground from the links, or benty sands, towards the sea. The upper part of them ...consist of little hills of a light sandy soil, which when cleared of weeds, and sufficiently manured, are found to produce good crops of grain and sown grass.

Taylor's Plan was printed in George Moir's lifetime - he died in 1793 - and the Plan shows fields under cultivation from the Powis Burn southwards towards the boundary with the town at Love Lane. Two loanings go eastwards through these fields on a line that has been followed in more recent times by Linksfield Road and Pittodrie Place. South of the 'laboured ground' was rough country where Love Lane (St Peter Street) petered no further. Much of this area, now bisected by King Street, was then straddled by the Whin Hill.

Not that long after George's Moir's death, work began on the North Turnpike. We think nothing these days of driving along King Street to the Bridge of Don and beyond but the Turnpike's construction was a long saga which lasted from 1797 when work began on the Balgownie to Ellon stretch, until 1830 when the new Bridge of Don was completed and made the whole thing relevant. Work on the stretch through the Spital Lands from the city boundary at Love Lane out to the Lady Mill, or St Peter Street to the King Street Mill pub if you prefer, got off the ground, in a manner of speaking, in 1804. It seems to have been a relatively straightforward piece of civil engineering, avoiding the problems of the section immediately to the south, where the Turnpike trustees had arguments with the Society of Advocates over access to their land and problems with levels between Jasmine Terrace and Love Lane where the high ground on the east side had to be levelled off, with much soil removed by horse and cart in 1803. The Whin Hill was taking its toll.

George Moir's successor, Alexander, sixth laird took a keen interest in soldiering. He was commanding officer of the new Gentlemen Volunteers, so it may have been he who originally gave land for a Rifle Range which occupied much of the rough uneven Whin Hill area, running eastwards to the Links. When the Militia Barracks was first mooted in 1861, the King Street-Love Lane site was favoured because it was 'at a convenient distance from the exercise grounds and musketry range on the Links'. The west end of the range was just across the road. In more modern terms, it formed a long rectangle starting at Pittodrie Lane at the rear of Nos 392-406 King Street, and running east almost to the shore, where targets were located. Another factor in the siting of the Militia Barracks had been the 'advantages of open space and free communication', for even by 1880 there were still many wide open spaces in King Street. Nevertheless, when the lease expired in 1881, the Secretary of State of War, who then was renting it at £32 per annum from the last laird, Henry William Knight Erskine, did not seek to renew the lease.

The Rifle Range continued to appear in the valuation rolls of the 1880s as part of the Spital Lands, but houses were now going up in this part of the King Street Road, and granite yards were opening up in the vicinity. The trams, using horse traction at this time, had been running as far as John Duncan's City Auction Mart at Nelson Street since 1880, and in 1888 came out as far as Merkland Road. The Rifle Range flitted, as did its neighbour, the Powder Magazine, erected in 1807 on the Gallowhills, near what became the east end of Errol Street. The Magazine lay a matter of yards outwith Spital Lands, but merits a mention. Like the leper colony, it had to be located within the burgh's limits where the magistrates, or in this case the Police Commissioners could exercise control, while keeping it as far as possible from 'the body of the kirk'. Indeed, the stone 'incised with ane cross', that marked the eastern extremity of the ancient Leper Croft lay near the Magazine. The latter was a common store; as well as the military, gunpowder merchants kept their stock here and whalers, when in port, stored their gunpowder in the Magazine to avoid any mischance in the busy harbour area. A small profit was made from the dues paid by these users. The Magazine was housed in a jail-like compound, comprising a quadrangular enclosure, granite- built and three feet thick, with two vaulted stores of stone and lime, each 41ft long, 20ft broad and 20ft high, plus three smaller buildings, all slate-roofed.

As the city expanded northwards, folk grew more nervous about its location. The Seven Incorporated Trades, owners of Trinity Cemetery being laid out behind the Magazine, presumably did not want to see their new graveyard filled precipitously. The Magazine was rebuilt in 1888 at a new site on the Links while its down-takings were used to build a public shelter on the old site near the Cemetery Lodge, much frequented by old men in its days, and still well within the living memory.

Returning to the Spital Lands, the charmingly named Dung Stance Road ran along the north boundary of the Rifle Range which though anonymous, can be seen on the Post Office map of 1880, (page 226), north of the Powder Magazine. It formed a junction with the King Street Road opposite the new Merkland Road, ran east for a distance then turned due north, to the Dung Yard, which again is on the map. This depository was also known as the North Dung Stance or the Police Dung Yard, being under the aegis of the Police Commissioners in charge of the cleansing of the city, and much else. The Dung Stance had been sited at King Street, but was complained of by the Board of Health as 'a dangerous nuisance,' so in 1852, the Police Commissioners offered to rent ground from Sir Michael Bruce and Dame Isabella for a Dung Stance, near the Gallowhill at £7 an acre. They initially declined, but later made the land available.

In those days of genuine horse power the sale of manure was one of the city's sources of income, albeit a modest one. Initially a sort of 'dung tacksman' was appointed, who made the highest bid for the 'police manure'. He would then sell the product to farmers and hopefully make a profit over the year. By the late 1880s, the Town Council - the Police Commissioners had amalgamated with them in 1871 - would appoint an agent 'for the sale of the city manure' at a commission of 10%'. James Cowie was one such agent. He already was a grain merchant and would have many contacts among North East farmers. Dung was collected from the city stables, and swept from the streets, (that was known as 'police manure'),

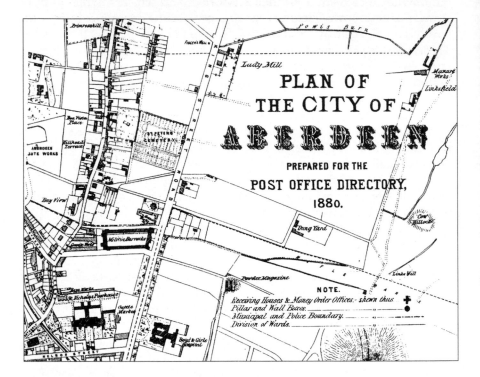

Detail from the Post Office Plan of 1880, showing from the foot upwards, the Powder Magazine, the Rifle Range, and the Dung Stance Road (unnamed), running from King Street to the Dung Yard. The Spital Irrigation Farm occupied the central portion, covered by lettering. Napier's Manure Works is top right, and the Lady Mill, top left. Newham Cottage sits opposite the Mill enclosure.

and the sight of a horse clip-clopping along King Street to the Stance, its cart piled high with manure must have been a familiar one, albeit deprecated, like much else in King Street, by Professor 'Homer' Geddes in a speech to Aberdeen Philosophical Society in 1874. The ground occupied by the 'Police Manure Store' was leased to the Council by Henry William Knight Erskine at an annual rent of £69 3s 0d.

We move northwards again, to another ferly, the Spital Irrigation Farm, which occupied the greater part of the east Spital Lands east of King Street, from the Dung Stance Road to what is now Linksfield Road. When researching *The Spital*, I kept on coming across this mysterious Spital Irrigation Farm, tenanted by Peter McRobbie the Sunnyside farmer. This was a puzzler. Irrigation, dimly remembered from distant geography lessons, was something they did in hot countries where rainfall was sparse; watering crops from man-made channels running through the fields. The Spital was not in a hot country. Moreover, to judge by the valuation rolls this was a fair size of a place. Too big even to fit into the Spital. Then the facts were gradually pieced together. The farm was not in the Spital at all, but far away in the Spital Lands; nor was it a farm in the conventional sense either.

The story begins in 1864 when the Police Commissioners instructed Mr Robert Anderson, Resident Engineer for the waterworks, to design a sewerage scheme, for the entire city. Anderson, at this time was busy planning a major waterworks scheme but the Commissioners thought they might as well kill two birds with one stone; if they had the water, they might as well have the sewers. The hard-working Anderson was quite agreeable to carrying out both tasks, though at one time there were murmurings, though to no avail, that he should have an assistant At this time there were but nine miles of sewers in Aberdeen, serving only the principal streets. The cesspool system 'with all its attendant evils' was much depended on. In his Report on the State of Sewerage of 1864, Anderson gives us some idea of his problems. He was faced with over 50 miles of streets to survey, and a total lack of information and records. The first ordnance survey of Aberdeen had not yet been carried put. Nevertheless, Anderson, one of Aberdeen's unsung heroes, designed the new scheme as required, and it was carried out under his direction during 1866-70.

Reporting to the Commissioners in February, 1865, Anderson produced two schemes for disposing of the city's sewage, one conventional, the other for 'sterilising a portion of the sewage matter by irrigation of the Old Town Links …'. One of popular theories of the day was that 'sewage, if properly distributed over land as manure would yield, even upon the poorest soils, large and abundant crops', and Robert Anderson had given a nod in that direction. Nothing further was heard of the irrigation system, until the sewers were being constructed two years later. Then Sir Alexander Anderson strode on to the scene. In 1867 he wrote to the Police Commissioners:

Gentlemen, I have lately had the opportunity to witness the effects of Town sewage applied to a crop of grass at an experimental farm at Barking ... There is no doubt that where capable of accomplishment at small cost, such an application may be made with profit.

Sir Alexander, Lord Provost from 1859-65, was both a controversial figure and one of the greatest civic heads Aberdeen has ever had. It was he who got the Cairnton water scheme underway in 1864, and now he had some practical ideas about sewerage. Robert Anderson, promoted to City Engineer, had originally suggested that the Links would benefit from irrigation through sewage, but Sir Alexander, now wearing his lawyer's hat, had spotted a more suitable area nearer town, that part of the Spital Lands from opposite the Militia Barracks to the Lady Mill. He acted for the new Spital laird Mary Anne Moir and her husband Colonel Henry Knight Erskine and he understood that they were amenable to having their fields fertilised in this novel way. Robert Anderson was able to confirm that £2000 could be saved by making sewage available for irrigation, at a cost of £9000 as against the original £11,000.

An intercepting sewer was now put in place, beginning at the south end of Bon Accord Terrace, sloping gradually towards the Spital Lands, winding its way via as many streets as possible including Union Street, Belmont Street, Back Wynd, Harriet Street, George Street, 'where there is a dense population', Spring Garden, the Gallowgate, under the GNSR by iron pipe on the lower side of Mounthooly Bridge, into field on the north side of St Nicholas Poorhouse, across the King Street Road to the gardens opposite the Militia Barracks, along the east side for a short distance, then across the Dung Stance Road, and the adjoining market gardens. The sewer terminated in a field above the Dung Stance, 150 yards east of King Street Road 'where (the sewage) will be distributed over the fields by proper channels for irrigation purposes'. Mr Bryce, manager of Edinburgh's Irrigation at Craigentinny visited Aberdeen, examined the proposed lands on the King Street Road which were already under cultivation, and pronounced them 'favourable both from their situation near town, and the nature of the soil', and entertained commissioners with a fascinating account of the development of Craigentinny Links.

Aberdeen's great and good went irrigation mad. That the new sewerage system could be used to achieve the production of wheat where there were tares, literally as well as metaphorically, had a blend of thrift, science, progress and self-help, that appealed to the Victorian mind. Police Commissioners assiduously studied articles in *The Times* about Barking 'where the great London sewers debouch' where grass, wheat and rye, red and white cabbage, parsnips, birdseed, strawberries as well as Italian rye grass for horses were grown. Robert Anderson visited Croydon, and saw open aqueducts dispersing sewage through sloping fields. Lord Provost William Leslie, while in England on harbour business took the opportunity to visit Hastings where sewage underwent a special deodorising process. When he came back the Commissioners called in Jimmy Brazier, Professor of Chemistry at Aberdeen University, and a renowned experimenter to carry out tests. They paid Brazier a fee £25, but no further action was taken. The entrepreneurial waste-products chemist, John Miller, founder of the Sandilands Chemical Works, visited irrigation farms near London which grew carrots, turnips, green peas, onions, rhubarb, mangel-wurzel and much more, and was able to reassure the Commissioners, to whom he gave his notes, and members of the Aberdeen Philosophical Society to whom he read a paper, 'that it was only on stooping down and bringing the nose to within a few inches of the surface we detected the well known ammoniacal and characteristic smell'.

And so the lease for 'the privilege of using the Town's Sewage' at the Spital Irrigation Farm was drawn up in 1869. It was initially to run for nineteen years. Messrs Murray, Urquhart & Co were awarded the contract to build the 'Aberdeen Irrigation Works' which they carried out for £379. Not less than 10 acres were to be brought into irrigation during each of the first five years, bringing 50 acres under irrigation all told. The rent the Knight Erskines paid for the sewage at £5 for an acre's-worth, was £50, in the first year, increasing to £250 as the acreage increased.

It was not all plain sailing. Mrs Knight Erskine complained of insufficient supply sewage in 1871, while the Commissioners argued that they had fulfilled the terms of the lease. Meanwhile in 1880 the Cleansing Committee attempted to improve the quality of the manure at the North Dung Stance - perhaps farmers had complained that it wasn't strong enough - by mixing it with a portion of 'the Town's Sewage'. William Henry Knight Erskine, granted permission for the sewage to be taken from the farm three times a week, for five hours at a time. In 1882, William Henry complained that the sewage had been diluted and would not pay more than £100 for its supply.

Mrs Katherine Trail, born in 1863 comments on the experiments 'in fertilising the fields by means of the town's sewage' in her *Reminiscences of Old Aberdeen*, and gives a picture of how the farm looked:

In my young days I remember the field to the south of Linksfield Road carrying quite a heavy crop of wheat. Between the fields and the pavement were high banks - the joy of children and the dread of their nurses.

Presumably the sewage was larded onto the fields from the irrigation channels by a long-handled spade.

In the Schedule of Particulars of 1883 the 'scientifically arranged Irrigation Farm' is much vaunted. It produced 'three or four rich crops of Grass more than two feet high' per season which were 'sold in the Ground at the rate of £8 per acre', presumably as fodder. No sign of strawberries or mangel-wurzels, however. The annual revenue was £475 against the sewage rent of £250. The Lands as we know were not sold at this time and in 1887, with the end of the nineteen year lease in sight, Aberdeen Town Council renewed their agreement to supply sewage, but only for five years and at a reduced rental of £100 per annum. In fact the farm and the sewage agreement lasted until 1899.

No sooner had the late nineteenth century traveller left the Sewage Irrigation Farm at the Links Field, than he saw looming up, the vast and dread shape of the Linksfield Manure Works, though no one every called it that. It was as much a euphemism as the Spital Irrigation Farm. It was located at the furthest corner of the east Spital Lands, in today's terms at the junction of Regent Walk and Golf Road. A small farm to the south, roughly at the east end of Linksfield Road was also part of the complex. This was Napier's realm. It was a knackery, still remembered by older Aberdonians. The manure in question was fertiliser made from the bones of slaughtered horses.

Charles Napier, 'manure manufacturer' - two generations of the family would have been involved - started off in West North Street around 1870. Ten years he had moved to the Links. Unlike its eloquent appraisal of the Irrigation Farm, the Schedule of Particulars of 1883 remains mute about the Manure Works. It simply states that Charles Napier is paying rents of £35 and £26 14s 6d for 'manure and farm' respectively. In July 1892, 'Messrs Charles Napier & Co, Slaughterers of Horses and Animal Manure Manufacturers' - a straightforward description of the work undertaken - sought permission from the Town's Public Health Committee for an extension to the 'Animal Manure Works at Linksfield'. The additions that Napier sought were substantial - four sheds, each 125ft long, walls of stone, ten feet high, the roofs slated. Shades of the Powder Magazine! The committee was pleased to recommend 'the enlargement of the building', but two years later Napier and his architect, John Rust Jnr, were back again seeking more additions, three buildings this time, each 88ft long, slaughter house, digestion house and engine house, with plans too, to improve the bone mill. The size of the place indicates the huge population of working horses then in the city, providing manure both while living and dead. No happy green fields of retirement for them. In 1905 there was a fire which must have been horrific. The whole place had to be rebuilt.

Planning applications relating to the knackery mention 'foul-smelling matter arising from the manure'. The smell was notorious, and Alex Slessor has a spine-chilling tale thereby. One morning, very early, many years ago he was at the Links putting down his name for a round of golf as you did at that time. Then he noticed, with some apprehension, a band of a dozen or so rats, their curious bluish pelts visible in the half light, making their way, in a very determined manner, towards Napier's. These were ships' rats which had come off the vessel *Idaho*, aground on the beach, and were setting off to investigate the interesting smells coming from the knackery. Alex never saw the blue rats again. There were many rats on the Links at that time, and the *Idaho* rats would have mated with the locals and lost their special colouring. By 1929, the land where the knackery stood was in the ownership of Aberdeen Town Council, and the building of the School Road Housing scheme was underway nearby. 'Smells emanating from the Linksfield Manure Works' were deemed likely to cause what was known in legal terms as 'a nuisance'. Napier's lease was terminated at Whitsunday 1930. That was not the last of the rats, however. Left behind after the knackery closed they infested School Road and a bounty of up to 1/- was offered for each rat caught.

Just beyond Napier's, the Powis Burn reached the city boundary at what is now Golf Road. That was the most northerly point of the Spital Lands. After that were the Lands of Seaton. At this point, we turn back south-westwards, following the Powis Burn upstream to the Lady Mill, built as a meal mill, the only mill which the Burn powered in its course. It was named after Dame Isabella - Lady Isabella Bruce - and erected on the King Street Road in 1832 to take advantage of increased traffic generated by the new Bridge of Don. The mill's southern boundary ran alongside the future Linksfield Road, an easterly continuation of 'old' Orchard Lane. This road would have been convenient for Spital dwellers and those in the southern part of Old Aberdeen. To build a mill beside a road that was already in use was only commonsense. But a fine, broad new road was created for the those in mid and north Old Aberdeen, terminating opposite the north end of the mill enclosure. It was called University Road, stressing the status of King's College as a university in its own right.

The mill's curtilage, the enclosure within which it sat, was extensive and surrounded with trees. A miller's house, Ladymill Cottage, sat nearby. A 'gangway' which is enclosed by handsome wrought-iron railings leads to its front door, passing over a semi-basement which transforms itself into a

The Old Mill Enclosure at King Street

Above, the extent of the former Mill enclosure, showing the west range, from left, the Lady Mill, now the King Street Mill pub, the tenement later shoe-horned in, and Ladymill Cottage, with filling station and flats beyond.

The mill from the rear. This gives some idea of the depth of the enclosure.

The mill workers' cottages.

◀ *Opposite, Ladymill Cottage, now No 490 King Street. To the right, the filling station and flats occupy the former site of the Excelsior Granite Works.*

full storey at the rear. Two mill-workers' cottages behind the mill are still approached by a country lane which leads off King Street. Beyond Ladymill Cottage, a grassy, tree-girt area carried extended south to Linksfield Road. The Mill is a pub these days, and one gets a good idea of the original layout from the carpark. The long mill building remains, though there has been some demolition to the rear. It was built of brick harl, and some of the bricks are now exposed. They are huge. If indeed they did come from Seaton Brick Works, the most likely place, this must have been a special order. There is no sign of a lade, but the Powis Burn flows north-eastwards in its culvert, through a wee valley between the Mill and Linksfield

The little valley of the Powis Burn, (in culvert), with Linksfield Academy, left and the Mill enclosure, right. The striking, multi-storey Seaton flats are in the distance.

Academy.

The Lady Mill later became a saw mill. It converted to the production of bobbins before the end of the nineteenth century, and for many years was run by J & J L Brebner, bobbin manufacturers. Offcuts were popular with local children. Jean Simpson recalls that the Mill cut circles of wood for 'beddies' in season and charged $\frac{1}{2}$d. George Elphinstone and his friends were interested in larger wooden circles which served as the inner wheels of their cairties.

By 1890 the curtilage of the Mill had been eroded, if that is not too strong a term to use. The granite merchant Robert Gibb, one of three Gibb brothers, each with his own granite yard, set up his Excelsior yard immediately south of the mill, well within the enclosure. It was a vast enterprise,

The bricks used in building the mill were outsized!

taking up the area which today is covered not only by the filling station on the King Street-Linksfield Road corner, but the new flats behind. Robert Gibb, an 'over the shop' man acquired Ladymill Cottage, now No 490 King Street, as his personal residence. A handsome, late nineteenth century tene ment, originally Ladymill House, but now Nos 496-498 King Street, was shoe-horned between Mill and Cottage. Built by Gibb for his workers it now houses a general merchant and the Bobbin Pharmacy. The mill-workers' cottages are still there at Nos 492 and 494, while the Mill itself is a pub, known these days as the King Street Mill. The mill was re-incarnated as the Bobbin Mill pub in 1973. It was the brain child of the millers themselves James and Kenneth Booth, both third generation craftsmen. They carried out the conversion themselves, making tables, chairs and bar stools from their own wood, and retaining original features wherever possible. Ken Booth was a folk singer, and in his day, the Bobbin Mill with its long, dimly-lit cosy interior, was a popular spot for folk music. It was later acquired by Alloa Pubs, who offer an impressive range of food and drink.

Chapter 18

Merkland to Linksfield
A Granite Merchants' Mecca

The King Street Road: Love Lane to Lady Mill
Aberdeen Post Office Directory, 1884-85.

In time, Rifle Range, Dung Stance, Sewerage Farm and Manure Works vanished as the city spread northwards and eastwards. The King Street Road was feued out as far as the Lady Mill, and new streets, running eastwards to the Links, were created, most of them on the line of existing cart roads. Progress was slow. The Schedule of Particulars of 1883 of the sale of the Spital Lands reveals that on the west side of the King Street Road, only James Hutcheon's Granite Yard on the corner with Love Lane (which became St Peter Street in 1888), John Duncan's fine new mansion, Zetland House, and St Peter's Cemetery, were in existence, plus one small house. As Katherine Trail wrote in her *Reminiscences, of Old Aberdeen;* 'Between the corner of University Road and King Street to the Militia Barracks there was only one cottage which still stands among all its more modern brothers.' This must have been Newham Cottage, where Mrs Newham took in lodgers. It was built before Orchard Street was laid out, and now No 475 King Street, still stands there, every bit as smart as its younger neighbours. Mrs Trail continues:

St Peter's Cemetery, then very much smaller than it is today, was the favourite goal of many of our walks. The gatekeeper was a great friend, and many a sticky sweetie found its way from his pocket to our mouths.

236

Newham Cottage.

She adds an interesting insight into King Street transport arrangements:

> For some time horse-drawn cars stopped at the cemetery gate, as the hill down to University Road was too severe a gradient to be tackled without an extra horse. Some years later this was provided, and the car terminus was extended to the north side of University Road.

Even today, that gradient remains quite noticeable.

On the east side, about sixteen feus had been given out by 1883. They were attractive urban cottages, with a name rather than a number. Among the early ones were Rosevale, Kent, Meadow, Beach Bank, Bayview, Ivy, Gleniffer. They are still there, between Nos 414 and 438 King Street, though some have either changed or lost their names. Marchmont, No 392, a fine house, was a little later on the scene. This was the first house beyond the old city boundary, the first in the King Street Road. Almost rivalling John Duncan's Zetland in size and style, it was built for Councillor Ernest Hutcheon whose family granite yard was across the way. In fact this stretch of the Spital Lands lying within the King Street Road was marked by Hutcheon's King Street Cemetery Granite Works at one end and Robert Gibb's Excelsior Granite Works at the other. Northwards of St Peter Street,

Ivy Cottage, home for many years of Alex Morrison, superintendent of St Peter's Cemetery.

the boundary between King Street and the King Street Road, the thoroughfare changed in character, becoming leafy and suburban. In December 1894, the King Street Road was 'abolished' by the Town Council and King Street now ran all the way from Castle Street to the Bridge of Don. To this day, however, and in spite of heavy traffic which continually pounds along King Street, the difference between the two sections of the road can still be observed.

The Irrigation Farm had tactfully commenced over a hundred yards behind King Street, beyond what is now Pittodrie Lane. When the Spital Lands were being marketed, it was stressed that when the sewage contract with the Town Council ended, the Irrigation Farm land would have a good feuing value. Henry William Knight Erskine doubtless envisaged streets where once the corn had grown high, set out neatly in grid fashion, full of new houses, all paying feu duty. This contract was due to end in 1899, but Henry William, impatient to get on with his urbanisation plans, yoked Smith & Kelly to lay out some new streets for him, from King Street eastwards, just for a short distance, though not into the bowels of the Farm itself, which was still going strong. In December, 1893, the team got permission to lay out a street on 'the east side of the King Street Road opposite St Peter's Cemetery, to extend in an easterly direction for a distance of 121 yards or thereby'. The street was to be named Pittodrie

Place, and it already existed as a cart track. Henry William was again making use of the family names, Erskine at the west side of the Spital Lands, and now Pittodrie at the east side. Pittodrie Place was not the favoured Council width of 50ft, but only 40ft 'the greatest width obtainable on account of there being houses already erected fronting King Street Road'. So that had to do.

The existence of the Irrigation Farm at a time when those streets on the east side of King Street were being laid out, explains a characteristic still evident today. Tenements and industrial buildings extend a short way eastwards, then stop. That was as far as they could go. Then the character of these roads changes for they were not developed until years later. The 1901 ordnance survey, shows irrigation channels still in place, one running west from the former Dung Stance then heading north to Linksfield Road, crossing Pittodrie Place *en route*. When Henry William wanted to extend Pittodrie Place in 1898 the continuation had to be built across the irrigation ditch.

The next street to be laid out also gave trouble. This was the Dung Stance Road, to the south of Pittodrie Place, like it, a cart road, and a busy one. Henry William had a customer here by 1894, another granite yard, Messrs Stott & Warrander, at the junction with King Street. The Dung Stance Road had to be widened. At this time a new road 'to be called Merkland Road East, to run 367 yards east from King Street, was sanctioned by the Town Council. It would 'for a certain distance involve the discontinuance of the existing Dung Stance Road.' Merkland Road East was not a new road at all. It *was* the Dung Stance Road, now improved, deodorised and renamed. It could be extended further than its neighbours at this early date, for it lay just south of the Irrigation Farm. In its early years it was often in a poor state of repair, and improvements were carried out in fits and starts over the next few years.

More roads followed. In 1896, a new street roughly on the line of the ancient cart road which led past the Links Field to the Links was laid out and called, quite appropriately, Linksfield Road. The following year, a fourth street was sanctioned by the Council. It appeared briefly in the Post Office directories as New Street, but eventually Henry William thought up a name for it - Pittodrie Street. In 1898, yet another new road was 'to be laid out on the property of the Spital running parallel to King Street, between Pittodrie Place and Linksfield Road'. This grand introduction heralded little Linksfield Place, a short cross street which was edging near the Irrigation Farm.

The City of Aberdeen Land Association, owners of the Spital Lands after 1900, decided to run the four roads, Merkland Road East, the two Pittodries, Place and Street and Linksfield Road straight to the Links. But over the next few years the Association's best laid plans had a disconcerting habit of going agley. Pittodrie Street, could not initially proceed through to the Links, because 'the Bon Accord Golf Club feu comes in the way'. Plans to continue Merkland Road East through to the Links were thwarted by the fact that someone had inconsiderately laid out a football pitch in its path. The Land Association regarded this merely as a temporary hitch. After all they owned the ground. (At time of writing the football pitch is still there and Merkland Road East still hasn't made it to the Links). Linksfield Road was planned to snake northwards and eastwards to the Manure Works, but Napier's proved unco-operative. The flurry of proposals presented to the Council by CALA in 1901 were withdrawn, then superseded by amended plans in 1902, by further amended plans two years later, and by even more amended plans in 1913. By the 1920s, the two Pittodries, Street and Place still hadn't reached the Links.

Ardarroch Road had made its appearance by 1907. It ran parallel to Pittodrie Lane though it was much wider and a couple of hundred yards further south, indicating that the Irrigation Farm had eventually given up the ghost. Even here things did not run as smoothly as CALA might have hoped. In December 1906, Mr P Tawse, contractor, agreed, rather ungraciously, to lay it out. As he advised Messrs Walker & Duncan, CALA's surveyors:

The price you offer me - £200 - is a very low sum indeed. I will undertake to do the work for this sum - this I am only able to do seeing that I have the great bulk of the material already on the ground in the form of surpluses from other Contracts.

Walker & Duncan, incidentally, had specified 'granite channels of blue or grey granite from Rubislaw, Kemnay, Persley or Cairncry quarries' which was to be supplied by Charles Ritchie of the Clayhills - now Portland Street. These cassie-paved edgings have disappeared from many of our streets, but a good example remains outside Marischal College, preserved between the old pavement and its extension.

How did these new roads develop? Merkland Road East was so christened by 1901, though that was a bit of a mouthful compared with Dung Stance. In spite of being sanctioned to proceed some 367 yards eastwards seven years earlier, it had managed to get only a little way beyond Pittodrie Lane, the little cross street, which ran from the old city boundary to Linksfield Road. Two distinctive flatted houses and a cottage, Merkland House, had appeared, then the start of a row of tenements, but there was nothing else apart from a rope walk behind Merkland Road East, just on the city boundary. This extended almost as far east as the gasholder. There was once a track here, the ancient 'cart road to the Gallow Slacks', but

Distinctive houses in Merkland Road East.

it had been superseded by the Dung Stance Road many years earlier.

By the 1920s, the rope walk had gone, and Merkland Road East had developed as far as east as Ardarroch Road. Like King's Crescent and Froghall, Merkland Road East and the area around, had become one of the city's Meccas for granite merchants. On the left, walking east from King Street was the yard of Robert Crofts & Sons Ltd, a well known family firm, and next, the Pittodrie Granite Turning Company, which carried out the highly specialised work of turning columns and producing granite rolls for paper-making. They later moved to Wellington Road. Next was the enduring firm of David Ruddiman, monumental masons. Established in 1895, it would have three generations of the family successively at the helm, Davids Snr and Jnr and John Ruddiman. David Snr had married a Cumberland girl, and the firm developed an extensive trade with England. Then came the yard of James Inglis. Beyond the Ardarroch Road divide, Messrs A & F Manuelle had opened their offices and yard here in 1903. They owned the Sclattie and Dancing Cairns quarries, and were also granite importers. They vanished relatively early from the scene, and their old yard was occupied for many years by William Gray & Co, timber merchants, one of a number in the area.

On the right hand side, were Alex J Wilson's Balgownie Granite Works, with the offices round the corner in King Street. In later years these were even more handily located, back to back to the yard, when Alex Wilson bought the old Hutcheon residence, Marchmont, No 392 King Street and re-christened it Balgownie House. It is still there, still serving as offices. Back on Merkland Road East and next door to Wilson's was John O Rettie's, Laurelwood Works. Rettie had started off as one half of Caie & Rettie but the partnership broke up and each man went his own way. The name Laurelwood came from Laurelwood Avenue which was near John Rettie's Kittybrewster home. He lived at Abbey Green, next door but one to Arthur Taylor's house in Ashgrove Road, shown on page 162. Many granite families were related through marriage and Rettie's daughter Margaret had married David Ruddiman Jnr. John O Rettie died in 1933 and his son Forbes (Fobbie) continued the

John O Rettie's membership of the Aberdeen Operative Masons and Stonecutters Society. Courtesy, Charles Rettie.

business with his younger brother, John, and one of his sisters, Elizabeth.

Moving further north, Pittodrie Street in the early days had little apart from a rope walk which ran across to Pittodrie Place. Again by the 1920s, it had vanished and the granite yards were there in force. On the left hand side after Pittodrie Lane, were D M Kinghorn, and Brookes Ltd, and across the road, William Edwards & Son, Ltd, where Harold Bishop of College Bounds had been a hand polisher. Next door was Alexander Lambie, who at one time was married to Hilda, of the legendary Jessamine clan. Sandy Lambie and Fobbie Rettie on a memorable occasion got themselves locked into the cellar of the Red Lion Bar where they had an unscheduled overnight stay. This was a favourite howff, but not that favourite. Sandy Lambie later sold his yard to Crofts, who based their Emerald Granite Works there. This made sense for it sat back-to-back with their Merkland Road East establishment. John A Sangster's St Clair Works, engineers and blacksmiths, were across at No 5 Pittodrie Street for many years. They manufactured equipment for the granite firms, as did the King Street firm of George Cassie & Son.

Further north still there was very little in Pittodrie Place at the end of the

Nos 5 7 Pittodrie Place. The latter was the home of the writer David Toulmin for many years.

nineteenth century, apart from an attractive house, No 3, on the left hand side and the tall tenements next door, Nos 5 and 7. On the right, side, were James R R Kennedy & Son granite sculptors and finally John Rettle's former partner, now operating as Caie & Co. In Linksfield Road, furthest north, James Coutts's yard was on the right hand, before Ardarroch Road. Such then was the Pittodrie granite 'pocket'. Here, and indeed throughout the city's yards, there was great camaraderie among members of the granite community, from the early years until the decline of the 1960s and 1970s. Retired granite merchants have many a tale to tell of lively nights out at the Northern Hotel. Before the war, many of the merchants lived 'over shop', in fine houses in King Street. The move to the west- end was a post war-trend.

Mrs Margaret Fraser, who now lives in Pittodrie Place, stayed with her in-laws in Merkland Road East after the war and still remembers the 'ching-chang, ching-chang' of the granite yards and the whistle blowing or stopping time. 'My husband recalls before the war at the corner of Merkland Road East and Ardarroch Road there was a factory which was called the Flock and Shoddy. They teased out old rags and stuffed mattresses. He remembers there was always a bit of a smell. By the time I came on the scene in '46, the corner was occupied by William Gray, timber merchants.' This would have been the yard originally laid out for the

Manuelles. Margaret Fraser continues; 'From the gable of No 40 down to Pittodrie Lane there were plots and a scrap merchant, Cunningham, and Gordon's Billiard Saloon.'

By the late twenties, a council development was going up east of Ardarroch Road, on the old Irrigation Farm lands. May Cooper, whose family lived in the King Street Barracks and whose tale of ghostly reminiscences was retold in *The Spital,* has written a fascinating memoir of her life there as a young girl. While still living in the Barracks, her father, Arthur Forbes, who had served in the Royal Engineers during the First World War, was working with Aberdeen Corporation Tramways, and, she says, always looking at ways of increasing his income. With this in mind, and with a view to serving the new community in the Pittodrie area, Mr Forbes, bought a small sweet and grocery shop located at the Bay of Nigg, dismantled and transported it to ground at Ardarroch Road between Pittodrie Street and Pittodrie Place, where he reassembled it.

The Huttie around 1930 with Alec Forbes and daughter Hetty.
Courtesy, May Cooper.

So popular was the shop or the Huttie as it was inevitably known, that Arthur Forbes gave up his job on the tramways to run it, gradually increasing his stock until he sold everything from groceries to ironmongery. May's sister Hetty served in the shop, while May, still at school, did the paper round. Life at the Huttie was not without incident. Syrup was filled from a barrel in the back shop 'One day,' writes May, 'we were horrified to see syrup oozing through from the back shop to the front. The tap hadn't been turned off properly.' The Forbes family were rehoused at School Road and May had to cross a waste tip before she could start her paper delivery. Pittodrie in those days was very much a community on its own, well away from King Street, and they got to know many of the locals. Some of their

The Huttie, with the addition of windows a year or two later. Hetty at the door with a customer. Courtesy, May Cooper.

customers were unemployed, and one favourite 'dodge' was to present a chit to buy groceries up to a certain amount. 'Sometimes they asked for Woodbines which were forbidden and asked us to enter something else in the grocery line instead'.

May's father was quite an entrepreneur. He became interested in a bookie's shop near the Huttie - he used to race his greyhound at the King's Crescent track - and went into partnership with him, leaving Hetty to run the shop. He was in business with Ron Davidson and Swifty Rennie, and involved in all sorts of amazing ploys, even bringing 'Syncopating Sandy' to Aberdeen where he stopped the traffic on Union Street after breaking the record for non-stop piano playing. May's husband, John Cooper, was foreman at the Granite Supply Association in Urquhart Road where imported granite required by local merchants was stored. He had followed in the footsteps of his father, one of the Aberdeen masons who had gone to Barré, Vermont in the early days.

Another who had gone to Barré, was Alexander Robertson who, on his return, set up his own firm, Alex. Robertson Sons, on the King Street-St Clair Street corner. He was succeeded by both sons and in 1936 by his grandson, Sandy, who after the war, successfully expanded the firm, taking over Taggart's in Great Western Road in 1951 and merging with his great rival,

This Pittodrie Street yard was originally that of Alexander Lambie, later Robert Croft's. In 1971 it was purchased by A & J Robertson (Granite) Ltd, and the photo dates from that time. The building with the attic window in the centre background was the office of William Edwards & Son. Sandy Robertson writes: 'The derrick cranes dominated all the yards and were the only means of lifting. The lean-to sheds originally were open to the front but had portable shutters in the winter to keep out the worst of the stormy blasts.' Courtesy, Sandy Robertson.

James Robertson & Sons of the Hardgate in 1963 to form A & J Robertson (Granite) Ltd, a neat combination of their initials. Then there came a gradual move to the Pittodrie area, where some firms were closing, and others had principals who were seeking an opportunity to retire. A & J Robertson bought William Edwards & Son Ltd in 1965 and the goodwill of George Kemp & Co of Gilcomston Park in 1966, moving the employees to Pittodrie Street. Caie and Co of Pittodrie Place was acquired that same year, and the staff taken over to Pittodrie Street. (That old Caie site and the neighbouring one, J R R Kennedy is now occupied by Douglas Metals). In 1971 A & J Robertson purchased Robert Croft & Sons Ltd, both sets of premises, at No 9 Merkland Road East and No 6 Pittodrie Street. The old businesses in the Hardgate and Great Western Road were sold off and all staff now moved to one site. In 1983, No 15 Merkland Road East, the one time premises of the Pittodrie Granite Turning Company, was purchased,

The Douglas of Pittodrie wall is a glowing patchwork of granites, a testament to its previous existence as a granite yard.

followed in 1989 by the acquisition of an open yard at No 8 Pittodrie Street where the Charles 'Scrappy' Ross had his famous 'Use your Brain, Hire a Crane' business.

No 9 Merkland Road East now houses the Robertson memorial show-room, the office block, and car park. The stone centre, which the firm inaugurated some twenty years ago is located at No 15. It supplies fireplaces, worktops and vanity tops, using, among other stones, marble, slate and of course granite - attractive imported granites from South America and South Africa. The stockyard and factory are at the Pittodrie Street site, fitted out with the most up-to-date equipment available. Gone forever are the days when masons' aprons and overalls were singed as a result of huddling round the brazier, in an attempt to keep out the cold. Sandy Robertson continues these days as non-executive chairman, though he has retired as joint-managing director, leaving his son Graeme, who must be Aberdeen's only fourth generation granite merchant, at the helm. Bill Robertson, who had been the principal of the old Hardgate firm had retired, and the firm was now wholly owned by the Alex Robertson family. Staff at time of writing number around seventy-five, five of whom are apprentices. Several former apprentices are still with the firm, or have rejoined it. Robertson's are largest manufacturer of granite memorials in the United Kingdom, and the largest retailer, with thirty-six branches

A & J Robertson's memorial display in Merkland Road East.

throughout the country. What is incredible is that A & J Robertson is now the only granite yard, not only in the Pittodrie area but in the whole of Aberdeen. Another great firm, John Fyfe, operates at Westhill, but its business has a different emphasis, and it is some years since it was locally owned.

Of the other Pittodrie firms, Rettie's closed about 1969 and sold the ground to Securior. Ruddiman's almost completed the century, closing

The Robertson Stone Centre in Merkland Road East left, and Knowles Fruiterers, the former office of David Ruddiman.

their yard at the far end of Merkland Road East in 1985. The ground, next door to Robertson's Stone Centre, was acquired by Knowles the Fruiterers. In Pittodrie Street, McKinnon & Co, of Spring Garden fame have been operating from what was once Sangster's Engineering Works since 1992. William Gray, the timber merchant, left the far end of Merkland Road East in 1994, and now conduct operations from Spurryhillock, Stonehaven and the Bridge of Don. The ground vacated will now be used for housing.

Of the personalities of the area - outwith the granite trade which was full of them - the North East writer David Toulmin is the best known. He gave up his job as a Buchan farm servant and moved to a comfortable flat at No 7 Pittodrie Place in 1972, where he lived for the next twenty years or so. D Toulmin and J Reid used to have their nameplates side-by-side on the door, but they were not bidies-in, (after all, his wife Margaret was there), just keeping the postie right, since Toulmin also received mail under his real name, John Reid. His move to Pittodrie Place co-incided with the publication, to much acclaim in the North East, of his first collection of short stories, *Hard Shining Corn*. Many of these had already been broadcast, or published in magazines, but they came as a revelation to those who did not already know Toulmin's work. Over the next seventeen years he published nine books including a full length novel, *Blown Seed*. What has emerged from his writing is a potent evocation of the hard world of

David Toulmin.

Buchan farm life in the inter-war years with its ruthless work ethic; tales of greed, jealousy, lust, vengeance, incest, of thrawn chiels and dour quines, where even the most intelligent and progressive of farmers were hard masters. But humour does break through and Toulmin is a master of the notoriously difficult skill of handling the Doric. Unlike some, he has not had to go furth of the North East to be able to write about it. In 1986 he was honoured by Aberdeen University for his contribution to Scottish literature.

Another writer living in Pittodrie Place, though further east, towards the Links, is Ethel Kilgour, who has produced two highly readable memoirs, *A Time of our Lives*, and *A March of Time*.

Still well-remembered from an earlier period is the organ builder,

E H Lawton's Organ Factory in Ardarroch Road, photographed in 1976 when the building was occupied by Clyde Factors. Lawton's house, Glenmallan, now demolished, stands behind.

Earnest Henry Lawton. A Sheffield lad, apprenticed to the famous Manchester firm of Earnest Wadsworth, he came north in 1895 to assist in building an organ for Mannofield Church. He saw potential in the North East, and in 1899, when he was thirty, set up a workshop in Pittodrie Lane. Orders came quickly, thanks to Lawton's flair for public relations, and the fact that the tycoon Andrew Carnegie was offering a fifty percent grant towards the installation of new organs in Church of Scotland kirks. In the years that followed, Lawton sold organs in many countries of the world, and enjoyed a particularly good trade with the African continent. In the 1920s, he even opened a branch in New Zealand. His Pittodrie Organ Works, by now based in Ardarroch Road, was a household name in the North East, and he lived 'over the shop', round the corner at No 32 Linksfield Road. The name of the house, Glenmallan, was inscribed in granite on the gable. Lawton, who travelled far and wide in the cause of his business, died in 1947 at seventy-eight years of age, after contracting pneumonia when the train in which he was travelling became snowbound. The building that housed his organ factory is still in use, but Glenmallan has been demolished. The site is now part of the Ardarroch Court housing development.

Linksfield Road, the most northerly of the four roads has always retained its 'feel' of the wide open spaces. By the mid-1920s, there was little sign of development. Robert Gibb's mighty Excelsior Granite Works occupied the north-west corner as well as much of the former Lady Mill enclosure, there was a sandpit rented out to Leith the contractors, on the north side, and a small group of tenements, Coutts' Granite Works and E H Lawton's house, Glenmallan, on the south side. Eastwards, on the old Irrigation land, were sports grounds with cinder pitches and waste ground. By the 1930s, three new developments had taken place; council housing, a primary school to serve the new population and a new sports ground.

The school, Linksfield Primary, opened in 1932 by Lord Provost Rust, was one of the earliest schools in Aberdeen to be built on the French *Ecole de Plein Air* principle. The emphasis was on fresh air and sunlight, the windows, at the rear with their views of green fields giving the impression of being out in the open air. After the war it became surplus to primary requirements. The new council houses in the Pittodrie area, with only one bedroom, were not suitable for families, and there were not enough children in the catchment area to justify its continued existence. The school building was used for a variety of purposes over the years, as an examination venue for Aberdeen University when the Elphinstone Hall was out of commission, as the School for the Deaf, as the Pre-Nursing College and latterly as an outpost of Aberdeen College. During this period the clear-cut design of the rear of the school was totally impaired by a an assortment of huts. It went the market in the mid- 1990s and at time of writing is under offer.

The area east of Ardarroch Road and between Pittodrie Street and Linksfield Road was acquired for municipal housing in the inter-war years,

Mrs Lumsden in her attractive garden in Pittodrie Place.

laid out in neat courts, and in the 1990s, underwent a thorough-going refurbishment. The gardens are neat and colourful. Most of the residents are elderly single folk or couples. The disappearance of Coutts's yard and a pre-cast concrete company from Linksfield Road has allowed space for modern housing here. Ardarroch Court, the site of the old Lawton house, is a particularly attractive development.

Linksfield Sports Ground, next door to the Linksfield Primary, was built in the 1930s, as a sop when Advocates' Park in King Street, a great favourite with supporters of junior football, was taken over by Aberdeen Corporation Transport. Linksfield lacked atmosphere, and despite being promoted to Stadium, did not attract the crowds. Pitch, cinder track and terracing deteriorated over the years. By the 1960s and 1970s, the ground was playing a poor second fiddle to other sports centres, particularly that at Sheddocksley, and plans to resurrect it as a greyhound track were vetoed by councillors.

The untimely death of ex-Aberdeen FC player Chris Anderson, vice-chairman of the Club, in 1986, was the catalyst that inspired Aberdeen District Council to transform the stadium into something worthy of bearing his name. At a cost of £1.5 million, and with grants from the Football Trust and the Scottish Sports Council, the stadium was transformed. It now boasts an eight-lane all-weather track, so tempting that it persuades you to get on to it and run. There are also all-weather football and hockey pitches and a new stand. Mrs Christine Anderson, Chris's widow performed the re-naming ceremony on 11 September, 1988, while the Olympic sprinter and gold medallist Alan Wells carried out the official opening; 'It's as good as anything you'll find at Meadowbank or Crystal Palace,' he commented.

The Chris Anderson Stadium, with the Seaton flats behind.

Chapter 19

Pittodrie

The best football team in Merkland Road East
Scotland the What?

For ten years, from 1888, Aberdeen Football Club, one of the forerunners of today's Aberdeen F C Ltd, played its football in the Chanonry. Their pitch was part of the former playing fields of the Old Aberdeen Gymnasium, a famous boys' school in its day. It closed in 1887 and the pitch was made available to the Club through the good offices of Mr John Clarke, the 'Gym's' last headmaster, and one of the pioneers of football in Aberdeen. In 1898, however, much of the 'Gym' site was sold to Miss Anne H Cruickshank, who wished to lay out a Botanic Garden there, in memory of her brother, as indeed she did. The 'Whites', as Aberdeen Football Club was known from the colour of their strip, found themselves cast into the wilderness yet again.

Established in 1881, the 'Whites', the first football club in Aberdeen, had moved from ground to ground in the early days in search of a permanent home. Now that search had resumed. Then someone suggested the Dung Stance. The idea seems a curious one in an Aberdeen that still had green fields and open spaces near its heart. The land occupied by the Stance was leased to Aberdeen Town Council by Henry William Knight Erskine, but someone must have known that there was a chance of availability. And so it was on 6 February 1899 that the Council's Cleansing Committee held the historic meeting during which the tenancy of the Dung Stance was handed over to the Aberdeen Football Club, with the consent of Mr Knight Erskine of Pittodrie and Spital.

It was a condition that Whites were to restore the ground to its 'former agricultural state', repair the cart road - at that time Merkland Road East extended only a yard or two beyond Pittodrie Lane - and 'remove or utilise the old rubbish heap at present on the ground'. Rent and rates were apportioned and it was agreed that 'the keeper of the North Dung Stance be allowed to remain in the occupancy of the dwelling house until Whitsunday next, rent free'. (The players found it a handy place to change after the keeper moved out). That February, the Aberdeen Football Club went to work with a will to make their new ground 'as perfect as it could be'. They levelled the width and 190 yards of the length, presumably first having disposed of any dung. They set out to terrace the east end 'a vast improvement on the antiquated style of spectators standing on the level'. They advertised for estimates and tenders. They organised a bazaar to raise funds. They needed at least £550.

By the end of summer 1899, the ground was ready for the new season and for the first time the name Pittodrie Park came into use. 'Dung Stance' though accurate would give rise to adverse comment, particularly when the team was doing badly, and 'Merkland' was not a contender for Merkland Road East was still new-fangled, at that time just a group of houses off King Street. The main access was from east, via the Links, or from the north, via Linksfield Road, crossing the paths of the incipient Pittodrie Place and Street, and of course the chap who owned the land was the laird of Pittodrie at Chapel of Garioch. Still the press observed of the name, 'it will never catch on'.

The first game 'at the best ground in the North by a long way' was played against Dumbarton on August 1899. There was a festive atmosphere with the pipe band of the 1st Volunteer Band the Gordon Highlanders providing the music. Tramcars, still several months away from electrification, were laid on from Market Street. Secretary Ellis 'was here there and everywhere attending to the large number of guests' who had accepted invitations. Baillie Lyon, a future Lord Provost, made a short opening speech and kicked off. 'The side that Baillie Lyon plays for in the municipal match is bound to lose,' wrote one commentator wryly. The Whites managed to win. 'Pittodrie' was still causing problems. 'By the way,' wrote a commentator, 'cannot a more suitable name be got for the ground? Pittodrie is hardly poetical and does not fall softly on the ear'.

There were other grumbles. The Press box was poorly positioned. You couldn't see part of the ground from the back of the stand, and its roof sloped the wrong way. Later the Town Council was to write to the Club about its unsatisfactory state. 'The Council should have saved their penny stamp', wrote one reporter. Any strengthening that they think necessary would be misspent money; it is seldom used. No one enjoys paying a sixpence to see what passes for football at Pittodrie. Whenever there is another game in town, the crowd are sure to be found at another enclosure'. The fact was that Aberdeen Football Club was the oldest in Aberdeen, and had the finest ground, but it was not the best team. Orion, the Stripes played at Cattofield and Victoria United, the Blues at Central Park both of whom were consistently ahead of Aberdeen FC in the old Northern League. Football talent in the city was spread too thin. It was difficult to get the best teams to come north. There was only one solution. Early in 1903, excitement was in the air. The talk was of amalgamation - and the Scottish League. The football public wanted. Dundee FC, an important voice, wanted it. But there was bickering among the Whites, the Orion and the Vics, and their finances were at low ebb. A 'local Carnegie' to put things on a sound footing was looked for but no obliging millionaire came forth.

Eventually on March 26 1903, a public meeting chaired by Mr John Clarke, now a lecturer in Education in Aberdeen University, was held in the Trades Hall. Amalgamation was agreed on. A limited liability company with a capital of £1500 was to be formed, the new company taking over at valuation the removable assets of the city's three senior clubs. But speculation was rife. Could they get a good enough team together by August? Could they get into the first division of the Scottish League? Above all, could they afford the £50 a week - wages of fourteen players to pay, plus management expenses - to run the club?

In spite of these problems, the new club came into being on 18 April 1903, with a wide constitution: It set out to promote the practice and play of football, cricket, lacrosse, lawn tennis, hockey, bowling, cycle riding, running, jumping, and the physical training and development of the human frame. What this meant was that Aberdeen Football Club Ltd had come to Pittodrie.

On the gloomy, threatening afternoon on 15 August 1903, the team of Aberdeen Football Club Ltd, wearing the white jerseys of the former Aberdeen club took the field for the first time against Stenhousemuir in a Northern League match. The huge crowd 'howled with joy' when the 'homesters' managed to equalise. Gate money was £106. In season 1904-05 the team, now 'promoted' to the second division of the Scottish League ran out in black and gold jerseys. This was condemned as 'rank desecration, enough to drive the old Whites supporters wrong in their minds', but by August 1904, the burning issue was whether the 'Black and Gold brigade' could lift the Second Division Championship and bring First Division football to Aberdeen. The answers respectively were no and yes. The promotion-relegation system didn't come into existence until the 1921-22 season, so although the Wasps as supporters were now calling them, finished the season at the middle of the Second Division, they managed to get themselves elected to the 'charmed circle' of the First Division at the third attempt on 22 May 1905. This achievement was not due to the skill of the players but to the perseverance and single-mindedness of their directors. It had been agreed to the extend the First Division from 14 to 16 clubs. Clyde and Falkirk who headed the Second Division were also applicants for promotion. Aberdeen and Falkirk were chosen.

The rush was on to make facilities at Pittodrie worthy of First Division football. There was trouble again with the stands. The defects of the 'new' one - the old Orion stand removed from Cattofield and resurrected - had not escaped the eye of the burgh surveyor who had condemned it on account of its worn and decayed wood, its lack of handrails, its precipitous and dangerous stairs, and the rough and unsatisfactory manner of its reconstruction. And if the stand was a death trap, the changing conditions were primitive, 'A decent clubhouse which would hold both the visitors and the homes teams at one and the same time would not come amiss', wrote one reporter. By the summer of 1905, however, improvements included a new pavilion with two large dressing rooms, and an ornamental front, and the very latest internal fittings.

The first real triumph came in March 1908 when the Wasps played Celtic in the semi-final of the Scottish Cup. Forty-three special tramcars were switched to the Pittodrie route that day, 20,000 paid £586 10s 11d to see the game, and the Broad Hill and the Gallowhill, another 'Miser's Hilly' were packed with non-paying spectators. The only drawback was that Celtic won 1-0.

More improvement were carried out at the ground during the Paddy Travers era. By 1928 the Club had a new stand and had purchased the ground. No longer could the City of Aberdeen Land Association threaten to continue Merkland Road East through the pitch. The Club was also free from debt, largely due to transfer fees which over the past ten years had added up to all of £30,000. One player during this era we have already met, Charles B Forbes, who had taught Maths at Sunnybank Intermediate in the 1930s, and subsequently became headmaster of Middlefield. The last amateur, he played for the Club in the 1920s and later joined the Board. The ex-Don, Archie Baird, a teacher himself when his playing days were over recalled of Mr Forbes: 'the fact that one of the Board had been in the 'trenches' went down well with the players and seemed to separate him from those directors who had never 'met an angry Ranger'.'

In the 1930s, the innovative trainer, Donald Colman, invented the 'dugout', not just a 'first' for Pittodrie, but for the whole country, and put the Wasps on a fitness and exercise programme the like of which had not been seen at Pittodrie before.

The new pavilion built in 1905.

Archie Baird recalls Pittodrie in 1938: 'My first memories were those of a star-struck football-mad eighteen year old, thrown suddenly into an environment I had dreamed about as a schoolboy. I then was a second-team player, just signed from Strathclyde Juniors in Glasgow. That meant I was paid £4 weekly of which £2 went home to my mother in, 25/- on board and lodging, in nearby Urquhart Street, leaving 15/- for my daily needs including entertainment. Fortunately these were modest - a couple of nights at the cinema. (Besides playing football, I was studying architecture). George Johnstone, Willie Cooper, Frank Dunlop, Matt Armstrong, Billy Strauss were names you read about, and if you were lucky, had their pictures in your collection of cigarette-cards. Now, I was rubbing shoulders with them at training, sharing their thoughts on the game, relishing their tips and advice.

'Pittodrie itself, though basic in every way compared with today's lavish stadium, fully lived up to my dreams. It was the first time I had ever been 'inside' a senior football ground. It had a romantic aura that I still experience today when I visit the place. The picture comes back of the home-dressing room with its rows of pegs. Above the wooden slatted benches that had carried the black and gold jerseys of Dons heroes over the years; the huge communal, tiled bath in the adjoining ablution room with its steaming, soapy contents awaiting eleven physically and emotionally exhausted players around 4.40pm on a Saturday afternoon; and the modest treatment room with its single 'heatlamp', redolent of the smell of embrocation and Johnson's Baby Powder.

'Our manager David Halliday was a kindly man, and in the way of football mangers of the day, more a motivator than a tactician and planner. The directors were a shadowy group, usually seen just before the kick-off,

Cloth caps, and other types of headgear at Pittodrie in 1934.

when they bestowed a good luck handshake or word of encouragement.'

A new era dawned on 18 March 1939 when Aberdeen took the field against Queen's Park wearing for the first time the red and white strip, no doubt with an eye to the Scottish Cup semi-final the following week. An appropriate choice since red and white, gules and argent, are the heraldic colours of the city. (I remember once observing to the then Chairman, Dick Donald, how smart the black and gold colours looked in old photographs. He replied dolefully that they ran badly when washed). This was the era of the cloth capped spectator, and Margaret Fraser, looking back to her days in Merkland Road East recalls 'the trams coming down the road on Saturday to the football and the men all with flat caps jumping off at our

258

Dick Donald.

door before the tram went round the loop into Ardarroch Road'.

By 1953 an account of football as played at Pittodrie was considered important enough to gain a place in the Aberdeen volume of the *Third Statistical Account of Scotland*:

> The weekly wage of each player is £10 or more in the case of better players...On payment of 1/6 or more if seats are required, the citizens of Aberdeen crowd into 'Pittodrie' on a Saturday afternoon. The spectators are composed largely of young and middle-aged men of all classes.

In 1958, and again in 1969, takeovers bids, the first by the architect and town councillor, Tommy Scott Sutherland, the second by a mystery six, later revealed as well known faces around Pittodrie, including ex-Dons, Don Emery and Tony Harris were much discussed in town. Both groups promised a new heaven and a new earth in the form of complete cover for the terracing, immediate flood-lighting, new talent on the pitch (as well as an electric blanket), new faces in the boardroom. Both bids failed. Indeed one wonders why the would-be new brooms even bothered, given that the

Granite portals, appropriate for the Merkland Road East entrance, around 1990.

shareholders were either the directors themselves or widows of former directors. The 1969 takeover bid was 'seen off' by the Chairman, Charles B Forbes, who after his playing days had become a director, and had run the Club during the war with Councillor George Anderson, of 'Anderson's Super Kream Ices' fame. Forbes was succeeded as Chairman in 1970 by Dick Donald, another ex-Don who played his last game in 1939. He was the son of Richard F Donald who among other things, had established his famous Dancing Academy in North Silver Street. By the time he was voted onto the Board in 1949, Donald was the boss of the family's widespread entertainments business. Archie Baird again:

Generation of Dons players will recall the fortnightly ritual at the Joint Station prior to away matches. The Shell was the meeting place. Players would arrive early: then the directors, most in sombre hue and attitude as befitted their position. Dick's arrival was more an entrance with his jaunty step, beaming face and the little impromptu tap-dance as he disgorged pocketsful of chocolate for the journey.

In 1899, the old Aberdeen Football Club had laboured to make their new ground 'as perfect as it could be', and set a high standard that would be followed over the next century. During the 1950s and 1960s the club went ahead with improvements and modernisation, cover for terracing at the Beach End and floodlighting in 1959. Each improvement at the time

Pittodrie Stadium in 1985, with Alex Ferguson.

seemed a culmination; with hindsight each was little more that the stepping stone to something better. Like that other great local institution, Aberdeen Harbour, there is at Pittodrie, a continual process of re-building, upgrading and improvement. In 1967, the ground was being groomed for the Dons' entry into European football. By 1971, £80,000 was spent on new turnstiles, better terracing and 1500 additional seats. Alas in February of that year fire destroyed part of the main stand, dressing rooms, sauna and offices, and valuable records were lost. Ten years on, Pittodrie was again in the vanguard, becoming the first all-covered, all-seated stadium in the country and two years later executive boxes were built into the rear of the Main Stand, though *aficionados* will tell you that while they enjoy the comfort of these executive facilities, the atmosphere in the crowd is irreplaceable. Further improvements including under-soil heating went ahead in the late 1980s contributing to Pittodrie's reputation of having one of the finest playing surfaces in the game. The ground now hosts Scottish international games. What would the keeper of the North Dung Stance think of it all! Sadly, ex-Don, Chris Anderson, who would have succeeded Dick Donald as Chairman, died in 1986, and it is Dick's son Ian, a former Manchester United player, who is now Chairman of Aberdeen FC.

Two visual developments in the Pittodric area, virtually synonymous, deserve comment. In the early 1990s we bade farewell to an old friend, a familiar landmark, the Gallowhills gasholder. It had nothing to do with

The Beach End and the Gallowhills gasholder in the 1980s with March Stone No 63 to the fore. The photoghraph on page 264 makes an interesting comparison.

Pittodrie *per se* but was always part of the scene. Then in 1993, came the erection of the Richard Donald Stand at the Beach End - it *is* the Beach End - named in honour of the late Chairman. The view from the Spital to the Links and Aberdeen Bay has been altered forever, and so enormous is the Stand that its great cantilevered maw appears to ready to gobble up the unwary pedestrian as he walks along Merkland Road East. It even gives the impression of following one as one drives around the Pittodrie area. Viewed from the Beach, however, it blends remarkably well with the sort of architecture currently *in situ* there, and in earlier times, would have provided a useful landmark for navigators. Aesthetics apart, the Richard Donald Stand has much more to offer than a view of the ground; it encompasses the Club Shop and function suites where you can hold receptions, exhibitions, even get married. Betting incidentallly, on a range of sporting events, is now possible from the ground.

Crowd control is admirable. Home spectators use the Merkland Stand at the King Street end - this used to be the 'Paddock', housing away supporters - the Richard Donald Stand, the Main Stand, and the South Stand. The latter Stand also now caters for the away support, who have a separate entrance. Seating arrangements are flexible, with larger segments being made available when the travelling support is likely to be heavy. Incidentally, the walk down Merkland Road East, the turn north into Merkland Lane, is identical with the old track to the Dung Stance .

The history of Aberdeen FC has an aura of *tout ça change tout c'est la même chose*. In 1898 the game in Aberdeen was described as a huge commercial enterprise. In 1997, the Club appointed financial experts Richard Ramsay and Martin Gilbert to the Board, who have brought their skills to the running of the Club. Again in 1898, the game at Pittodrie was condemned for roughness and brutality, and there were complaints about 'disgusting language from the spectators'. In 1903 one commentator advised the directors of the new club to let the players know who was master; 'Football players are but kittle cattle to deal with, and if they have a fault, it is that of having too high a sense of their own importance.' In more modern times, Tommy Pearson's decline and fall as manager during the early 1960s, was paralleled by that of Willie Miller thirty years later. 'Dons' Prospects not so Bright,' wrote 'Merklan' in the Bon-Accord Annual of 1934. He could have said exactly the same thing during the 1995-96 season when the Dons came within a whisker of being cast out of the Premier Division, and in the 1997-98 season.

Pittodrie Stadium is in good shape, Aberdeen FC Ltd is skilfully managed, sponsorship is in place, and there is little left to ask for. Warts and all, there remains enormous pride and interest in the Club throughout the North East. Fans are on a knife edge for much of the season; but when the team is doing well, the whole city glows. By the way, 'the Dons' only means one thing in these parts. When a statement was issued by Aberdeen University staff at the time of the fearsome cutbacks of the 1980s, enjoining everyone to 'Defend the Dons', there was genuine puzzlement. Surely in Miller and McLeish the Dons already had just about the best defence money could buy.

The Dons have always been a cyclical team and that cycle was high under Alex Ferguson, who was manager from 1978 until 1986. During his 'term of office', Aberdeen won the European Cup Winners' Cup, beating Real Madrid 2-1 in Gothenberg on 11 May 1983. There were incredible scenes of rejoicing at Pittodrie during this tournament, especially on that memorable occasion on 16 March, when the Dons, playing out of their skins defeated Bayern Munich 3-2 in the second leg of the quarter final. As my father, a Dons' supporter almost since 1903 remarked; 'to think I have lived to see this.'

Teddy Scott and Alex Ferguson.

The last word must be devoted to the immortal Teddy Scott, whom we left at Sunnybank in 1954. He was signed by Aberdeen FC that year, and has been a servant of the club ever since, as player, trainer and now as kit manager. Speaking of kit, the strip is redder these days, red shorts having replaced the white, though an element of white does remain. Fortunately Teddy has no runny Wasps' jerseys to contend with these days!

A Footnote on the Pittodrie March Stone.

On 6 August 1698 during the Riding of the Marches, 'the magistrates and councill, accompanied by certain of the brethren of guild...' took the ancient 'cart road to the Gallow Slacks', which pre-dated even the Dung Stance Road. At its end they found 'an eard-fast march stone, marked with ane sauser and ane key', marking the city boundary, the freedom boundary and the Spital Lands boundary. If any of the successors of the above gentleman follow this path today - they would be better to walk down Pittodrie Street - and go round to the back of the Richard Donald Stand in Golf Road, they will find the stone, or at least its modern counterpart there, March Stone No 63. Or hopefully they will before the end of 1997. The March Stone, apparently not so 'eard-fast' as its ancestor, 'went missing' earlier that year, but a replacement was immediately ordered.

The Richard Donald Stand in 1996. The gasholder has gone, as has March Stone No 63, dimly perceived beside the traffic restriction sign. A replacement stone should be in place by late 1997. This is the same site as shown on page 261.

Postscript

More About The Spital

Round About Mounthooly stirred many memories. More memories have been aroused since the publication of *The Spital* and readers have written to Denburn Books with a host of stories about the area. Many related to the *Spital Lands* and have already been incorporated into the text. Quite a few, however, are about the Spital itself.

Mr Stanley D Rennie lived in King's Crescent which really is a part of the Spital. His home, No 25, and the house next door, No 23, at the junction with Jute Street, were mirror images, with a common oval lawn. 'I recall pedalling my small tricycle round and round it,' he writes, until a loud rapping on the window of No 23 would indicate old James Rae's displeasure, (he owned the Crown Granite yard opposite), and send me in retreat until next time!

'My father, Alfred Rennie, was a locomotive driver with the GNSR and then the LNER, retiring in 1935. Depending on one's political sympathies at the time of the General Strike of 1926, he was liked or disliked for being the general secretary of the Aberdeen Strike Committee. He was at that time a great admirer of Russia and was known among some of his workmates as the 'Bolshevie Driver'. In later life his views mellowed.

'He was a very keen amateur wireless fan who was forever constructing and revising wireless sets, from the days of the crystal set to thermionic valves. To satisfy his hobby he had two largish sheds erected in our back garden; one for building and the other for testing his radios. To ensure that he would get the best possible radio reception, he had erected near the bottom of a long back garden, an aerial mast of 3-inch diameter steel tubes screwed end-to-end with supporting stay wires. The mast towered above all surrounding property and must have been at least fifty feet above the level of Jute Street. From its top an aerial wire was slung for about a hundred feet to a mooring on the house chimney stack.

'With livestock marts in King Street (John Duncan's City Auction Mart) and Kittybrewster, it was a weekly event for cattle to be driven along Jute Street, King's Crescent and Advocates Road, or in the opposite direction. This was a signal for all to take cover and keep garden gates shut, because on occasions bewildered animals managed to get into our garden.'

And Mr Rennie recalls the 'battles' that used to take place between the children of the two neighbouring streets, the 'Crescenters' and 'Juters'. 'There was much sound and fury and hurled insults, but little damage or injury as the winners pursued their foes.'

In *The Spital* reference was made to a dance hall in King's Crescent, near the site of the old leper colony. It appears in the old valuation rolls, but none of our contacts in the area could recall it. Mrs Jean Simpson comes to the rescue. 'I remember the dance hall in King's Crescent. On our way home from Girl Guides my sister and I took turns of peeping through the keyhole to watch the dancers, wishing we were old enough to join them.'

Mrs Jean Simpson, née Nelson, was born at No 90 the Spital in 1921 and

The Nelson family, Jean, Andy, Gladys, James and Hazel at the front of No. 90. Courtesy, Mrs Jean Simpson.

lived there until 1938, in one of the houses owned by Willie Weir. His Spital farm was behind their house, in Merkland Place. (He had the farm at Sunnyside as well). The Spital farm had a farmhouse, a byre which held about eight cows, and the Weirs had a machine for cutting the turnips into quarters which were then fed to the cows. There was also a stable, hen houses, various outhouses, a midden, a dairy and garden. One of his cows, a special Jersey, provided milk for the new babies in the area, especially those who were poorly. Jimmy Yule, whose family lived in Elmbank Road, remembers being sent to get milk for his young sister Lottie in the early 1930s.

Jean Simpson recalls: 'To get to the dairy, you would go through the lobby of No 94, through the back

Mrs Nelson with the family at the back of No 90 The Spital. Willie Weir's farm can be seen at the back, left. Courtesy, Mrs Jean Simpson.

garden, collect the milk, drink some of it on the way back, then top it up with water from the tap at No 94!' In the dairy, the milk separator was worked by hand. There was a milk cooler, a steam jet to sterilise milk cans and the butter churn which was also worked by hand.

Jean used to help Willie's mother with the cheese-making. Rennet was added to buckets of milk and the following day, the curds were lifted into a large zinc bath to be crumbled down, then packed firmly into muslin-lined wooden tubs. 'During school holidays I often made the butter and helped Mrs Weir to crumble the curds.' In the farmhouse, the lobby and kitchen floors were slate and the room off the kitchen where the cheese was stored had an earthen floor and no window.

George Elphinstone herded cattle for Willie Weir, bringing them round from Sunnyside, down Merkland Road and into their byres at Merkland Place. Harold Bishop recalls: 'the Weir family cultivated a lot of fields in the University area. We picked tatties and did carrot weeding for them as loons at 2/- a day.'

Willie's vegetable round and his horse Sandy are still well remembered. Mrs Margaret Fraser recalls 'the long gone happy days of Willie Weir, a man of few words and a kind heart. He trundled round with his tattie cairt and his ever-present lovely Airedales.' His round took him to Merkland Road East where she stayed at the time, and he also came to St Peter's Street when she and her husband went to live there. 'Both my late father and myself bought Airedale pups from Willie. They were tough, strong and well-adjusted. They had to be quick-witted to escape Sandy's flying hooves. I loved the quiet good-tempered horse, and many a jammy piece he got from me. '

Jimmie Smith in his shop at No 47 The Spital. Courtesy, Mr J Smith.

Jimmie Smith, who retired in 1995, had the shop at No 47 the Spital. He would open at 4.45 am (not 5.30am as quoted in *The Spital*!) and closed at 8pm. This was his routine for fifteen years with never a day off. His sister came in for a hour or two in the morning to let him do the banking and go to the wholesalers.

When Jimmie was renovating the shop he discovered what seemed to be traces of an earlier resident using it as somewhere to live. 'Behind the panelling, as you enter the shop, was an old-fashioned window, a double window with a bolt at the bottom for keeping it closed, bricked up on the outside. Behind the panelling on the opposite wall, was an open fireplace.' He used to set out a seat in the front shop for elderly customers. 'The shop was run in a family style,' he recalls. 'I had some very good paper boys who would also deliver milk and rolls to customers in the morning. We also delivered their messages free of charge with their evening papers. '

Jean Simpson can still see in her mind's eye, the gypsy-style caravans that came to Merkland Place, with their small ponies. Gordon Cardno and his family lived opposite, in Hillhead Terrace, and she remembers her mother buying a hen from his grandmother for 2/6d. 'Mr Glass, the fishmonger, lived at No 88 the Spital. He delivered fish on a wheelbarrow and later by horse and cart. Ex-Lord Provost Hogg's wife stayed in the house at the top of the lane between the Red Lion and Miss Mitchell's shop.'

Donald's cooked meat shop, where the famous ice-cream was made as well, was at No 122, at one side of St Peter's Gate. 'They had a restaurant there, the room to the left, entered through a curtain. They sold soup and pies, very popular with local workmen. On a Sunday the Spital folk who didn't have ovens would cook their beef, cover it with pastry and then take it to the Donald's to be baked.' Milne the Shoemaker went into this shop

after the Donald's and Harold Bishop's brother, Bill, served his time there.

Finally, a memory of Jean's that testifies to the sheer number of folk who used to live in the Spital. 'A bus used to go over the Spital every working day, collecting girls for the Grandholm Mill. Crowds of masons walked up and down the Spital on their way to work in the morning - they started at 8am - and back again at 5 pm, and their boots crunching on the cassies.'

◀ *This photograph of demolition in the Spital, to make way for the Council development of the early 1970s, was loaned by Mrs Hilda Robb, the last matron of Primrosehill House. Jean Simpson provides the commentary below:*

The building in the photo was at the corner of St Peter's Gate, at the opposite corner from Donald's shop. The shop was a newsagent's owned in the 1920s and 1930s, by a Mr Anderson. I remember when I was a child I bought small books of fairy tales from him which cost 2d each. All the tenants of the house except one, entered at the back of the building. Those on the upper floors had to go up a flight of stone steps and their doors were on a balcony which ran the length of the house. I can only remember the name of three of the tenants: Page, Dow, and Mrs Taunt who was a dressmaker. The tenant at the front of the house had to come along the pavement, round past the shop to the back of the building to get to their toilet and wash house.

Footnote: The new Central Fire Station at Mounthooly-Kings Crescent, which received planning consent in 1992 after much local opposition, eventually came in to operation in late 1997. The story of its birth pangs was told in *The Spital*.

Select Bibliography

Books consulted

Anon, *Freedom Land Marches*, nd
Burnett, John George, (ed), *Powis Papers, 1507-1894,* Third Spalding, 1951
Carter, J J & Pittock, J H, (ed), *Aberdeen and the Enligtenment*, AUP, 1987
Coutts, James A (ed) The Book of Powis, 1906
Douglas, Francis, *A General Description of the East Coast of Scotland*, Paisley, 1782
Forbes, Margaret, *Beattie and his Friends*, Constable, 1904
Gibson T A E & Wood, G K , *Courage Remembered*, HMSO, 1989
Kennedy William, *The Annals of Aberdeen*, London 1818
Keith, Alexander, *Eminent Aberdonians*, Aberdeen Chamber of Commerce, 1984
Mackenzie, Hugh, *City of Aberdeen;The Third Statistical Account of Scotland*, Oliver & Boyd, 1953
Mackinnon, Lachlan, *Reollections of an Old Lawyer*, D Wyllie & Sons, 1935
McPherson, J M, *Primitive Beliefs in the North-East of Scotland*, Longmans 1929
Mercer, James, Lyric Poems, 1794, 1806
Milne, John, *Aberdeen, Topographical, Antiquarian and Historical*, Aberdeen Journal, 1911
Munro A M M , (ed), *Records of Old Aberdeen* , New Spalding, 1899
Rait, R S , *The Universities of Aberdeen*, Aberdeen 1895
Reid, John S, *Mechanical Aberdeen*, KMP/JSR, 1990
Simpson, WD, (ed), *The Fusion of 1860,* University of Aberdeen/Oliver & Boyd, 1963
Stewart, J, (ed), List of Pollable Persons within the Shire of Aberdeen, 1696. Spalding, 1844.
Tayler, A & H, *Jacobites of Aberdeenshire and Banffshire in the Forty-five*, Milne & Hutchison, 1928
Taylor, Dr J, *A Medical A Treatise on the Fir-hill Well*, 1800
Thomson, Michael, *Silver Screen in the Silver City*, AUP, 1988
Trail, Katherine, *Reminiscenes of Old Aberdeen*, D Wyllie. 1932

Booklets, Pamphlets
Anon, *Sunnybank Football Club; The Story of 1953-54*
Diack, William, *The Rise and Progress of the Granite Industry in Aberdeen*, Reprinted for the Quarry Managers' Journal, 1949
Henderson, Stephen, *The Story of Primrosehill*, 1995
Hopkin, Archibald *The Aberdeen Pub Companion*, 1975
Pratt, Jim, *The Music Hall*, City of Aberdeen 1993
Tinsley, Joseph, *Aberdeen Churches 'Twixt Gallowgate and Powis, 1987*

Reference Books
Aberdeen Post Office Directories
In Memoriam, William Mitchell 1900; James Henderson, 1896; Charles McDonald, 1892; Wm Kay & Sons, Aberdeen:
Scotland of Today, Part II Historical Publishing Co, 1889, James Cocker & Sons

Periodicals
Aberdeen Chamber of Commerce Journal
Industry in the North East of Scotland:
No 19 'Roses', Spring 1960
No 32, 'Paint and Allied Products', Summer 1963

Leopard Magazine
Atiknson, Geoffrey, 'Ronald Center: The Music and the Man', June 1986
Baird, Archie, 'Dick Donald', September, 1976
Forrest, Vivienne, 'Embattled Heritage', February 1986
Wright, Philip, 'E H Lawton', September 1967

Monographs
Cooper, May, 'Memories of King Street Barracks' nd
Geddes J D , 'Local Aspects of the Fine Arts', Aberdeen Philosphical Society, 1874
Ritchie, John, 'The Aberdeen Granite Trade' nd

Newspaper Articles
Casely Gordon, 'Linksfield What Now?' Evening Express, 16 May 1969
Morgan Diane, 'The Pittodrie Story', Press & Journal 28 & 29 September 1971
Morgan, Diane, 'The Buchan Writer and the Orra Loon' The Scotsman: 22 July, 1972
Morgan Diane 'Yokit tae the Darg...' The Scotsman 27 December, 1989
News Cuttings
Cuttings on the Spital Lands by courtesy of George Gordon; Cuttings on the air-aid of 21 April, 1943 by courtesy of Laura Galloway

Aberdeen City Archives:
Deeds relating to Orchard Cottage
School Log Books: Sunnybank Public School 1906-24: Sunnybank Intermediate School 1924 - 39, Sunnybank Primary School 1939 - 81
Valuation Rolls: 1855-56, 1883-84, 1900-01, 1901-02, 1925-26, 1932-33, 1945-46

Aberdeen City Libraries: Aberdeen Endowments Trust; Minutes and Proceeding of the Trustees 1911-1931;
Aberdeen Town Council Minutes from 1883;
News Cuttings on Froghall,Linksfield, Lord Provost Rust

Aberdeen Endowments Trust: Accounts 1910, Minutes 1936-38:

Aberdeen University Special Collections: King's College Land Rentals K84, 1791-1815; Walker & Duncan Papers, MS 2626

Index

Abel, A & W,197
Aberdeen, Andrew, 8-9, 10
Aberdeen Building Co, 184
Aberdeen Endowments Trust, 26-7, 29
Aberdeen Football Club Ltd, 255- 63; fire, 261; foundation, 255; ground improvements, 256-8, 260-2; strip, 255, 258; takeover bids, 259
Aberdeen Football Club, (Whites), 253-5
Aberdeen Philosophical Society, (Wise Club), 43- 6
Air-raid, (21 April 43) 99-100, 115-7
Anderson, (Sir) Alexander, 228
Anderson, Chris, 111
Anderson, Robert, (city engineer) 227, 229
Ardarroch Court, 252,
Ardarroch Road, 240-2, 250, 258
Arthur, Andrew, 184
Balgownie, (Marchmont) House, 237, 242
Bandeen, Elizabeth, 138, 145
Ba(e)verlay, James, 8,
Baird, Archie, 256-8, 260
Bank Cottage, 61, 62
Barré, Vermont, 153, 245
Beattie, Prof James, 17 18-9 23, 44-5
Bedford Place, 25, 79, 81, 84
Bedford Road, l, 12, 36, 76, 78, 92, 95, 102, 105
Begg, Tommy, 149
Belmont FC, 121
Birkbeck, John, 142-3
Bishop, Harold, 47, 88, 242
Bisset, James H, 73, 74, 214
Booth, Charlotte, 89, 94
Booth, J & K 235
Booth, Jack, 188
Bowes-Lyon (Bain), Connie, 98-9
Brebner, J & JL 235
Bruce, Sir Michael & Dame Isabella (Moir), 12, 72, 130, 210, 225
Bruce, Doreen, 178, 182
Bryce, Mary (Duncan), 109
Burness, John , 206-7
Burns, Robert, 206-7
Butchart Centre, 172, 190, 195
Byron, Lord, 19

Caie (granite merchants), 242, 243
Campbell, 'Prinkipal' G, 44
Campbell, Tess, 97
Cardno, Gordon, 138, 211, 269
Carter, Hubert, 98
Center, Ronald, 82-3
Central Fire Station, 269
Chalmers, Billy, 123, 124
Chalmer(s), Robert, 9, 125,
Cheyne, Andrew, 158-9
Chris Anderson (ex-Linksfield) Stadium, 252
City of Aberdeen Housing Association, 92
City of Aberdeen Land Association, (CALA), 14, 38-9, 40, 85, 86, 91, 94, 138, 239, 256
Clark, Edith (Farquhar), 108, 163, 186, 187, 192
Clark, GC, 163, 165
Clark, John, 172-3, 176
Clarke, John, 253, 255
Cocker, Anne, 186
Cocker, James, & Sons, 67, 130, 137
College Lane, Wynd, etc, 76, 78
Collie, Helen, 9-10,
Colman, Donald, 256
Comper, Rev John, 201, 219
Cooper, Henry, (manufacturer), 71, 215-6
Cooper, May, 244
Cooper, Willie, 110, 257
Courage, Baubie, 34-6
Coutts, George, architect, 74
Coutts, Jimmy, dairyman, 190
Craig, Arthur, 'in Sunniesyd', 8
Crane, Major Henry, 67-68, 89, 90, 83, 85, 216
Crawford, Fred, 15, 94, 117
Croft, Robert & Sons Ltd (granite merchants), 241, 246
Crown Cottage, 58, 65, 193
Davidson, Robert, 66
Deans, John, 121
Deer Cottage, 63
Donald, Iris, 28
Donald, Richard, ('Dick'), 260
Donald's, Spital, 269

Donaldson, Tommy, & Isobel, 86-7, 94, 111
Douglas Metals, 246
Duncan, John, Rev, 74
Dung Yard/Stance, 225-7, 253, 254
Dung Stance Road, 225, 226, 239, (See also Merkland Road East)
Dungers, 64
East Back Gate, 173, 223
Edwards Wm, (granite merchant) 165, 244, 246
Ellis & McHardy, 102
Elmbank House, 68-71, 85, 103
Elmbank Road, 81-82, 94
Elmbank Terrace, 5, 10, 73, 74, 75, 89, 90, 91,
Elmfield Avenue, 79 , 81
Elmfield Farm, 13, 74
Elmfield House, 66-68, 85, 89,
Elmfield Terrace, 90
Elphinstone, George, 186, 187, 188, 192, 201-203, 267
Erskine Road, (see also Bedford Road) 76,
Erskine Street, 73, 75, 80, 81
Farquhar, J J, 107
Ferguson, Alex, 263
Firhill(well) Cottage, 46, 48
Firhill(well) Lane, 46
Firhill, Little, 7
Firhill Place, 10, 33, 46, 47, 48, 65
Firhill Road, 5, 33, 38,
Firhill, the (Hermitage Hill etc), 7, 92
Firhill Well, see Gibberie Wallie
Fisher, Norman, 196-97
Forbes, Arthur, 244-5
Forbes, Charles, 86, 11, 256
Forbes, Harry P, 86-87, 111
Forbes, Junius (Ernan Granite Yard), 144, 154-5, 166-7
Forbes, Rev Patrick (Old Prosody) 35,
Froghall Cottages, 128, 150
Froghall Farm, 125, 128
Froghall Housing Scheme, 139-41
Froghall, Lands of 5
Froghall Lane (see also Terrace), 125, 128
Froghall Nursery, 128
Froghall Plotties, 138
Froghall Road, 135, 136
Froghall Terrace, 125
Fraser, Alexander,
Fraser, Christian (Moir), 6,
Fraser, GM 40
Fraser, Margaret, 242, 258, 267

Gallow Slacks, 171, 240
Galloway, Laura, 92, 93
Garden, R Connon, 158
Gemmel, Margaret, 95
Gerrard Dorothy, 138, 211,
Gibb, Robert, (Excelsior Granite Yard), 234-5, 237, 250
Gibberie Wallie (Firhill Well), 7, 11, 21, 30-41; damage to, 35; removal 40-1, 91
Gibrie (gingerbread), 34
Gillan, John, 149
Glebe Hill, 7,
Glenbervie, Lord, 18, 21
Glennie, Jim, 116-7, 143
Gordon, Harry, 109
Gordon, George, 29, 180
Great North of Scotland Railway (GNSR), 12, 72, 75
Gregory, John 44
Greig, George, 86
Halliday, David, 258
Harper, Mrs (Causeyton), 82, 87
Hay family, (Orchard House), 177-8, 196
Henderson, James, 68-9, 71
Henderson, Stephen, 52, 54
Hermitage Avenue, 5,
Hermitage, the, 104
Hogarth, Thomas 67
Hogg, Norman & Elizabeth, 52, 268
Hope Terrace, 57-8, 65
Hultie, 244-5
Humanity Manse, 33
Hutcheon, (King Street Granite Works), 237
Inverurie Highway, old, (See also Elmbank Terrace), 1, 10
Jute Works, 38, 112, 131-3, 137, 151; as housing colony, 141-3;
Kennedy JRR, granite merchant, 217, 242, 246
Kerr, Billy, 147-9
Kerr, Jackie, 54-5
Kerr, Tony 149
Killah, George & Mrs, 14
Kilgour, Ethel, 249
King Street (Road), 181, 183, 224, 227, 236-9
Kittybrewster, 12, 74
Kittybrewster Station, 73, 75
Kittybrewster Road, see Oldtown, Road to
Knight Erskine, Col Henry, 46, 72
Knight Erskine, H W, 13, 72, 75, 78, 83, 84, 85, 135, 182, 183, 184, 211, 238, 239, 253
Knight Erskine, Mary Anne (Moir), 13, 46, 72, 210

Knowles, Jimmy, 118,149
Lady Mill, (King Street Mill), 181, 183, 224, 231-5
Lambie, Alex, (granite merchant) 249-50
Lawton, EH, 249-50
Leighton, John, builder, 178, 214
Leslie, William, 118, 131, 229
Liberty Occupational Health, 56
Linksfield Manure Works, (Napier's Knackery), 230-1, 240
Linksfield Primary School, etc, 251
Linksfield Road, 239, 240, 250
Linksfield (Chris Anderson) Stadium, 252
Macandrew, Daniel, 46, 47, 48, 61, 133
Macdonald, William, mason, 61
Mackenzie, J Russell 78-9, 80
McCall, Steve, 188
McDonald, Charles, (Froghall Granite Works), 79, 136, 153-4, 159, 217
McDonald Court, 159
McKenzie, James, 192, 193
McKinnon, Wm & Co 249
McLaren, Alice & Ian, 97; Ian, 165,
McLeod, Ronald, 94
McRobbie, Alex, 12, 13, 14
McRobbie, Peter, 12, 13,
Maitland family, 95
Manuelle, A & F (granite merchants) 241
March Stones, 67, 91, 127, 136, 264
Marshall, Andrew, 57-8
Martin, William 57-8
May, Andrew, 118-20
Melvin J L, 137, 144
Mercer, James, 16-23,
Mercer, Thomas, 17
Merkland Place, 15,
Merkland Road East, 239, 240, 241, 242
Miller John, (Sandilands), 131, 136, 229
Mitchell, Adam, builder, 214
Mitchell, Dr, (ASB), 25, 106-7
Mitchell, Robert, builder, 79-80
Mitchell, William, postmaster, 71-2, 85
Moir family, 205, 210
Moir, George, 19, 176
Moir, John, of Barnes, 6, 8
Moir, William, burgess, 5,
Morocco, Alberto, 110-1
Murray, Rev J Gordon, 106-8, 119
Newham Cottage, 236
Nicol, Graeme D, 56
Nimbrie Jean, 9-10
Northern Bowling Green/Club, 188-9

Old Aberdeen Heritage Society, 194
Oldtown Road to, 10, 12, 13, 75
OMS , 56
Orchard Cottage, 174-8, 193-5
Orchard House, 173-9, 196-7
Orchard Lane (new), Susie's Close, 177, 181
Orchard Lane (old) 173, 178 180, 183, 192, 199, 223
Orchard Place, 174, 178, 179. 181, 183, 184, 197, 198
Orchard Road, 184, 188, 189
Orchard Street, 181, 183, 185, 199, 210
Orchard Walk, 174, 179 192
Orion, (Stripes), 255
Parleys ,(Parliament Cakes), 34
Paterson, W Dove, 80
Paton, Misses of Grandhome, 23-24
Peterstown, 75
Pickiltillum, 127, 136
Philip, James, (mason), 162
Pittodrie Granite Turning Co, 238, 246
Pittodrie Lane, 238
Pittodrie Park/Stadium 254-2
Pittodrie Place, 238
Pittodrie Street, 239, 240
Play House, 43, 173
Police Commissioners, 72, 225, 227
Poll Tax, 8-9
Powder Magazine, 224-5
Powis Burn, 6, 7, 33, 104-5, 231
Powis House, (Community Centre), 7
Powis, Lands of, Estate, 6, 12
Pratt, Adam, 58
Presslie, Ann, 201
Primrose, Margaret, 49
Primrosehill Centre, 5, 54-5; Children's Home, 51-4; House 48, 49, 50,
Red Lion Brae, 10, 11, 33,
Red Lion Inn/Tavern, 10, 33, 43, 46, 48, 50, 242
Reid & Leys, 28
Reid, (Sir) George, 216-7
Reid, Prof Thomas, 18, 43-4
Reith & Anderson, 76, 92
Rennie, Stanley, 110, 146, 265-6
Rettie, Charles, 59, 62, 91
Rettie John O (granite merchant) 242, 248
Reynolds, Sir Joshua, 45
Rezin, George and family, 49
Rifle Range, 224
Robb, Mr & Mrs, (Primrosehill) 52-5
Robertson, A & J, (Granite) Ltd 245-8
Robertson, Graeme, 247

Robertson, Ken, 69, 103
Robertson Sandy, 245-8
Rocklands Cottage, 95
Rose Cottage, 179-180, 190-2 195
Ross, Charles (Cranes), 247
Ruddiman, David, granite merchant, 241, 242, 248-9
Rust, James, 156-7
Rust, John Jnr 74, 230
Rust, Margaret, 157
St Machar Sports Ground/Centre, (Sunnybank Bowling Green), 38-9
St Margaret's Convent, 132, 133, 145, 201, 219
St Martha's Home, 132, 145
St Peter's Cemetery, 181, 205-221; War Memorial, 220-21
St Peter's Chapel (Spital Kirk), 5, 181
St Peter's Place, 181, 183 199-203
St Theresa's Chapel, 192-195, 198
Sandpits, 7, 36, 92, 105, 251
Sconce Well/ field, 174, 176, 180,183, 195
Scorgie family, 184
Scott, Mrs A (Nina Milton), 14, 93
Scott, Dennis 15, 59, 94-5
Scott, Teddy, 12, 263
Scottish Enlightenment, 45
Sharp, Ian, 117-8
Sheriffs, James, 11-2
Shirras, Joseph, 64, 90, 137
Sinclair, Councillor George, 36
Sinclair, Vic, 199
Slessor, Muriel & Alex, 28, 83, 86, 98
Simpson, Bobby, 123
Simpson, Jean (Nelson), 15, 184, 187, 188, 266-7
Skakle family, 134
Skinner, Bishop John, 207-9
Smith, Alex, 50
Smith, Jimmie, 268
Smith & Kelly, 80, 83, 84, 183, 238
Smith-Shand, Anna (Stuart), 24-5, 83
Smith-Shand, James, 24-5
Souttar, James, 129, 184
Spencer, Isaac, (Coatings Ltd), 5,151
Spital Irrigation Farm, 227-30
Spital Lands, 5; boundaries, 14, 78
Stalker Family, 134, 151
Stalker, GM , 165-66, 167
Stankyaird, (see also Froghall Farm), 9, 125-6
Stephen, Billy, 121

Stephen, Molly 138, 145, 150, 151
Stewart, D C, builder, 104
Stronach, Alex, 24,
Sunnybank Estate, 83, 84
Sunnybank FC, 121-4
Sunnybank House, 21-9, 84, 85, 86; as 'Homey', 27-9, 65
Sunnybank Place, 81, 83
Sunnybank Place families, 96-98
Sunnybank Road, 39, 40, 65, 84, 86
Sunnybank Road (old), 33, 61,
Sunnybank School, 86, 106-119
Sunnybank Skating Rink, 86
Sunnypark, 129-130, 137
Sunnyside Farm, 6-7, 10-12, 13, 14, 33, 104-5
Sunnyside Gardens, 105
Sunnyside, Lands of, 5, 6, 16,
Sunnyside Road, 14, 25, 38, 86
Sunnyside, (old) Road to, 10, 14, 81, 83, 84
Sunnyside Terrace, 91
Sunnyside Walk 84, 90. 95
Sunnyside witch: see Jean Nimbrie
Sutherland, TS, 92, 259
Taggart, James, 51
Tait, George, 188
Tarry Briggie, (Froghall Railway Bridge), 5, 94,127
Taylor, Arthur, 160-65
Taylor, Dr J, 30-33
Taylor, Mr & Mrs, (Primrosehill), 52
Tester family, 193
Thom George, (Albion Granite Works), 167
Thom, Jim, 123,124
Thomson, James 110, 114
Toulmin, David, 249
Trail, Katherine, 33, 229, 236
Trinity Cemetery, 225
Walker & Duncan, 85, 86, 89, 240
Walker Medal, 29
Watkins, Albert, 48
Weir, Willie, 15, 104, 199, 266-7
Weston, Elizabeth, 51,144
Whin Hill, 224
Wilson, Alex,(granite merchant), 241- 2
Wise Club, see Aberdeen Philosophical Society

Zetland House , (John Duncan), 236-7

What the Press said about 'Footdee'

Footdee book tops sales list.
Aberdeen Press and Journal

A model of what a local history should be.
Scottish Book Collector

She writes with warmth and affection.
Bob Smith: Leopard Magazine

ISBN 1 898645 01 9

ISBN 1 898645 02 7

What they said about 'Mounthooly'

200 pages of tightly written fact and anecdote, leavened with archive phot-graphs and documentation...a book that does Aberdeen a great service.
Aberdeen Press and Journal

The second in a ground-breaking series...Diane Morgan has rescued from impending oblivion, the story of Mounthooly and its people
Scottish Local History

What they said about 'The Spital'

Another best -seller from Diane Morgan
Evening Express

The Spital is a very good read. It is also a first class reference book.
Leslie MacFarlane,
Aberdeen University Review

ISBN 1 898645 03 5